Praise for *The Sportsca*

T0266417

"In *The Sportscaster's Daughter*, Cindi nav g
bittersweet past, the ties and pains of family, her parents' divorce, and life and love in the shadow of a famous father. This is a clear-eyed, affecting look back, and in the end our heroine emerges into the light."

> **—Cullen Thomas,** author of *Brother One Cell*, memoir teacher at New York University and Gotham Writers Workshop

"*The Sportscaster's Daughter* cozies up to you and breaks your heart. It's a long, deep look at family dysfunction in the suburbs and the devastation of an unrequited love for a family. You'll find echoes of Karr and Walls. Read it."

> **—Stephanie Jay Evans,** author of *Faithful Unto Death*

"Cindi Michael's memoir does not end on the last page. *The Sportscaster's Daughter* lingers. It makes you question how a young girl, barely out of middle school, assumes the role of family caretaker . . . and survives. As the daughter of a celebrity sportscaster, Michael engages the written page as if it were her last chance. Woven delicately, this memoir will break your heart until understanding and forgiveness emerge. Then you will cheer."

> **—Julie Maloney,** Director of Women Reading Aloud

"*The Sportscaster's Daughter* is a compelling story about the special love a daughter has for her famous and at times unapproachable father. This is the true story of Cindi Michael, a strong, hardworking young girl who is at first surrounded by her father's love, and then, for inexplicable reasons, is cast from the house to live in isolation, confusion, and heartbreak. Cindi does not give up. She is a fighter. This is an important story of a daughter's love for her less-than-perfect father, about overcoming the childhood pain of being raised by parents who have no tools to help themselves, let alone guide their children to healthy relationships."

> **—Leslie Nack,** author of *Fourteen*

THE SPORTSCASTER'S
DAUGHTER

a memoir

CINDI MICHAEL

SHE WRITES PRESS

Published 2016
Printed in the United States of America
ISBN: 978-1-63152-107-2
Library of Congress Control Number: 2016935559

Cover design © Julie Metz, Ltd./metzdesign.com
Interior design by Tabitha Lahr

For information, address:
She Writes Press
1563 Solano Ave #546
Berkeley, CA 94707

She Writes Press is a division of SparkPoint Studio, LLC.

For us, so that we may heal.

Author's Note

This memoir is based on my memories. I relied on decades of journal entries, letters, and newspaper articles to support my memory for factual accuracy. Names of some minor characters have been changed to protect their privacy.

CONTENTS

CHAPTER 1

Digging for Baby Clams

Dad, left, working the phone lines at WFIL

MY FATHER WOULD SAY I was selfish, a liar, a manipulator, that the family was happier without me in it. Eventually, he didn't even acknowledge that I existed, and he never mentioned my name again.

I, on the other hand, could never pretend that my father didn't exist, because I saw his face everywhere. He was a famous sportscaster, his show broadcast around the world. I tried not to watch him, because it hurt; but sometimes, when missing him was unbearable, I'd secretly watch him on TV. Hearing his familiar voice and seeing his hazel-green eyes, the same as mine, gave me hope.

I have wished I had the hatred to curse my father for disowning me. It might make it hurt less. But I never did like to disagree with him; because with my father, you were either with him or against him, and I'd rather have been with him. Always. The sad reality is that no matter how I have lived my life or what I have accomplished, the child in me comes slinking out, wondering if my father was right all along.

So many people have idolized him—important people like presidents and professional football players. Doesn't that prove my father was right? Doesn't that make me an undesirable, unlovable person?

Being disowned is like being caught in a rip tide. From the outside, my present life is the sun glimmering on the surface of the ocean—beautiful, soothing, a seemingly charmed life. I keep the daily pain locked away in order to survive.

Even at the beach—my place of peace—with my own family, there is a constant worry that all this will one day be taken from me, whisked away like my once happy childhood. My son and I hold hands to jump the waves together, laughing as the sea sprays our faces. I revel to watch my daughter dive into the waves, the furthest one out; I have given her those wings, or more accurately, those fins. My husband, meanwhile, has to gently coax me further into the ocean, because even though I am a strong swimmer, I distrust joy. Will I pass all my old family crap to my own children, dragging them into the ugly vortex, continuing the cycle?

The few people who know my story blame my father and stepmother for my disowning. My husband falls into this group of people, and there are some days I can believe him, in my head anyway. But in my gut, I'm not so sure. I search for what I might have done differently, moments when I might have altered the course of events that led to my father casting me out.

If I can just get past the murky depths where I doubt myself, when I can barely breathe, there is the ocean's solid floor filled with happy memories of my childhood, when my father loved me. He'd watch me dig for baby clams, and share my joy at the bright colors: pink, purple, amber. He gave me my wings, then clipped them, plucked them, and ultimately tried to amputate them.

My father, George Michael Gimpel, was born in St. Louis, the son of a butcher. My mother, Patricia Ann Gallagher, was the daughter of an assistant chief of police, and my great grandfather an FBI agent during the prohibition. They were all devout Catholics, and I think that explains some things. Dad's side of the family was German, which probably explains some more.

Dad couldn't wait to get out of St. Louis. Whether to get away from his father—Pop to me—or because he dreamed of a bigger life, I'm not sure. I only knew that Pop used the belt on his kids, something Dad vowed never to do. My father even changed his name, shortening it to George Michael, a better name than George Gimpel for someone hoping to be famous.

Dad was an aspiring disc jockey so we moved around a lot. My older brother Brad was born in Milwaukee (radio station WRIT). Then they moved back to St. Louis (WIL) where I was born. Then to Littleton, Colorado (KBTR). Then to Cherry Hill, New Jersey (WFIL) in 1968. I sometimes wonder how my mother managed uprooting to a new city every year with two toddlers and whether my father gave her any credit for this. I was born only fifteen months after my brother, a rhythms baby, my mother said, a mistake.

When I was little, Dad was the music director and a disc jockey at WFIL in Philadelphia, the top rock 'n' roll station in the area; he worked the evening shift. They called him King George. In one of the photos used for autographs, he was dressed in a royal robe and crown. I was used to hearing my father's booming, deep voice on the car radio (56 AM) and over the loud speaker at the supermarket. Sometimes, he would dedicate a song to me; my favorite was "Playground in My Mind." "My name is Cindi, when I get married, I'm gonna have a baby or two." Sitting on his lap once, at the kitchen table, I asked him what he wanted to be when he grew up. To me, playing records seemed too much like fun, not what fathers did in their jobs.

My earliest memory of my father is in Colorado, where we lived when I was three. We went to a park with teepees and a petting zoo, and I got to feed the goats a bottle of milk. I stood there holding the bottle, probably cute with my freckles, dimple in the right cheek, sun-blonde streaks in my auburn hair, surrounded by goats. When the goat finished the bottle, it nudged me for more, but I didn't have any more, so the goat began chewing on my pink sweater, and I shrieked in terror. My father scooped me up in his arms, away from the hungry goat, and his deep voice boomed with laughter. With his laugh, I stopped crying. It was the first time he rescued me.

In Cherry Hill, New Jersey, in 1968, we lived in an idyllic neighborhood, Downs Farm. Every neighbor was like an extension of our family. There was a whole pack of us—Steve Struthers, three houses up on the right, Danny Kohs diagonal across the street, Roy and Kristi Lemieux to the left, Brendan McConnan across the street, and Jacqueline Pointer just past the elementary school. All of us kids could travel from one yard or house to the next, playing all day. There was a creek behind our house that fed into a huge concrete tunnel. We'd run through the tunnel, propelled by a fear that a big gush of water might drown us midway through at the deepest, darkest point; then laughed with the thrill when we safely came out the other side into sunlight. A majestic weeping willow hung over the edge of the creek, and bushes of honeysuckle trailed the sides. I can still taste the sweetness of the white flowers that we'd sometimes pluck and suck on. I think back to those happy years and look for clues that explain why I lost my family.

Like the year our cat had kittens. The mother cat slept in this big, black suitcase lined with towels, while the kittens nursed with their eyes closed. We gave most of them away, but I got to keep one. It was my dad who helped me pick his name, Curiosity. When Mom and Dad were sitting in bed having their morning coffee, Curiosity would pounce on Dad's big toe as if it were a mouse to catch. One day, Curiosity followed me to kindergarten. I kept pleading with him to go home, but he wouldn't listen. As I walked to school on the sidewalk, every few feet I turned around and scolded my kitten. He'd linger further back, but as soon as I turned around and started walking again, he ran to catch up to me. Finally, I tried ignoring him. When the school bell rang for us to go inside and I no longer saw him, I thought Curiosity had gone home.

Then shortly after class started, Curiosity tried to climb in through the school window to get to me. The teacher shooed him out and knocked him off the window ledge. I hadn't liked my kindergarten teacher before that day and liked her even less when she slammed that window on my helpless cat. He was only trying to find me!

Later that morning, we had to go the school nurse to get measured and weighed. My friends and I were all standing in a line through the nurse's office when I spotted the crossing guard sitting in the main office holding my cat. I tried to tell the teacher that it was *my* cat, but she told me to be quiet and to stay in line. It seems even in kindergarten, I could not find a voice to speak up for myself.

When I got home from school, I looked everywhere for Curiosity, hoping he had come home by himself. I told my mom the whole story and begged her to go talk to the crossing guard. She didn't. I don't think she even called the school, and I never saw Curiosity again, my kitten who used to sleep on my belly.

As a mother myself now, when my daughter lost her turtle, I hung flyers in supermarkets and stuffed mailboxes. It's only now that I wonder about my mother and father who couldn't bother to call the crossing guard about a lost cat. Was that a clue that the cracks in their relationship had already formed?

My mother would say it was all the pressure of having to be thin and pretty, as a rock 'n' roll DJ's wife, even though my sister had just been born. With my mother's big blonde hair, blue eyes, and shapely figure, when she walked into a room, heads turned. Call her a flirt or just friendly. Both were true.

My sister Michelle was born when I was five, June, 1970. Dad, Brad, and I went to the hospital in the blue Ford Mustang to bring her and Mom home. In the car, she lay in Mom's arms, her eyes never opening. When we got home, I sat on our living-room sofa, and my mother laid my baby sister in my arms. I remember being surprised that she was so much heavier than my doll. I don't know if I loved my sister from the start or if it was a feeling that grew. I only remember that she had an endless stream of cloth diapers that I had to fold and stack, neatly and precisely.

There is a picture of Michelle in the baby carriage on our porch in Downs Farm. My mother is standing behind the carriage and I am next to it, with my arm outstretched and a hand on the handle, standing as far to the side as possible while still being in the picture. I would not let go of my sister or be pushed aside. My father didn't want me in the photo and told me to move out of the way. It was my mother who told him it was okay. But I could see in my father's face that he was annoyed. I had moved like he told me to, but not all the way. Was this the first sense, a feeling unnamed, that my father's love was not a given?

Even now, I feel a spark of triumph for that little girl who stayed in the damned picture. Oh, how my stubbornness must have irritated the crap out of my father, more so if he recognized that I inherited it from him.

I try to remember my mother from before their divorce, but the images are so fleeting, like the seeds of a dandelion blowing away in the wind. There was one night when I was five, I was sick and threw up in bed. I remember so clearly. My father came in with my mother and raged, "If she gets sick one more time, she can clean it up herself!" My mother tried to argue with him. "She can't help it, George." I didn't get sick again that night.

My mother was tired all the time the year Michelle was born. One day, she set the kitchen on fire, having forgotten her hair rollers boiling on the stove. When I came home from school, the once-white cupboards were completely blackened. At some point, my mother was hospitalized for exhaustion. She later told me it was because she dieted too much after Michelle was born. Dad didn't want a fat wife.

My mother could be tough, though. When Nancy Sinatra had released a new song, the record promoter told Dad he had to play it; that, if he didn't, he would blow up our house. Dad didn't know what to do. He had never accepted payola, a big part of the music business at the time when DJs were paid money to play certain songs. But this was different. This was about Dad's wife and kids. My mother told him, "You tell Nancy Sinatra and her record promoter to go to hell." My mother would not be threatened or bullied. As a daughter of a police chief in St. Louis, she had seen a thing or two of bullying. So, Dad didn't play Sinatra's song, and our house didn't get blown up. I'm still impressed that neither of them caved under such a personal threat.

Downs Farm in New Jersey had its own swim club, which was the center of our social life in summer. Only people who lived in the neighborhood were allowed to join the club, and everyone pitched in to take care of it. Mr. Kohs, Danny's dad from across the street, painted the sign that marked the entrance along Walt Whitman Boulevard pastel blue with white trim. Brendan's older brother was a lifeguard at the pool, and Mr. Bush, who lived next door to us, built the new deck. Mr. and Mrs. Bush were the only old people in our neighborhood. Even though their children were grown, they always had the best lights at Christmas. At Christmas time, our family would drive through the neighborhood and vote on who had the best lights. The Bushes always won, and it was always unanimous.

Tuesdays in summer were when I missed my dad the most, because that was family night at Downs Farm. Families would bring coolers and picnic baskets to the pool, and the club would stay open late. We never stayed for family night, though, because Dad worked the evening shift at WFIL. Just as families were coming back to the pool for the evening, my brother, sister, and I drudged out of the club to head home with our mother, while I looked longingly at the other families who were eating dinner with their fathers.

Brad and I were on the swim team, so, we were always at the pool. We had practice every morning and, afterward, hung out with our friends, playing Sharks and Minnows or Marco Polo. For Michelle, there was a big toddler pool, only a foot deep. Dad got to come with us on the weekends. Most of the day he worked on his tan, dozing on a lounge chair; but a high point was when Dad would finally go into the water with us. He'd stand in the deep end, near the diving well, and I would wrap my arms around his neck, unable to touch the bottom. Sometimes he'd swim breaststroke across the pool, carrying me on his back, and I trusted him not to let me go under. When Dad wasn't working on his tan, he'd play tether ball with us or join the other adults in volleyball. It all seemed so perfect.

One summer, the swim team won the championship at Tri County, and to celebrate our victory we threw the head coach, Mr. Lyons, into the pool, fully clothed. My eight-and-under girls relay team came in first place, and when they presented our medals we stood on the blocks just like in the Olympics. Dad took picture after picture and declared he would build a special display case for all the medals I won that season. Pride felt a lot like love to me.

The following summer, we moved up to swimming fifty meters—two laps. Mastering the flip turns was all about timing and holding your breath long enough not to choke mid-summersault. We were at an away meet, in an unfamiliar pool and, as I came into the wall, I turned too soon. I tried to push off the wall but felt nothing. Not having the wall to push off slowed me down, so I swam as fast as I could to catch up. As soon as I got out of the water, my teammates were outraged at the official.

"He wasn't even paying attention!" Jacqueline Pointer shouted.

"Yeah, he was talking away to some other person. He couldn't have seen anything, but he's saying you missed the wall," my other teammate echoed.

I didn't yet know that I had disqualified my entire relay team.

My disqualification became the talk of my teammates and their parents, and my teammates began to ridicule the official. "Maybe we should all chip in and buy him some eye glasses!" I overheard Dad defending me to the other parents.

The truth was, I had missed the wall. I didn't know it was illegal. I didn't know I should have gone back. But once silence steam rolls into a lie, there's no stopping it.

I said nothing, and Dad never asked me what happened. He defended me, though. I have sometimes wondered since then if he was supporting me, or if he didn't want to confront his own embarrassment from my mistake. In my father's world, mistakes were something to be avoided, not lessons to learn from. That summer, I learned that silence can be a lie.

When I was in second grade, we moved into Alluvium as soon as school let out for Christmas vacation, December 19, 1972. We were officially house number three in the new subdivision in Voorhees, New Jersey, twenty minutes from our old home in Downs Farm. The Oliveris were the first, the Parkers number two. The Oliveris had three boys and the Parkers two girls, our new friends.

Like with everything else, our neighbors helped us with the

move from Downs Farm to Alluvium, first with the garage sale, then the packing, and finally with piling things into a pick-up truck to haul across town. Brad and I now had our own bedrooms. Each of us were thrilled that we didn't have to share any more, me even more so because I got to choose a pink carpet. The master bedroom even had its own fireplace. It was Mom and Dad's $63,000 dream home, customized throughout the construction.

Jill Parker was a year older than me and lived across the street. She went to a Catholic school, as I had at Downs Farm; but so few people lived in Alluvium that there was no bus, so I started at E. T. Hamilton, a public school within walking distance. My new friend Jill came over to play, and we were playing in my room when Michelle, two years old, tried to join us. I didn't want her there and told Brad to play with Michelle. It seemed only fair; he didn't have a friend over and I did. Brad disagreed, and our argument escalated. I closed my bedroom door to keep Brad and Michelle out. He tried to force the door open, so Jill and I sat on the floor and pushed our backs against it. Brad and Michelle pounded on the door.

Dad came storming down the hallway and shoved it open. He picked me up by my arm and leg and tossed me down the hallway. I bounced down a few stairs before landing on top of my brother.

Jill ran down the stairs, climbing over us, and raced out the front door. I don't remember being spanked. I only remember being airborne.

Brad and I were grounded to our rooms for the rest of the day. Neither of us was seriously hurt, on the outside. I sobbed into my pillow and eventually dozed off. At one point, Mom came into my room to put laundry away. Michelle tagged along and asked why I was sleeping and why I wouldn't play with her. I pretended to be asleep, full of loathing for her. It was her fault I had gotten into trouble.

With nothing else to do that afternoon, I lay on my bed and discovered a tattered book with a blue fabric cover on my headboard. I escaped into my first *Nancy Drew*, a happier world than real life.

It's surprising that Jill ever came over again after that afternoon, but thank God she did. She became my best friend, and Mrs. Parker became a second mother to me.

I have wondered about that day when my father so lost his temper. Was it a clue? Did he sense he was losing my mother, despite having given her a new home?

When the first snow came that year, we had to find a new hill for sledding. In Downs Farm, we had sled down Carolina Avenue, a nice steep street, but Alluvium was flat. We drove around the unpaved roads until we found a hill at the back of Alluvium where construction hadn't yet started. Dad loved sledding as much as Brad and I, and we rode double-decker down the hill with Dad stretched on his stomach on the wooden sled and me on top, gripping his shoulders as the snow flew in our faces. My father was at his best when he played with us. Whatever demons were chasing him, demanding perfection and success, took a respite. Dad just laughed. When he played with us, perhaps our laughter drowned out Pop's whisper in my father's head, "You'll never amount to anything."

In the spring, when they poured the sidewalk, Dad took a stick and wrote in the freshly poured concrete at the foot of our driveway.

"Daddy, what are you doing?"

"Writing in the sidewalk."

"Is that allowed?" I knew writing on the door in the school bathroom was a bad thing. I wasn't sure about sidewalks.

"Of course. It's our sidewalk."

I contemplated this. "I thought the sidewalk belonged to everyone."

I walked over to see what he had written. *George and Trish, 1973*, circled with a heart.

I still wasn't sure if he'd get in trouble or not.

My father's love for my mother also showed in the special things they did together. That spring, Mom and Dad went to Mexico together, just the two of them. She convinced Dad to go parasailing even though adventure terrified him. He would go fast on a sled that he could steer, but flying above the sea, strung to a boat that somebody else controlled, was not his idea of fun.

On their trip, Mom shopped for unusual things to sell in a store she was planning to open; and our garage became filled with tables and chairs made of animal hide and bouquets of big, paper flowers. Our new Golden Retriever kept barking at the hide chairs, smelling a predator. The retriever didn't last long: he kept tearing up the freshly laid sod which drove my father nuts. If there were an eleventh commandment in our house it was, don't mess with Dad's grass. Dad eventually gave the dog to a friend and record promoter, Red Richards. Red lived on a farm where the dog could run free, no worries about sod.

Dad always had a house project going. That first spring in our new house was when he laid the brick walkway and brick patio. His masterpiece was the brick housing unit for the grill.

It was hot that Easter, and it wasn't particularly smart that the Easter Bunny hid the big chocolate-covered coconut eggs outside. By the time we got home from church, they were mostly melted, and we found the last one hidden in a corner of the brick grill. Do I remember this clearly because of my father's look of annoyance and probably an angry exchange—in hushed tones—between my parents so we wouldn't suspect anyone other than the Easter Bunny? The friction must have passed quickly, though, because we spent the rest of that Sunday at the beach, a place where we were always at our happiest.

Another day, Mom was getting ready for their weekly date. I sat on the floor of the bathroom watching her do her makeup, a liquid pastel blue eyeliner, and Dad told me, "Nobody does make up better than your mother." She let me have a try, and the coolness of the liquid shadow on my eyelids surprised me. With my freckles, upturned nose, and eyeglasses, I wasn't pretty like my mother, blue eye shadow or not.

My father loved my mother, of this I'm certain. They went out on a date most weekends and took trips, without us children, to special places like Mexico and Disneyland. What I hadn't yet learned, though, was there are different kinds of love. My parents' love for one another was the flammable kind; and my Dad's, conditional. I never saw them fight until the summer of 1973, the first summer in our new house, and, once they started, it got ugly fast.

CHAPTER 2

Through the Windshield

IT WAS ONE OF THOSE early days of summer at the end of second grade, 1973. Our babysitter, Joan, had taken my brother and sister and me to the Philadelphia Zoo. Mom and Dad had a day out on their own, shopping or something.

We had decided to have one last look at the polar bears, when it started to drizzle. So, we hurried back to the car. Brad and I scurried ahead as Joan pushed Michelle in the stroller. Brad climbed into the front seat of Mom's new car, a navy blue Ford Mustang, declaring dibs because he was the oldest. I thought it was obnoxious, as usual, that he didn't wait for Michelle and me to get in first, forcing us to navigate over him into the back seat of the two-door sports car. Seatbelts didn't exist then, so we sprawled across the back. I kicked off my flip-flops and dangled my feet out the triangular rear window. As we drove along the highway, the wind cooled my feet, soothing the blister between my toes that were not yet used to summer flip-flops.

Eventually, I swung around to sit on the hump in the middle of the car for a while, and leaned forward to join in on the conversation between Brad and Joan. Plus, looking out the front window kept me from getting car sick. Michelle sat beside me. Having just turned three, she was tired from the day out and was dozing off.

We had only been driving twenty minutes when I saw a white car coming down the hill toward us, spinning like a Tilt-a-Whirl.

It was mesmerizing, until the crash. The silence that followed the explosion lasted only a moment, a slow motion of confusion, things out of place, my sister no longer beside me, the front end of the car no longer there.

"GET OUT OF THE CAR! GET OUT OF THE CAR! OPEN THE DOOR! OPEN THE DOOR!" Joan shrieked.

Brad's door wouldn't open. He pushed and kicked. Finally, we climbed out Joan's side, and shards of glass dug into my bare feet. My right leg would not support the full weight of my body. Brad and I hobbled to the guardrail on the side of the road. I looked over to the car to Joan. She was leaning over Michelle, who was on the hood of another car.

Two elderly ladies came over to Brad and me and offered us paper towels, me for my leg, Brad for his face. We were both bleeding.

The police quickly arrived. A policeman came over to get me and I tried to follow him, but I couldn't walk. He scooped me up and put me in the back of the police car. Joan was in the front, cradling Michelle. Brad was taken away in an ambulance.

The police car sped away, its sirens blaring, ear piercing. I begged him to turn them off and pressed my hands to my ears. "Please, they're too loud!" The sirens were one loud scream and the policeman couldn't hear me.

At the hospital, Michelle and I were laid on tables next to each other. Several nurses hovered over my sister.

She kept crying and screaming. "I want my mommyyy! Mommyyy! I want my mommyyy!"

Her cries hurt me more than my leg. I called over to her, "I'm here, Michelle. Sissy's right here. I'm right next to you."

But Michelle couldn't see me through the nurses. She couldn't hear me above her wails.

Eventually, one of the nurses pulled a thin curtain between us. I stretched my arm to grab it, to let my sister know I was still there, but I couldn't reach her.

One of the nurses rushed into our room and demanded, "Where's the babysitter?"

"She went to check on the boy."

"We need to have a look at her."

Joan came running in. The paper towels she was holding to her chin were soaked in red. She had lost most of her front teeth when her face hit the steering wheel and would need twenty-two stitches.

The nurses eventually wheeled Michelle, still screaming, out of the room, leaving me alone in eerie silence. In my shorts and T-shirt, I only had a thin sheet over me and I began to shiver. Mr. Campbell, our new next-door neighbor eventually came. I asked him where they had taken my sister. He wasn't sure, but he told me my mom was with her. They had called my daddy at work, but he wasn't yet at the radio station. The hospital had reached Mom at home, and Mr. Campbell had driven her to the hospital. I told him I was cold, but there was nothing he could do.

Eventually, the hospital took X-rays of my leg. I sat in a wheelchair in the emergency room, waiting to find out if my leg was broken, not sure where my brother and sister were. Whenever the double doors to the waiting area swung open, I caught a glimpse of Joan's boyfriend, Billy, talking to my dad. I knew they were both worried, and I didn't want them to worry, so I tried to smile the next time the door flapped open. Later, Billy said to me, "You were laughing," dragging out the word, *laaaughing*. I was scared of Billy, so I didn't correct him. Whether it was his pockmarked face or that he had been to Vietnam or his once-long black tresses that had been reduced to fuzz that scared me, I don't know.

But I wasn't laughing. Being in the hospital wasn't fun, and I wasn't happy. I was scared and cold and tired under the bright fluorescent lights shining down on me. But I didn't want Daddy and Billy to be scared, too. I wanted them to know I was okay. How is it that at the age of eight, I already knew how to force a smile for the benefit of others?

Brad and I were released late in the middle of the night and went home with Dad. Nothing was broken, just bruised. Joan was sent home, too. But Michelle had to stay, and Mom stayed with her.

The next morning, Brad and I went next door to Mrs. Campbell's for breakfast, and she made us bacon and eggs. It was unusual for us to eat at our neighbor's house. I sometimes wonder if, in those days, my father didn't yet know how to cook or if this was simply a gesture from a neighbor in the face of a family crisis.

Dad said that Michelle had gone through the front windshield. He wouldn't say anymore. Later, he told us that when the hospital called WFIL, they had reported to him that only one of his daughters was alive. They didn't know if the other would make it. Initially, he hadn't known which daughter was fighting for her life. He had raced to the hospital, not knowing which of us he might lose.

A few days later, Dad took Brad and me to swim practice. Our teammates were swimming in the diving well when we got there. It was supposed to be a fun practice, not regular laps, and they were playing Sharks and Minnows. I tried to swim, but my arms hurt in places I hadn't realized were bruised.

It turned out that Michelle had a severe concussion. Her right eye was swollen shut, and the doctors weren't sure the eye was still there. They would only know for sure when her eye reopened, which could be months. Mom stayed with her at the hospital day and night. Children weren't allowed to visit intensive care, so Brad and I weren't allowed to see our sister. After the first week, Dad took us to the hospital to stand outside on the grass and wave to Michelle from there. He told us to count up seven floors and to look for Mom and Michelle in the hall window. I counted up and saw nothing. Then they were there, two silhouettes. I waved and waved, jumping up and down to be sure my mother and sister saw me. Neither waved back.

"She doesn't see us," I whined.

Finally, my sister waved back.

After the hospital, Dad, Brad, and I went to the junkyard to find Mom's car. It was totaled. I wondered if my flip-flops were still there and what else we might find.

We walked around the piles of cars, some stacked on top of others, like crumpled metal accordions. Finally, we found what had been our navy blue Mustang. Not much was left. The passenger side of the windshield had a large sunburst.

"But, Dad, if she went through the front windshield, why isn't there a big hole?"

Dad couldn't answer, and something in his look told me to leave it alone. Michelle's head had made the sunburst, of that I'm sure. Years later, when a reporter called my father an embellisher, I thought back to the accident as the first time when things didn't quite add up. Had my dad exaggerated the tragedy or was it the hospital that called him at work and told him Michelle had gone through the windshield?

I found only one flip-flop.

Michelle was in the hospital for two weeks. When she came home, her eye was a swollen plum and still closed. Her eyelid opened by August, and her eyeball was still there, but the bruise remained for months. Except for her funny-looking eye, Michelle seemed fine.

My mother later traced the beginning of the demise of their marriage to this car accident. Dad became so angry. He'd shout and curse, who would do this to his children, to *him*? When Mom stayed at the hospital with Michelle, Dad felt she was not paying enough attention to him.

One morning that summer, I noticed a hole in the wall in the downstairs bathroom. When I asked how it got there, nobody wanted to say. Forty years later, my mother told me it was from when Dad slammed her head against the wall after she admitted to having feelings for David Kohs, the eighteen-year-old son of our former neighbor. Even the priest had come to the house to intervene. I don't remember the fight. I only recall the hole in the wall.

That August, 1973, was the first time we went to the Admiral Motel in Wildwood Crest, New Jersey. Before that summer, whenever we went to the beach we stayed at the Sands Apartments in Ocean City. However, Wildwood had more restaurants, a boardwalk with better games, and the Admiral Motel was right on the beach, with a kids' club, mini golf, and a Little Miss Admiral contest.

What I remember most about that vacation is how much talking Mom and Dad did. They would sit in the motel bedroom, talking until late in the day. Brad, Michelle, and I weren't allowed to go to the beach without them, so I busied Michelle with mini golf, the merry-go-round, and splashing in the baby pool. Each time I went back to the room to see how much longer before they came out, they'd say, "Give us twenty minutes." I'd leave them then, taking Michelle in tow, to wait on the concrete balcony and stare out at the ocean. Michelle wanted to jump in the waves. I wanted to do anything but keep waiting.

One day that week, Mom entered Michelle and me in the Little Miss Admiral Contest, a pageant I did not want to be in. I thought it was stupid: Michelle with her bruised eye and me with my upturned nose and freckles. Mom put lipstick and dangly earrings on me and took off my glasses. It didn't make me any prettier. Even worse, none of the other girls had on makeup. I was eight; everyone else was younger and still cute.

We had to write on an index card our age, our town, what we wanted to be when we grew up. I said a teacher, Michelle said a school-bus driver. Neither of us won. Over the next few years, Michelle would come in second place multiple times, a natural beauty, always cute. Even the first summer, she had pranced in front of the judges, put her hand behind her head in a pose, and flashed an adorable smile. She had spunk. Whatever spunk I had had, I lost it that summer.

CHAPTER 3

Whispers in the Night

THAT OCTOBER, MOM WAS taking a trip to Mexico by herself, to shop for her new Mexican-furniture boutique, for which she had not yet found a location. There was talk of Brad going with her but, in the end, my parents decided he couldn't miss that much school. So Dad, Brad, Michelle, and I drove Mom to the Philadelphia airport and walked through the terminal to her gate. Beautiful in her white trench coat, she turned and waved, then she was gone, outside to the tarmac to board her plane. We stood in the middle of the bustling airport and stared at the empty doorway, as if she'd change her mind and come back.

My father pulled us into a huddle. I waited for him to say something, but all I heard was a guttural choking sound. I looked up to see him crying for the first time. Nobody said anything. This moment still haunts me.

On the way home from the airport, we went shopping for furniture. Dad was moving into his own apartment. We badgered him with questions. Why were we moving to an apartment when we had just built a new house? Daddy didn't answer.

We picked out a plush brown sofa, with chrome armrests. The chair and ottoman were big enough for Michelle to sleep on and, there in the showroom, she snuggled up on her makeshift bed to be sure it was comfortable.

Mom stayed in Mexico for three weeks. When she returned, she and Dad sat us at the kitchen table and told us they were separating. I didn't know what the word *separating* meant. Dad told us we would see him every weekend. He promised he would always have root beer in his apartment, and we could drink as much as we wanted. I had never had root beer. Would I like it? I wondered.

Dad found an apartment in Blackwood, New Jersey, in the Village of Pine Run, only twenty minutes from our home in Alluvium. Our house felt empty without Dad sitting at the bar in the kitchen planning his playlists, without the constant music of Motown beating through the stereo. The only place emptier was Dad's apartment. The walls were bare of Mom's paintings.

Back at school, now in the third grade, I told my friend Tracy Fogarti that my parents were separating. She said her parents had done the same thing and were now divorced. These were new words to me. *Separated. Divorced.*

Knowing someone else whose parents were separated made the change at home less strange.

I'm not sure when the word *affair* entered my mind. It was another word I didn't understand. My father never directly said that my mother was having an affair, at least not to me. Instead, I overheard conversations and gleaned hints from how he introduced songs on the air. I still hear the words by Gordon Lightfoot's "Sundown": "Sundown, you better take care, if I find you been creeping round my back stair." I pictured a man creeping around our back stairs, a man whose name I overheard in whispers, the reason my father left us.

The whispered conversations had started one night during Mom's trip to Mexico. Dad was sitting in the kitchen talking with friends, probably our neighbors the Toops. Mrs. Toop sometimes substituted at my elementary school; she was my favorite sub because she laughed a lot and had shiny blonde hair.

But that night, there was no laughing. I had come down the stairs from my bedroom and heard them talking quietly at the kitchen table. Dad's voice, normally booming, was soft.

"They say the husband is always the last to know," he said. "Somebody saw them coming out of the elevator at the wedding."

The conversation stopped when they noticed me. I quickly ducked into the hallway bathroom, pretending I had heard nothing.

The man's name had not been mentioned. That came the night he broke my father's arm.

One night, Brad, Michelle, and I were all asleep in our rooms at home, when the upstairs hall phone kept ringing. Finally, I stumbled out of bed to answer. It was Dad.

"Let me talk to your mother."

"She's not home. She went out."

"Who's babysitting?"

"Nobody. She said we'd be okay. She was going to wait until we fell asleep and then go out."

"Cindi, that can't be right. I woke you up. You must be half asleep. Go downstairs and check."

I was eight, Brad was nine, and Michelle three. Were we too young to be left alone?

I knew Mom wasn't home, but Dad insisted I check. So, I set the phone on the carpet and went downstairs. The house was dark. Nobody home.

I ran back upstairs and picked up the phone. "I told you, Dad. She's not home."

"I'll be right over."

It was a Saturday night and Dad was just finishing his shift as a DJ at the Coliseum, a local disco. He told me not to wait up for him, so I went back to bed.

I have no memory of the rest of the night. All I remember are bits and pieces from overheard conversations.

Dad stopped at the Country Club Diner for coffee to go. Our neighbors, the Oliveris, were leaving and greeted him. But Mom, then thirty-four, and her boyfriend, David Kohs, age eighteen, walked in. The air in the diner's lobby grew tense.

As a DJ in the rock 'n' roll industry, my father's livelihood depended on his youth and how hip he was. It would have hurt him less if Mom had an affair with Dad's best friend.

Dad shouted at Mom for leaving us alone at night. The Oliveris stopped the argument from escalating. Dad came back to the house and waited. I wonder if he came with his coffee or if he left the diner empty handed, the coffee forgotten.

When Mom returned home with David, there was a fight in the foyer. Dad grabbed the bronze sculpture of a naked woman off our entry table and hit David with it, supposedly breaking David's back; and David broke my father's arm.

I don't remember the fight. I only know this last part for sure, because the next day, my father's arm was in a cast. Dad told me later he thought he had seen me at the top of the stairs on the landing, watching the fight, but I don't think so. Brad maybe, but not me. I would have known to stay hidden.

In the hospital later that night, the scuffle almost resumed, until the nurses separated Dad and David in the emergency room.

Sunday was our day to be with Daddy. We always spent it with him alone. The morning after the fight, when he came to pick us up, he arrived with new friends, two nurses who lived in his new apartment complex. We kids were more interested in the cast.

"You should see the other guy," Dad joked.

I didn't know who the other guy was; and I had never seen "the other guy," not once. Besides, I was more excited about doodling on Dad's cast, preferably with a bright pink marker.

For decades, I believed my mother had an affair with an eighteen-year-old boy. It was a truth I never questioned.

In my late thirties, I asked my mother about David and their affair. She had come up from Florida to New Jersey for a visit, and we met for lunch at a quiet lakeside restaurant. She said, "We didn't have an affair, not by today's standards."

I stared out at the lake, an old irritation rising up. At the time,

I assumed she couldn't admit her mistake and culpability in ending the marriage. Her denial became one more divide between us. I assumed she wasn't facing reality, but rather than pressing the issue, which would lead to a fight, I commented instead on how pretty the lake was in winter, with the sun shimmering on the unfrozen ripples.

It was only after my father's death, when I began questioning everything I once believed about my childhood, that my mother and I had another discussion about David. We were talking on the phone, she in Florida and I in the dead of winter in New Jersey, when she repeated what she had said before.

"We didn't have an affair." She admitted to a crush, a longing, but nothing she had acted on until after Dad moved out.

She had, however, looked at another man. She had laughed with another man. She probably kissed him, too, but I stopped her before she got too specific about the details. Was my father the type of man to end a marriage, to break up a family, for a *kiss*? Even now, I don't want to face that answer.

Mom started dating David after Dad moved out. I don't know what Dad did or didn't do with other women after that. He kept it to himself. So, in my eyes, he was the innocent victim, still in love with my mother. Mom was the one to blame, I felt, because she had hurt my father.

I believe my mother now, but for much of my life I didn't. My unquestioned allegiance to my father remained, even after he disowned me.

A year after Dad moved out, he accepted a job at WABC in New York, replacing Cousin Brucie as the nighttime DJ. Dad had us kids for the weekend at his apartment in Blackwood when WABC insisted he come to New York that day to sign the contract.

Dad took Brad, Michelle, and me with him and turned the trip into an adventure. We took a seaplane from Philadelphia and landed on the Hudson River in front of the Statue of Liberty! Brad had been taking flying lessons and was the most excited about the trip. I felt nervous in such a small plane, not understanding how it wouldn't sink when we landed, but the Statue of Liberty, so magnificent from the sky and then right next to us on the water, filled me with awe.

Dad signed the contract, and we took a train back to South Jersey, not nearly as exciting as the seaplane but another new experience.

Shortly after, Mom and Dad tried to get back to together, and Mom went up to North Jersey with Dad to house hunt while we three kids stayed home with a babysitter. They found a contemporary house in Franklin Lakes. Mom described it as a house made of glass. "So many windows to look out to the woods."

I worried about bathroom privacy in "a house made of glass" but was excited that we would all live together again. I told all my friends and teachers at school that my parents were getting back together and that I would soon be moving. Then Dad called one day after school. I answered the kitchen phone.

"Let me talk to your mother."

"She's not home."

"Where did she go? When will she be back?"

It still made him angry that she left us alone so much, going to parties and out with friends even though it was during the day.

"She went swimming, at the pool at Echelon."

"Oh, yeah? Who with?"

Dad tried to sound lighthearted. I guess it was odd that she would go swimming without us. "Um, I think David. David Kohs." To me, David was just Danny's big brother, our old friend from Downs Farm.

Could a different answer that fateful day have changed our lives forever, had I understood about David? There was something in my father's voice that made me uneasy. "Maybe I got it wrong?" I said, wanting to make it right.

When Brad got home from his friend's house, I asked him, "Do you remember who Mom went swimming with?"

Brad didn't know and shrugged off my questions, like he always did. He never bothered with the details of our home life.

After that phone call, there was no more mention of moving to Franklin Lakes.

However, Dad still had to buy the house. The sellers wouldn't let him out of the contract. Because he could no longer sell our house in Alluvium, he had to borrow $40,000 from his new employers at WABC for the down payment. And he had to live in the house. He stayed there, alone, for two years. He never even furnished it. He only took what he had in the apartment. The formal living room, dining room, and what would have been our bedrooms remained empty.

When I asked Daddy why he couldn't live with us and why we weren't moving to Franklin Lakes, he said Mom didn't love him anymore. "She loves David."

CHAPTER 4

Worlds Apart

Dad and me, Christmas in Franklin Lakes, 1975

THE SEPARATION MEANT the end of my parents' marriage and the end of my childhood. The first year my parents were apart, Dad lived only twenty minutes away. The second year, he lived two-and-a-half hours away in a suburb of New York. But more than distance divided us—the time with my father was a world apart from the chaotic home life with my mother.

Dad took us to fun places like Ringling Brothers Circus, the Ice Capades, and the new amusement park, Great Adventure. He cooked us mouth-watering hamburgers and homemade apricot Danish drizzled with fresh icing. Plus, he was always on time to pick us up. It seemed to me that Dad was trying to be a good father.

Even when his girlfriend, Pat, visited the same weekend, she slept on the sofa. He met her when she was in college and worked as a "boss chick" one summer at WFIL in Philadelphia. A boss chick was a combination cheerleader and secretary to the disc jockeys, who were called "boss jocks." The key qualification for a boss chick was that she had to be beautiful, and Pat was. She had dark-brown hair, smoky-blue eyes, and an olive complexion—the exact opposite of my blonde-haired mother.

One weekend after Dad had accepted his job at WABC, he was packing up his apartment in Blackwood, New Jersey, to move to New York. Pat was there to help pack. As Brad, Michelle, and I were not helpful packers, we went next door to his friend Joanne's. We loved Joanne. She looked like Marlow Thomas, with a smile and Hershey kisses every time we saw her. Joanne offered to take us to the playground, so I ran back to Dad's apartment to ask if that was okay.

When I burst through the door, Pat was reclined on the sofa, with Dad on his knees behind her, kissing her on the neck. That's how I knew Pat was more than a friend.

While Dad was trying to be a good father, my mother didn't even seem to try to be a good mom. She never cooked. I got so bored of Tang instant orange drink for breakfast that, to this day, I cannot stand the smell of it. Mom was never on time to pick us up from a friend's house or a school activity. So many times, I was the last child after gymnastics, with the teacher waiting with me impatiently in the dark outside the school. I felt so guilty that I finally dropped gymnastics.

In the morning, if we missed the school bus, Mom didn't bother to get out of bed to take us to school, so we simply missed school that day. It took me only a few times to learn to never, ever wake up late—because I loved school. It gave me a sense of normalcy.

Mom would do things I knew were wrong, like "borrowing" money from advertisements I sold for the annual swim-team program. She never paid me back, and I felt ashamed about the ads that didn't make it into the program. Was it okay for my five-year-old sister to flip through a *Playboy* magazine, or see the movie *Jaws*? As Michelle stood outside the theater, crying in fear, I suspected it was *not* okay.

It bothered me that Mom never reminded Michelle to brush her teeth before going to bed, so my sister went to sleep with bubble gum that invariably got knotted in her hair overnight. I could usually get the gum out with peanut butter, but one time it was so bad that Mom had to cut off most of Michelle's hair. Her hair was so short that summer that nobody could tell if she was a boy or a girl. That summer, when Dad took us to Great Adventure, the photographer dressed Michelle in a boy's outfit, with a gun and vest. Nobody bothered to tell him she needed a frilly petticoat.

I couldn't say precisely what was wrong with my mother. It was usually only through other people's eyes that I knew things weren't right. For example, when my friend Jill was no longer allowed to sleep over unless we had a babysitter, which was rare, and Mom always went out at night. Mrs. Parker told me one day that when I walked to the bus stop in the morning, it looked like I had the weight of the world on my shoulders. I hadn't realized that the tumult in my heart showed on the outside. It wasn't so much that I felt sad inside but I worried that, if I didn't take care of my sister and me, who would? I didn't worry about Brad. He just went off to play with his friends.

In the few pictures I've seen from that time, 1974 through 1976, I notice that I didn't smile. I remember that I cried over silly things, like not being able to spell *friend* for a spelling test. How could I explain, to anyone, that I was hurting inside and why?

Once, when with Dad for the weekend, he took Brad, Michelle, and me out on the WABC music boat for a ride around Manhattan. We went swimming off the side of the boat in the Hudson River; Dad had chiggers for a week, and my back got badly sunburned and blistered. When Dad drove us back to South Jersey, he told me to keep my T-shirt on during swim practice. When I showed up to practice the next morning and coach told me to take off my T-shirt before diving in, I fought to keep the tears in. Coach asked me why I was upset. I simply shook my head and said, "I have to keep my shirt on."

I still cry at the wrong times, when an old pain hits me, unexpectedly. A few years ago, my son's best friend's parents were going through a divorce. I was standing with the boy's father at the baseball field when his other son, five years old, called him on his cell phone. The boy had woken up and was scared because his mom wasn't home.

The father looked at me, like, *What am I supposed to do?*

"Go!" I said.

He was worried his wife would get mad. "Go!," I repeated. "It's not about what your wife thinks. This is about your *son!*" I am normally reticent; my intensity made this father pull back as if I'd shoved him.

That evening, I cried for the little girl in me who had not cried so very long ago. Like a bear woken early from its slumber, I will be irritable for days, not able to pinpoint the reason for the dull ache that has stirred inside me. As a mother myself now, my daughter will invariably assume I'm annoyed with her, and I hate how easily the past poisons the present.

In the first couple of years after Mom and Dad's separation, I often felt embarrassed about the clothes I had to wear, clothes from a thrift shop. I reassured myself that my pants were still not as short as Lily Mann's, a girl in my class whose clothes were shabbier than mine. Though, kids teased both of us about our pants—"floods."

My short pants didn't bother me nearly as much as a particular sweater dress I sometimes wore to school. It was like a tunic, except with no leggings, so it was far shorter than a real dress. All day, I'd be nervous about my underwear showing, especially when I sat down or had to pick something up from the floor. I didn't think I was dressed too badly until my fifth-grade teacher, Mrs. McMillan, asked me to stay after class and discreetly handed me a brown paper bag with some of her hand-me-downs. Did it look like I had needed clothes? I wondered, puzzled. But I did like her yellow sweater with ruffled sleeves; it was beautiful, so I shyly thanked her.

One Sunday afternoon, Mom had to go see an interior design client and she left my brother, sister, and me at the mall all day rather than at home. Then she forgot the mall closed at five on a Sunday and didn't arrive until long after the doors were locked, the lights turned off, and the sky black outside.

I didn't cry while we waited in the dark and as the hours dragged on. Instead, I distracted Michelle so she wouldn't cry. I kept her happy, playing patty cake and hopscotch endlessly. I called Dad from a pay phone, but he lived hours away and said to call Joanne, his old neighbor, just a few minutes from the mall. But Joanne wasn't home and I was running out of coins. Brad, meanwhile, hung out in the arcade that was still open.

Mom showed up hours later, so we got home safely but I was mad and scared. Guilt slowly replaced my fear, because I was beginning to hate my mother.

In those first years of my parents' separation, I liked my mother less and loved my father more. I felt like the bad child who was breaking the fifth commandment ("honor thy mother and father"), because I didn't always like my mother, and I certainly did not honor her.

After Dad moved to Franklin Lakes, Mom drove Brad, Michelle, and me the two-and-half hours to his house each Friday after school, and he brought us home on Sundays.

As soon as I turned ten, Mom allowed us to take the Trailways bus from South Jersey (exit 4 on the Turnpike) into the Port Authority in New York City, where we hailed a cab to Dad's work.

"The ABC building, 54th and 6th, please," I announced proudly.

The cab fare was just over three dollars; with a tip, no more than five. One time when Michelle and I went to visit Dad for the weekend, without my brother, I didn't realize I'd given the driver a twenty instead of a five. I told him to keep the change. The driver only thanked me and didn't tell me, a child, that I had given him too much. Brad, with his street smarts, would have noticed. Dad just laughed it off. "No wonder he was so happy with your tip."

Sometimes the bus to New York was sold out, and Mom never got us there early enough to be first in line. One Friday night they were oversold with only two seats left, but Brad, Michelle, and I made three. All the times we took the bus, I sat with Michelle, because it was always my job to take care of her. My brother never wanted to. But that night, he sat next to Michelle, and made me sit on the floor. Brad said it was only fair, because he was the oldest. It made me mad, especially as I had worn a dress to look nice at Dad's work and the floor of the bus was dirty.

Thirty years later, I wonder that my parents let us venture into

New York on our own. But growing up, my siblings and I never thought that what we did was unusual. It was part of the routine and the reality of having separated parents.

Dad DJ'd from six to ten P.M., Monday through Saturday, so we always went to work with him on the weekends when it was his turn to have us. Dan Ingram was on the air before him, and Chuck Leonard came on afterward. Chuck was a tall black man. With his bell-bottoms, he reminded me of the guy on the TV show *The Mod Squad*.

Sometimes Brad and I walked over to the Joy Deli, two blocks from ABC, to get sandwiches for dinner. For Dad, we always brought back the "two teas, lemon on the side" that he needed for his radio voice. One night I had left my Diet Pepsi in the mini fridge in the TV lounge, and someone took it. Dad told me to go confront Mr. Pigg, the DJ in the other studio, WPLJ that played hard rock. I thought Dad was teasing, making me call him a pig for taking my soda. But that was his name, Tony Pigg. Mr. Pigg's studio was small and dark, so different from Dad's big and bright studio. With their long hair and jeans, even the WPLJ disc jockeys seemed different from the WABC DJs. Dad would never wear jeans to work. He always wore a turtle neck or a shiny, collared shirt and slacks.

Music was my Dad's life, whether at home or at work, and so it was woven into my memories. Some homes have bookshelves. Ours had a record case that Dad built himself to hold all his albums. The unit stretched along the entire living-room wall, filled with shelves and shelves of albums. Promoters and musicians sent Dad their music, hoping he'd play their songs, so he had a big collection. One of the rooms in Dad's house, probably what would have been Brad's bedroom if our parents had gotten back together, was filled with cardboard boxes of albums, stacked three high, that Dad had never unpacked from his apartment in South Jersey.

There are times now when I am driving by myself, and tune into XM radio, that the music of the seventies takes me back to those nights spent in the studio with my father—a time when I still felt his love. But it is the unexpected moments and songs that catch me off guard—a Friday night at home cooking in the kitchen, and my husband will hook up his iPod to the stereo and the Moody Blues or Barry White will blast out. "Pool party music," he happily declares. I have to stifle a yelp of unexpected longing. I don't dare voice this thought, though. I keep the hurts bottled up, so Keith doesn't hate my father or feel disappointed that he can't fill the hole my dad has left.

While I loved the rock and roll music Dad played, the evenings in the studio could be really boring. We kids couldn't dance or sing along. We had to be quiet. I usually busied myself coloring my Precious Moments coloring book. Mrs. Parker had taught me how to crochet, so sometimes I crocheted while in the studio. I once crocheted a blanket for Michelle in shades of pink, and when I finished that, I made a yellow sweater vest for my mother, a hint that there was a time in the early days of their separation when I still loved her.

Whenever Dad was on the air, there was a big red light like a police siren, on his desk that lit up. He used a stopwatch to time his intros to a song, and sometimes he'd dedicate songs to people. Once in a while, he'd talk about our mom. "Barry White, he's got the kind of voice every man wants to have when he's callin' up his ex-wife negotiating alimony." He'd give the cue with a wave of his finger to the engineer to amp up the music and Barry would sing, "You're my first. You're my last. You're my everything!"

The song from Lou Rawls made me sad, though. I could hear Dad's loneliness in the song's words. "You'll never find another love like mine."

But Dad never talked about Mom, never asked what she was doing. I sometimes wonder what kind of person has that sort of discipline. But was he stifling it? Perhaps he was cutting off his feelings entirely. It's only now that I realize this is how my father coped with his pain. At the time, it seemed that Dad was being a good parent and trying not to put us kids in the middle of him and my mother.

Mom, on the other hand, grilled us after every visit. It wasn't interest in us. What I couldn't figure out was if she loved David (as my father had told me), then why was she crying all the time? She went out a lot and sometimes a man would come home with her and sleep over.

Early one Saturday morning, I tried to stop Michelle from going into Mom's bedroom. As I ran to catch Michelle, too late before she barged in, I saw the naked man heading into the bathroom. I saw his *thing!*

I had never seen this man before and never saw him again. That morning, I had to sit next to him at the breakfast table while Mom made him breakfast. It bugged me. She *never* cooked, and here she was pretending in front of this stranger like she always cooked.

"Do you like your eggs cooked in bacon fat or butter?" she cooed to him.

Yuk.

I wrote in my diary: *My mom wants me to wear the same bummy thing as last week. Then she says, wear what you want. I don't care. Well, I know she doesn't care. She cares more about men. Daddy said no man is going to sleep with you in the bed he bought, and a man did with nothing on, and when he left he said I love you, and then they went out. I don't want a new Dad.*

Despite Dad's unusual job and having to go to work with him, it was the weekends with him that seemed normal, not the times at home with my mother. We went grocery shopping and did laundry at the Laundromat, since Dad didn't own a washing machine. It was Dad who taught me how to make a bed, fold the sheets, and how to clean. His upstairs hallway was dark brown linoleum tiles. So it was important to spray the dust mop first, then make an even zigzag across the floor. He taught me to tilt my head to see if the shift in sunlight showed any dust I may have missed. I followed his instructions perfectly. This mundane lesson became a significant point in my life, because cleaning played a role in my final disowning.

When we were with Mom, I felt alone. With Dad, I felt support. I would remind Michelle to brush her teeth, comb her hair, and she shouted back. "Don't tell me what to do! You're not my mother!"

Then Dad would scold both Michelle and my brother. "She's better than the mother you got, so don't talk to your sister like that!"

Mom hated that I was beginning to favor my father and did what she could to turn me against him, frequently bad-mouthing him.

In the fifth grade, at age eleven, I had my first experience in a school play, in the chorus for *The King and I*. It was not a big part, but the one thing I was good at was memorizing lines. For the scene reenacting the story of Uncle Tom's cabin, I could recite all the lyrics perfectly, louder than any other actor.

I called to ask Dad if he would be able to come. He hesitated. He certainly hesitated. Finally, he said, no, he had to work that night. I knew this of course. But my mother was relentless.

"You think he's working? He's not working. He's going to Florida with Pat!"

So the night of the play, I did my performance and, as soon as we got home, I ran upstairs to my bedroom and turned on the radio. My father was not on the air. My mother had been right, and I hated her for showing me that my father had lied to me; not only that he had lied, but that seeing me in a play wasn't as important to him as his girlfriend.

Mom started to prod us about whether or not Pat was pregnant. It had something to do with a song Dad had dedicated to Pat, Paul Anka's "You're Having My Baby." I didn't understand anything about the birds and bees, but I understood it had something to do with sleeping in the same bed.

Whenever we were at Dad's and Pat came up to visit (she lived two-and-a-half hours away in Philadelphia), Pat slept on the sofa. I swore to my mother that Pat slept on the sofa.

My mother scoffed at me, "You're so naïve!" (Well, jeez, at ten, let's hope I was naïve!)

So one weekend, I devised a plan to prove that Pat always slept on the sofa. Saturday night, Dad and Pat were going out with his neighbors, who had two kids Michelle's age. As the neighbors had a babysitter, she would watch us too, and then Brad, Michelle, and I would spend the night next door. So on Friday night when we got to Dad's, I slept on the sofa and the next morning I put the sheets and blankets folded just so and stacked in a particular order in the big red trunk in Dad's living room.

Sunday morning after we got back from the neighbor's, I checked the trunk to see if the sheets had been used by Pat. They had not.

They were still folded neatly, just as I had left them. I stared at those sheets for a long time, wondering what it all meant.

Then, because I had to defend my father, I told my mother about my trick, only I lied to her. I vowed that the sheets were crumpled and disorganized, proof that Pat had slept on the sofa.

For all the times my mother made my father look bad in my eyes, it only made her look worse for revealing him to me. I didn't want to know.

I could measure the further demise in my parents' relationship by how we spent the holidays. For the first Thanksgiving after their separation, my parents tried to have dinner as a family. Dad was living in his apartment so he went to Philly for the Thanksgiving Day parade in his own car. We normally went together. As a DJ, Dad would be in the parade in WFIL's double decker bus.

One year, Dad ran to the side of the parade where we were watching, grabbed baby Michelle from Mom's arms, and showed her proudly to the people lined along the streets. The first year they were separated, we were late and missed the parade. When we got back to the house in Alluvium, my parents immediately started fighting. It got worse when Dad saw that Mom had cooked the turkey upside down.

The first Christmas they were separated, Dad was a pushover with the tree in his apartment. We had two trees that year, one at home and one at Dad's apartment. Dad let us get one of those trees sprayed with white to make it look like fresh snow. Michelle and I lobbied for a pink one, but Dad drew a line at the white one. It made a "royal mess," as he said, but it was so pretty. That Christmas, I gave him a photo album so he wouldn't miss us so much. Dad was into pictures. He had just started a job with the Flyer's hockey team as a freelance photographer.

The second Christmas post separation, I was in fourth grade, nine years old. We spent Christmas day with our mother and went to Franklin Lakes afterward. Dad had a tree, but it felt all wrong. Santa hadn't come to his house. My gift to him that year was a bottle of

Scotch, Johnny Walker Black. At least Mom was still willing to help me get him a gift. He gave me a suede purse in the shape of a sunflower, with a bottle of Charlie perfume and five dollars tucked inside.

The third year after their separation was the worst. Even though Dad and Pat were dating, my parents decided we would spend Christmas as a family. Mom drove us up to Franklin Lakes. On Christmas Eve, my brother, sister, and I went into work with Dad, while Mom stayed behind at Dad's house so she could wrap presents. At least, in theory.

I had been in the TV lounge down the hall and was about to go back into the studio. The "On Air" light was not on, so I started to open the door to go in when I saw my father pick up a carousel of eight-track music tapes and throw it across the room. I quickly backed out of the room.

At first, it wasn't clear why Dad was mad. Brad and I tried to find out from the engineers as they came in and out of the lounge or the WPLJ studio. Someone said the engineer on duty messed up the timing on the intro, missing Dad's cue to start the next song, and making him talk into the song's lyrics. Another said it was that he had put the wrong song on, so that two ballads were played in a row. Dad *was* a perfectionist and could get mad at stuff like that.

Eventually we learned that it was Mom's fault. After a while when it seemed safe to go back into the studio, Brad and I picked up tapes from the floor, carefully putting them back in the rack in numerical order.

Dad eventually muttered, "Your mother called Pat."

Mom apparently went through Dad's phone book and started calling everyone with a female name. Eventually, she found Pat's number. Pat called Dad on the radio station's hotline, blaming him, cursing his ex-wife. When we got home from the station that night, the presents were not wrapped. My parents fought well into the night.

The next morning, Christmas Day, Mom was still wrapping. We had to keep Michelle in Dad's bedroom. Dad, Brad, and I sat on the bed trying to distract Michelle. There was no running downstairs to see if Santa had come or not. I still believed, wanted to believe, but

I wanted Michelle to believe even more. Eventually I offered to go downstairs to help Mom wrap, just so we could start the day. Dad said no. I silently understood he wanted me to keep believing. He needed Christmas to hold its magic, as much as we did.

When I got back to school and to CCD that year, the nun told me Santa wasn't real, the final way to ruin Christmas. My parents never spent another Christmas or Thanksgiving together. Thank God.

The summer after fifth grade, my mother rented a beach house in Avalon with some other single friends. It was a big beautiful Victorian house with a sweeping porch, only a block from the beach. I was disappointed I would not be able to still do swim team at Downs Farm, as we had all the summers before. I would miss seeing all my old friends and the little bit of stability Downs Farm had brought me. But my mother didn't give that any thought. She rarely thought about what I wanted to do, and this beach rental was only about what she wanted.

Most of her friends came down on the weekends only, so during the week, Brad, Michelle, and I each had a bed to sleep in, but on the weekends, we had to sleep on the floor of Mom's room or any other free place. One weekend there was a big party to which friends and boyfriends of all the divorcees renting the house were invited. The mothers marinated hot dogs in a garbage bag. Another girl, the daughter of one of my mother's new housemates, said she would never dare eat that for fear of food poisoning.

There was a man passed out in the hallway. Walter. I heard from the other adults that he was Mom's boyfriend, but I never met him. Someone said, "At least he made it until five o'clock." I stepped over his body, sprawled across the floor, and worried that he might grab my ankle as I walked by. What kind of person sleeps in the middle of the floor?

As the party wore on late into the night, the loud music, the crowded rooms, I looked for a quiet place for Michelle and me to sleep. Outside on the upstairs porch seemed the quietest. I tucked my sister in on the porch swing, then settled myself on the floor beneath her.

At some point during the night, Walter came out onto the porch. He told Michelle to get off the swing. He was going to sleep there. He called her a "broad," and swatted her on the butt to move.

This didn't seem fair to me. We were there first! Nevertheless, I took Michelle's hand and the two of us went to find another place to sleep.

When we visited my father the next week, I complained to him about Walter stealing Michelle's sleeping spot in the night. Dad rarely quizzed us about Mom and her friends, but about this, he wanted to know. Did Michelle have underwear on when Walter swatted her? How exactly did Walter touch her? I insisted it was a quick swat to say scoot, nothing worse.

While we were visiting Dad that week, Mom called him and asked if Michelle and I could stay with him in North Jersey. Her roommates said we were cramping their style. Brad was not a problem for her, because he always went off fishing.

So that summer when I was eleven, Michelle and I lived with Dad for five weeks. It was a longer-than-usual visit, too long to be sleeping on the sofa, so Dad took us shopping for beds. Michelle and I excitedly picked out a bunk bed.

Michelle and I also spent a few days with Aunt Alice, my Dad's aunt on his mother's side, and some cousins in Queens. Aunt Alice used to have her own TV show in the 1950s, known to viewers as Nancy Craig, something to do with cooking. Apparently, she was a trail blazer.

In the last year, as things declined at home with Mom, Brad and I often asked Dad if we could come live with him. The first time I got the courage to ask, Dad was driving and I was in the back seat, where he couldn't see me.

"Daddy, do you think we could come live with you?"

"Aww, honey, you know I'd like that, but it's not possible. I work a lot. Who would take care of you?"

In addition to DJ'ing evenings for WABC, Dad also did play-by-play for the Islanders hockey team, and he traveled with the team all over the country.

I did understand, really. My question was more wishful thinking than a possible future. Of the few children I knew with divorced parents, all of them lived with their mothers. Children did not live with their fathers in the 1970s. It was Mom's job to take care of us.

The last week of that summer before sixth grade, we were supposed to have our beach vacation with Dad in Wildwood Crest; but this year, Pat was joining us, sleeping in a separate bedroom, of course.

Dad, Michelle, and I drove to Avalon to pick up Brad. When we arrived at Mom's beach house, she pleaded with Dad to take us out for a family dinner. He didn't want to. He wanted to get to Wildwood Crest. I wanted to get there, too. The Admiral Hotel always had something fun going on. We might be missing the pizza party or the dance competition. Dinner with our parents was not a happy alternative.

I wondered if Mom just wanted to be taken out for a nice dinner, like they used to when they were married. My father didn't say yes for our sake. By that point, we hated when our parents were in the same room together. I wonder now, did he say yes because he still loved her?

Mom suggested The Sea Breeze at the south end of Avalon and on the waterfront. I had never been there before and immediately admired its elegance, with white tablecloths and linen napkins. The most breathtaking aspect was the view. Windows wrapped around the entire dining room, with spectacular views of the ocean.

The bickering started as soon as the waitress took our orders. Brad with shrimp, Michelle with spaghetti, and Dad apparently selected green beans almandine.

"You never used to like green beans almandine," Mom muttered in a low voice. She blinked her eyes rapidly, something she did before blowing up.

Dad sighed. There was nothing to say.

He changed the subject to a brighter topic. Would Michelle

win the Little Miss Admiral contest again? Who would be best at mini golf? But for Mom, these were not necessarily brighter topics, because she would not be joining us.

I was sitting on the opposite side of the table from my parents, so I don't know what else they were talking about. Dad could have been criticizing Mom for any number of things—giving Brad too much freedom over the summer, partying too much, not getting a stable job. Mom could have been digging at him that he didn't pay enough alimony or sent the checks late, checks that I sometimes found shoved in her junk drawer in the kitchen.

Our food eventually arrived. There was a buzz of restaurant chatter in the background.

"Does Pat cook you green beans almandine?" she hissed.

She picked up her plate and hurled it at my father. She stood and reached for Michelle's plate and hurled it through the air. Brad hurriedly ate his shrimp before she grabbed his plate, too. I was on the far side of the table, so my plate was too far for her to reach. She shouted "son of a bitch" as each plate flew through the air. The plates shattered on the floor around our table as my father tried to deflect them with his hands. Then my mother turned and marched out of the restaurant, deathly silent.

Dad sat there, covered in food and broken plates. It was not the first time Mom had thrown things at him, but it was the first time in public.

After a moment, he stood and, in his booming disc jockey voice, apologized. "Ladies and gentlemen, I'm sorry for disturbing your dinner. As you can see, my wife and I are going through a difficult divorce." He sat back down.

Meanwhile, Michelle was gulping air. Finally the wail came, loud and shrill. Dad told me to take her to the bathroom and clean her up. Some of the food had landed on her.

In the bathroom, Michelle kept sobbing, "But what did Daddy do? Why did Mommy get mad at him? What did Daddy *dooooo*?"

I kept repeating quietly, "He didn't do anything wrong. It's okay. It's okay."

I cleaned Michelle up the best I could, and a waitress came in to help us. I waited until my sister quieted before heading back upstairs to the dining room. As Michelle and I walked back to the table, I studied my feet to avoid the stares of the other people in the dining room. My father and brother were alone at the table, debating what to do.

"Maybe she hasn't left," Brad said.

"Christ, what if the car door is unlocked?" Dad groaned.

I envisioned all kinds of destruction in the parking lot.

"Somebody needs to check if she's gone," Dad said.

"I ain't going," Brad said, shaking his head.

Dad looked to me. I shook my head no.

Brad cut me off before I could speak, "You're already standing. You should go."

Both were staring at me. I could never outmatch my brother's logic and wished I had sat down more quickly. "But what if she's there? What do I say to her?"

Dad tried to make it sound like no big deal. "Just see if she's there, see if the car is locked."

I always did what I was told.

My heart raced as I stepped out of the restaurant. I didn't see her orange Ford Pinto, the new car she had gotten after the Mustang was totaled. I hesitated near Dad's white Grand Am. What if she was hiding on the other side? She could jump out at me. I stayed on the sidewalk and squinted to see if the door lock was down. It was. I raced back inside the restaurant.

Dad paid the bill and we left. As we drove down the highway to Wildwood Crest, we kept a look out for Mom's Pinto. The fight could be continued at the Admiral Hotel. She knew where it was.

At one point, I thought I saw her car far in front of us, but nobody else could see it. Dad tried to make light of things. "Cindi, not even the Bionic Woman can see that far!"

As we drove, Dad asked Brad quietly, "How do you deal with her?" Brad had lived with her most of the summer.

He shrugged. "I get used to it." Maybe Brad was used to it, but maybe it was also that he steered clear of her and often went off fish-

ing or to friends' homes. To this day, he is the one with the best relationship with her.

When we got to the Admiral Motel, Dad told the owner, Gene, and
his girlfriend, Margaret, all about the scene at the restaurant. By then,
he had made it an exciting story, almost funny. How Brad had raced to
finish all his shrimp before our mother could grab his plate! I didn't find
it funny, though. I never have. At what point, I wonder, did I become
such a serious person?

Pat got stuck in traffic, and we waited on the pool deck for her to
show up. Dad kept singing in a rich slow baritone, "Lonely days, lonely
nights, where would I be without my woman?"

When Pat finally pulled up in her blue Chevy Nova, Brad and
Michelle raced over to tell her the exciting story.

I try to remember my mother from before the separation. Did I
love her? Was she normal? I have driven to the apartment we rented
in Ocean City every summer until I was seven and stood on the
deck where she and I once fed the seagulls together. I have tried to
remember the good times, but they are beyond my reach, like shad-
ows in an underdeveloped photo.

Who am I to judge her, anyway? Haven't I, too, thrown a plate,
smashing it to shards when my own daughter, then seven, refused
to clear it from the kitchen table? After such bursts of anger, I feel
shame for days, convinced I will damage my kids. I got the throwing
gene from both my parents, after all. It is only my husband who can
talk sense to me: I didn't throw it *at* anyone, and not in a restaurant,
and there were a dozen things that had built up to my outburst. It's
easy for him to dismiss my fears. He's never thrown a plate, and for
that matter, neither have his parents.

CHAPTER 5

Escape

THE NIGHT WE TRIED to escape from our mother was a Sunday in October 1976. I was eleven and in the sixth grade. We had been with Dad for the weekend, and he had just dropped us off at home in Alluvium. There was the usual tension with Mom after a weekend at Dad's. Whenever we first got back home, it was safer to retreat upstairs to our rooms than to linger downstairs in the kitchen or TV room. Downstairs, Mom might bitch about Dad or grill us for information.

Brad usually went straight to his room to work on one of his model airplanes. He was really good at building them, painting them carefully, and then placing decals precisely to match the real planes. His model of the Starship Enterprise was my favorite.

The sky was already black that Sunday night. I was in my room, doing homework, when I heard their voices, a fight brewing. I went to the doorway of Brad's room, to see what was going on. Mom was yelling at Brad to unpack his suitcase. Michelle was hovering near Mom. Brad was intent on gluing one more piece of his model airplane and said he'd unpack when he was done with the model.

Mom wanted him to unpack "RIGHT NOW!" She smashed the plane and started throwing things at Brad—books, other model planes, anything within reach on his desk.

His yellow plastic lamp flew across the room and flashed blue as it struck Michelle in the face. I grabbed her and pulled her out of the way. We ran down the hallway. Michelle and I hid in Mom's room, behind the stone fireplace that divided the bedroom area from the makeshift office with the balcony overlooking the living room below.

I shushed Michelle and reached for the phone to call Daddy. Would he be home yet? *Please, please, please answer.*

Finally, he answered.

I whispered hurriedly, "Daddy, she's going crazy! She's throwing things. Michelle got hit in the face with a lamp!"

Dad tried to calm me down. I heard Brad shouting in the hallway.

"Let me call my father! I want to call my father!" There was another phone in the hallway, just outside Brad's bedroom and mine.

I whispered to Dad, my heart racing. "Wait. Shhh." I was trying to listen to hear whether or not Mom would let Brad call. "I have to hang up."

"Cindi, wait, don't—"

If Mom knew I was on the phone with Dad, what would she do? I quickly hung up, before getting caught.

Michelle and I cowered in the dark corner, waiting, trying to hear what was happening in the hallway. I shushed Michelle to keep her from crying too loudly. Her cheek was red where the lamp had struck her.

Mom was still screaming at Brad—but we could hear Brad calling Dad on the hall phone.

When I heard Brad hang up, I called Dad back. He was going to call my friend Jill's mom, Mrs. Parker across the street, to come get us.

Michelle and I stayed hidden, listening in fear of what our mother might do next.

Eventually the fight between Brad and Mom subsided, and she called for Michelle and me. I didn't want to go, but I was more scared of what would happen if I didn't. I gripped Michelle's hand, keeping her behind me as we cautiously went into the hallway.

The shrill ring of the hallway phone made me jump. Brad grabbed the phone from the cradle on the wall. The three of us stood in the hallway, scared to move, scared to bolt, trying to keep a safe distance from our mother who had Brad cornered in his bedroom doorway. I eyed the stairs as a way for Michelle and I to bolt. Brad simply nodded his head in response to whatever Dad was saying, holding in tears, then hung up.

Mom told us to get ready for bed. She started past my sister and me, and I hurried Michelle into her bedroom out of my mother's path. We pretended to get ready for bed.

As soon as Mom was downstairs and out of earshot, Brad, Michelle, and I met in my bedroom. Brad explained that Mrs. Parker couldn't come get us. She was worried about meddling. But if we could get out of our house and across the street to hers, she was willing to take us to the bus station and put us on a bus to New York to meet Dad.

Brad and I studied the roof outside my bedroom window overlooking the driveway. The drop to the driveway was not that far. If we clung to the beams that jutted out, we could drop onto the gravel drive. One of us would have to help Michelle onto the roof and drop her down. Brad and I squabbled about who should go first.

I heard Mom's footsteps coming up the stairs. I hurriedly put my robe on over my clothes, so it would at least look like I was ready for bed.

We had to wait for Mom to go back downstairs and to stop checking what we were up to.

The night wore on. We couldn't go to bed, and we were too scared to climb out the window. I thought Brad should go first, because he would be strong enough to catch Michelle. Brad thought I should go first, even though I am afraid of heights.

Finally, Dad called again and Mom hovered while Brad talked to him on the phone in the hallway. Brad just kept nodding his head, but he had a defeated look. When he hung up and Mom was out of earshot, Brad said Dad told us to stay there. To calm down. To do exactly as our mother told us to do and to not provoke her.

My sister slept in my room that night, afraid to sleep in her own bed.

We went to school the next day, like we always did, but nothing was the same. I didn't laugh or play with my friends at recess. I was afraid of my mother, and my father couldn't help us.

On Thursday, Mom announced we would be spending the week-end with our father. It wasn't his turn, so the change in schedule con-fused me, but I didn't question her, not wanting to make her mad.

We took the bus to New York Friday night, then took a cab to the ABC building as we often had. It was like a normal visit. But the next morning things were different.

Dad said he needed to talk to us. So Brad, Michelle, and I sat at the table in the plastic orange chairs in the empty would-be dining room in Dad's house in Franklin Lakes. The sun shone through the floor-to- ceiling windows, and outside the fall trees swayed in hues of yellow and red. Dad asked us if we wanted to live with him. He made clear that he worked a lot and his schedule would not change. We would only see him for a short time after school and on Sundays when there wasn't a hockey game. But he would never leave us alone. We would find a babysitter together. Brad and I would get three dol-lars allowance a week. He did not promise unlimited root beer, as he had done when my parents first separated.

Dad's last condition was that either we would all come live with him, or none of us would. "You three kids have to stick together," he said.

Dad enrolled us in new schools that week and took us shopping for clothes, as we had only been prepared for a weekend visit. We went to court the following week at Camden County Courthouse in South Jersey. I saw Mom in the hallway, outside the courtroom. She looked sad, with her shoulders slumped and her eyes red. I knew it was because of us. I didn't go hug her, though. I didn't know if we were allowed to or not. I didn't mean to hurt her. I just didn't want to live with her anymore.

Mom and Dad and the lawyers went into the courtroom while Brad and I waited in the hallway, sitting on hard wooden benches and watching people's feet clack hurriedly along the tiled floor. Michelle didn't come with us to court that day. In the court transcripts, Dad said she was sick. But now, I wonder if he thought she was too little to be much good to him in court.

The judge ordered each of us to talk to a court-appointed psy-chiatrist, Dr. Yaskin, on the same day. Dr. Yaskin's office was dark and filled with tall book shelves, so I felt trapped, even though he stayed behind his desk.

He asked me *why* I didn't want to live with my mother. I couldn't answer him. I told him I didn't like the way she made me clean the whole house, usually by myself. But I didn't share any other stories with him. How could I have known the difference between what was normal and what was not, which stories mattered and which didn't?

When I came out of Dr. Yaskin's office, Dad asked, "Did you tell him about when she left you alone at the mall, after it closed?"

I shook my head no.

"Did you tell him about Walter slapping Michelle on the bottom?" No.

My father asked about more instances, and I stared at the white tiled floor. I knew then I hadn't done a good job of convincing the important stranger why I wanted to live with my father.

I can look back on the psychiatrist session now and lament how awful child psychology was in those days. Where were the brightly-colored walls to make me feel comfortable? How about a safe, open-ended question like, "What's your favorite breakfast?" *Not Tang, but that's all there is!* Instead there were just the point-blank, brutal ones: "why don't you want to live with your mother? Do you love your mother?"

We waited for the judge's ruling in the diner across the street from the court house. Dad's lawyer finally came over and broke the news: Dad could have Brad and me; Michelle belonged with her mother.

I blamed myself. I hadn't given enough details. I hadn't said enough bad things about my mother.

I saw the pain in my father's eyes. A few moments passed before he said firmly, "No. The children stay together." I assumed this meant we would have to go back to our mother's house.

Instead, the lawyer negotiated more with the judge. If the neighbors testified that our mother was unfit, the judge would reconsider the ruling. Michelle, too, had to talk to Dr. Yaskin, who eventually declared Michelle was "ambivalent" about where she wanted to live. *Duh!* She probably just evaded answering his questions, as any six-year old would do when faced with a lose-lose outcome. I suspect to each of his questions, she shrugged and replied, "I don't know." She wasn't ambivalent. She was smart. And *adamant* about staying neutral.

In the weeks that followed, two neighbors wrote affidavits about how we were often left alone, shabbily dressed, how the lights in our bedrooms were on past midnight, and other details as evidence of our mother's neglect.

I hated picturing these neighbors saying these things about my mother and how she had to face them every day, knowing what they thought about her. Couldn't the neighbors have been left out of this ordeal? My mother lost not only her children that week, but also her dignity, her ability to pull into the driveway in her orange and white Ford Pinto and walk proudly into a house that once was to be her and my father's dream home.

My father was granted sole custody, making him even larger in my life than he already was.

That first custody hearing in October 1976 marked the first of many hearings, affidavits, and complaints over the next four years. I never got to say good-bye to my school friends from South Jersey. Dad took Brad and me to our old school late one afternoon to clean out our lockers. I found my last social studies project on the top shelf—a stone tied to a stick that was my idea for a tool a caveman might have once used. It was a project I never even got to present. While we were at the school, we saw our old principal, Mr. Brittingham, and got to say good-bye to him. Mr. Brittingham had moved from the fourth and fifth grade school up to the middle school the year before, when Brad started junior high. In fourth grade, when Brad and I once missed the bus and our mother wasn't home, I had called the school to ask if someone could please come get us. It was Mr. Brittingham who came to get us, and I suspect such a kind gesture was as forbidden then as it is now.

Our sudden move to live with our father started in trauma, but it marked the beginning of what I have always thought of as my family's golden years.

CHAPTER 6

Our Golden Years

HE TRIED SO HARD to be the perfect dad. It's the way he was then that showed me how to be a good mother to my own children. It is the memories from these years I relish most, memories that have allowed me to forgive him, to overlook the years of rejection.

He often said, "I may not have any money, but I am the richest man in the world, because I have my children."

Dad had been trying to sell the house in Franklin Lakes. It took two years. He bought a smaller house in Oakland, the next town over, on the busy, windy Breakneck Road. Dad sometimes called it "Break Your Neck Road." We moved a few weeks after Dad got custody of us. The house was a contemporary, California-style home, with cedar siding and an open carport for a garage. The garage was Dad's first project; with all the snow in New Jersey, he had the carport enclosed. In the two years he had owned the big house in Franklin Lakes, he never once attempted a house project; but that house was a bitter reminder of Mom and Dad's failed attempt at getting back together. At Breakneck Road, Dad nurtured the house as much as he nurtured us.

The house was nestled in the woods. There was so much shade that there was no lawn, just woodchips all around the house. Our bedrooms were on the ground floor and smaller than in Alluvium or in Franklin Lakes. My new bedroom held a twin bed and a dresser, with barely enough room to walk between them, and I had to stand to the side to open a drawer.

Dad wallpapered the far wall with a mural of a lush forest and waterfall, which made the room seem bigger. In Michelle's room, Dad took all her favorite posters from the Ringling Brothers circuses he had taken us to over the years and collaged them, filling the wall with tigers, elephants, and beautiful ladies on the trapeze. Brad's mural was of a skier.

Dad's bedroom was upstairs along with the kitchen and family room. Under the cathedral ceiling, he hung square mirror tiles, having Rickels Hardware store cut the squares into perfect triangles to cover the apex.

Dad was as organized with running the house as he was with his radio playlists and memorizing the roster of the opposing hockey team. With little time to grocery shop, he made a menu that lasted the whole month, planning both breakfasts and dinners. His schedule got even busier that year when he also started doing the weekend sportscast on ABC's Channel 7.

He warned us when we asked to come live with him that we would not see him much during the week, so it was always a treat when we came home from school and Dad was still getting ready for work. Normally he left the house by three thirty to avoid getting stuck in traffic at the Lincoln Tunnel. On the days he left a little late, we'd hang out with him in the bathroom while he shaved. I'd watch him in the mirror and tell him about school. I loved the smell of his Old Spice, a scent that filled me with pangs of longing the first time my son learned to use deodorant. The half hour wasn't much time, but it was more than what we had before we lived with him.

Our babysitter, Jane, was always there before Dad left. We were never left alone, so different from when we had lived with our mother.

Even though Dad didn't get home until just after eleven at night, he always got up with us in the morning. Mother never had. We ate breakfast together most mornings. When Dad thought everyone needed to lose weight, he'd serve us pink grapefruit. He'd slice each wedge for us so we could scoop the wedges out with a spoon, then sprinkle sugar on top, clearly undoing the idea of low calorie, but still.

If Brad or I had a test, Dad made us a hot breakfast, usually pancakes or French toast. His French toast was one of his specialties. He'd buy this special country-style bread then leave the slices on the counter overnight, something about the slices of bread hardening just enough so the French toast wouldn't come out soggy. He topped it off with a slice of butter on each piece of bread, while they sizzled on the griddle. We could add syrup and sugar. For pancakes, regular sugar was best. For French toast, powdered sugar was better.

One morning before school, Dad and I had a fight. I don't remember what it was about. I never talked back, but I hated when he "talked" to us; they weren't really "talks," but more admonishments of how we had done wrong and disappointed him. I would feel so guilty for the slightest infraction: a messy room, a bad grade, not looking after Michelle when we visited Mom. I didn't want to let my father down, ever. When I did, it felt like I would lose his love; that would be the end of my world. There were times I said to our babysitter, Jane, that I wished my father would just hit me. I thought a smack would hurt less than his talks and that the pain of disappointing him would subside more quickly, but he never hit me, not then.

This particular morning, the fight ended with Dad shouting, "If you don't like it, you can go back and live with your mother!"

I didn't reply. I kept everything inside. I never wanted to go back to live with my mother. I ran out of the house and up the driveway to catch the mini school bus, stifling my tears.

The sadness stayed with me throughout the school day. *Would Daddy really send us back to live with Mom?* At some point during the afternoon, a voice came through the loud speaker.

"Mrs. Goldberg, please send Cindi Michael to the office."

A couple of the kids snickered. "Ooh, Cindi's in trouble."

I knew they were teasing, because I never got in trouble. If anything, I was usually the teacher's pet.

I made my way through the halls, down the stairs, and rounded the corner. My father stood outside the office, in his black turtleneck and camel sport coat. He stood alone in the white hallway. I hesitated.

He came over to me. "I came to say I'm sorry. I didn't want the hurt to stay all day until I saw you tomorrow." He hugged me tightly.

I cried on his shoulder, breathing in the comfort of his after-shave. "I'm sorry, too, Daddy. I love you."

"I love you, too."

It's the only time I remember him saying he was sorry. As I grew older, he never again apologized. But on that day, he did and it mattered and I never forgot.

In 1976, there weren't many fathers who didn't work during the day, so school field trips were the domain of mothers. My dad was different. He came on my sixth grade class field trip to the Maple Farm. Everyone wanted to be in Mr. Michael's group; because, one, he was a dad and, two, he was cool. He could talk sports or music with anyone. All my classmates wanted to know how to win a WABC prize giveaway, whether an album or a moped. The visit to the maple tree farm was boring, but having my dad there made it special. I was so proud of him, and so glad my new friends liked him.

One weekend, after visiting Mom, I had left the script for the school play at her house. I called her as soon as I realized back at home Sunday night. I had the lead and was still memorizing my lines. We visited Mom every other weekend and it would be hard to do without my script for two weeks. Could she mail it?

The next day, after school, I was in Mrs. Goldberg's room, when I saw someone who looked like my mother walk by: a tall, blonde woman, head held high.

I ran over to the door and looked down the hallway. "Mom?" She turned. It was her.

"What are you doing here?" I asked.

"I brought your script."

I felt guilty. She drove two hours just to bring me my script? She was unpredictable like that. She would make a big gesture like this, then leave us alone at the mall past closing.

My teacher said quietly, "I better get Mr. Simon."

Mr. Simon was my guidance counselor. I thought my mother was in trouble for not signing in at the front office.

Later, I heard Dad shouting at her on the phone. "You caused a panic at the school! You're not allowed anywhere near the school!"

I didn't know the judge had made this rule. I knew, though, that there was no panic. Dad was exaggerating. It didn't change the fact that it was my fault, though. I had gotten my mother in trouble.

Oakland, New Jersey, is in the middle of the Ramapo Mountains. One of the best things about Oakland is the Recreation ("rec") fields in the middle of town, cradled by tree-lined hills.

On any given spring day, there were three or four softball and baseball games going on simultaneously. It was the place to meet friends, cheer them on in a game, and hang out.

The first spring we lived with Dad, he signed Brad up for baseball and me for softball. It seemed almost every kid in town played. There were about eight different girls' teams per grade, and we were assigned to different colors. My first year, I was on the Blue Sox.

Neither Brad nor I had ever played before. Swimming was the last organized sport for both of us. After a few practices, Brad said he wanted to drop it. I told Brad I stunk at softball, too, but that he should stick with it. My dad hated failure. More than that, he hated quitters.

Dad leant me his glove. It was big for my little hand, but it was soft. Dad oiled it to keep it that way, making it easy to wrap my hand around the ball. He stood at the side of our house in the wood chips, teaching me how to throw.

When we practiced batting, Michelle was the outfielder and Brad the catcher. This was not a big deal for Michelle, because I could never hit the ball. Dad and Brad laughed at how pathetic I was. I laughed, too. I was terrible, but determined. Determination is one of the better traits my father blessed me with.

Eventually, at the side of our house, I could catch, throw, and hit. But put me in a game and I struck out every time.

Some games were weeknights, and Dad had to miss those, but he was always at the Saturday morning games. When I struck out, I couldn't look at him. He was disappointed. Most of the time, they put me in the outfield, where I could do the least damage.

By eighth grade when I was fourteen, I stopped being so nervous and, when I made contact with the ball, it could turn into a double.

Donna Duke was on my team. She was a freshman in high school, but with her big boobs and makeup, she looked a lot older. She'd flash my dad a wide smile as she strutted past him, "Hello, Mr. Michael*llll*," the *l* rolling slowly across her tongue.

Pat thought Donna had a crush on Dad. I thought that was weird, but Pat was only just out of college herself. However, I assumed Dad was just popular with everyone.

Donna was a slugger. When her ball went foul, flying into the next field, she shouted "Heads up!" so nobody would get hit in the head from behind. It became a running joke in our house. "Cindi," Dad would say, "you should have shouted 'Heads up' with that foul!"

But there was something about Donna that my father admired. She was bold. She was a good softballer. I was quiet. I wished I could be more like Donna Duke.

The real tragedy of my softball career was that it peaked the year my Dad didn't come to a single game. I was in ninth grade, on the Green Sox team, alternating between catcher and short stop. In one game alone, I caught at least three foul tips and got three players out. My coaches gave me the game ball that day, and I even made it to the All Stars that season. I wondered if I played better that year because my father wasn't there, and I didn't feel the pressure.

When I think about little league baseball, I think more about Brad, even though he only lasted a few days. I can still picture his face at thirteen as we stood along the fence. He didn't look happy. He looked beaten. I see now how all the dads are at their sons' baseball practices. By middle school, all the boys know what to do and most have been playing for years. Up until that spring, had Dad ever thrown a ball with Brad? Sure, he rode the waves at the beach with us, but I don't remember Dad ever taking Brad to a ball game or throwing a ball with him except to help me practice that first year he got custody. I've heard that Brad now coaches his own sons' little league teams. I wonder if that's why Brad gave up that spring: because our dad couldn't be there. Because our dad never showed Brad how to play.

For so much of my youth, I judged my brother. I thought he did things intentionally just to piss our father off. I wonder now which one of us has had it harder. My brother has endured a lifetime of my father's look of disappointment, of never being quite good enough.

In seventh grade, when I was twelve, I got the lead part in *Pygmalion*, playing Eliza Doolittle. Dad couldn't come to the evening performance because of work, so he came during the day to the school assembly. From behind the curtain, as we readied for the performance, I could see him, the lone parent in the cafeteria. He sat to the side by himself, at one of the tables. My classmates and the teachers filled the chairs of the auditorium. This was the first play my dad would see me in. I could do the weird scowl in the way that made everyone laugh.

My voice projected a perfect Cockney accent, and later, a snobbish London one. "The rain in Spain falls mainly on the plain."

When he drove us home after the assembly, Brad in the front seat, me in the back, I asked, "So what did you think, Dad?"

"I thought it was great. You did great."

Brad chimed in, "I thought you said it was boring."

Dad swatted Brad on the leg to shush him, but the damage was done. It was not enough that I got the lead. It was not enough that I could memorize all my lines. To impress my Dad, I needed to show star potential.

But in seventh grade, I just wasn't there yet.

Once we moved to Maryland, he never came to another play.

Things may have been idyllic in Oakland, but they were anything but when it came to dealing with my mother. Instead of getting better after she lost custody of us, she got worse and I dreaded visiting her.

We were supposed to see her every other weekend. This meant leaving my father, leaving my friends, leaving normalcy. Mom usually went out on a date or with friends when we visited. So why were we there?

Even though Dad told her not to, Mom continued to grill us about him, about his girlfriend Pat, about everything. She knew the judge originally had ordered Michelle to live with her, and she continued to prey on this hope of getting at least one of us back. No way would Brad or I ever change our minds, but Michelle was only six. Mom worked on Michelle, trying to convince her to come live with her.

"If you were a good girl, you would tell the judge you want to live with me. You are so naughty, such a naughty little girl."

When Michelle was in second grade, she took up soccer. The team traveled by bus to neighboring towns. I don't know why Dad and I didn't go to this particular game. Maybe it was too far. Maybe it was that Mom was coming up to watch Michelle, and by this point, it was safer if Mom and Dad weren't together, even at opposite ends of a soccer field.

I was in the kitchen baking or writing a poem, my new-found hobby. Dad was on the kitchen phone, when he suddenly slammed it down, his voice loud and etched with fear. "Emergency call coming through!" He picked the phone up on the first ring. "George Michael," he barked.

It was a woman, a stranger who was with Michelle. My sister had been crying alone at the soccer field for more than an hour. Mom had driven off to get a cup of coffee and had left her dog with Michelle. The dog was not allowed on the bus, so when the game was over Michelle didn't know what to do.

My father sped through the town until we found the soccer field. When we pulled into the parking lot, people were standing with their backs to us, watching the game. Michelle faced the parking lot, looking for Dad's white Grand Am. Her tear-stained face was red and swollen. Her little body shuddered with each breath. She still held the leash for Mom's dog. In that moment, I hated my mother. Absolutely hated her.

Michelle broke into a fresh bout of tears when Dad and I walked up, and he spoke to the woman who had been watching her.

It was then that Mom pulled up. She said she had gotten lost. Dad was livid.

Dad had me take Michelle to the car. I couldn't hear their angry words, but I could see them fighting.

As we drove back to Oakland, Dad told Michelle it wasn't her fault. She couldn't have known what to do. He did not vent about our mother to us.

When we got back to Oakland, we stopped at the Grand Union grocery store to pick up a few groceries—and saw Mom in the parking lot. She needed money for the Turnpike tolls. Dad refused to help her. Michelle offered to help. "I have some money in my piggy bank."

"After what she just did to you?" I said to Michelle, flabbergasted. "Why do you want to give her *anything?*"

Michelle's voice was small. "But how will she get home?"

Michelle could so quickly block out any memory that hurt. I know it was her way of surviving. There have been many times I wished I could be more like Michelle. I often said, "If only somebody would give me a lobotomy, I'd be perfectly fine."

But then I think about the happy memories that have kept my love for my family alive all these years. Would I have to lose those, too?

And then I have to wonder: did Michelle really block memories out, or did they linger vaguely, like an odorless gas that slowly poisons its helpless victim?

One day Michelle came home from school and told me she hated school. "The other kids are making fun of me. They're teasing me about my bald spot."

"What bald spot?"

I looked at the top of her scalp, and sure enough, she had a bald spot the size of a quarter.

The spot got larger as time went on, so Dad finally took her to a doctor. The doctor said it was from nerves. He could insert a long needle into Michelle's scalp to make the hair grow back almost immediately, but Michelle screamed at the sight of it. So Dad opted for the cream, and it was up to me to rub it into my sister's scalp, three times a day.

I can still feel Michelle's bare scalp, the edges of the roots where she still had hair. I blamed my mother for this, so much so that years later, I would remember Michelle as having developed her bald patch when we lived with our mother. Life was bad when we lived with my mother but perfect when we lived with my father, right?

As I realized the mistake in my memory decades later, I wondered if Michelle was also stressed by trying to be perfect for our father. I thought about a remark our babysitter Jane had made to me about a drawing Michelle had once done, a drawing of our family. In it, she was very, very small and on the edge of the paper. My Dad was very large and in the center. Jane, who was a college student majoring in early child development, said this drawing was not right. Michelle should be in the middle and larger. There was something wrong with Michelle's view of herself, Jane said. I tried to argue with Jane that the drawing was just to scale. It didn't mean anything. It was only in high school that I, too, felt lost in my father's larger-than-life shadow. He was our everything.

Once, when I was in seventh grade, Dad and Pat took a trip to Florida together before they were married; Jane stayed with us. Dad had told all of us not to tell our mother about the trip.

Michelle could not keep the secret. She was seven. Then Mom showed up at Dad and Pat's hotel.

He was still furious when he got back to New Jersey. He confronted all of us in the upstairs kitchen. Michelle admitted telling Mom where he had gone on vacation. He slapped her across her bare arm. I didn't know how to stop him. When the blue hand print appeared on her arm, I blamed myself. I should have intervened. It's been thirty years, and the fact that I could not protect my sister still hurts. It's one of the few moments in my life when I could clearly say, "Dad was wrong."

For Christmas that year, Michelle made Mom a special present in school. The children hollowed out oranges and stuffed them with cinnamon and cloves. Michelle put the oranges in a red net that could be hung anywhere, a homemade air freshener. Mom did not like Michelle's present, not at all. She hissed, "I bet you *bought* Pat something nice." My mother was such a jerk. I assured Michelle it was beautiful, and it smelled wonderful.

But I wasn't there for the scene that probably traumatized Michelle the most. She went by herself to visit Mom for the weekend. Sunday night, Mom called to say she couldn't drive Michelle home. She had thrown her back out. Dad had to work so he couldn't drive to South Jersey to get her; and Michelle was too young to ride the bus alone. So, Michelle would have to miss a day of school. But one day turned into two, and on day three, the school called Dad saying an elementary school in South Jersey had requested Michelle's school records. Mom had enrolled Michelle in a school down there . . . and was refusing to return her.

The lawyer couldn't help. The police could not forcibly remove Michelle from Mom's home without a judge's order, and that would take time. That Dad had sole custody meant the police could only help if Michelle happened to be outside when they pulled up. I don't know that it was a good thing that she was.

Dad told us later that Michelle was playing outside when the police cars pulled up. They frightened her, and she started crying, thinking she had done something wrong.

I hated my mother for traumatizing my sister like this, and loved my father for keeping us together.

But it is the image of my sister's face, afraid and caught in the middle—then and now—that has allowed me to forgive her for the pain she has inflicted on me in the years since.

By eighth grade, when I was thirteen, I did not want to visit my mother anymore, and we had a final fight the weekend she moved into a new townhome. When she lost custody of us, her alimony had been reduced and she had to sell the house in Alluvium.

I was unpacking what would be Michelle's and my new bedroom, and I asked Mom where she wanted me to put something. She got mad, as she often did, and started screaming. She threw the curling iron across the room. Other things flew past me as well. I froze until her tantrum passed. When I got home to my father's after the weekend, I told him I did not want to visit her anymore.

He insisted that I had to keep visiting her. "She's your mother."

Mom called incessantly. When she was mad about something, eight times an hour. The judge eventually issued an order about how often she was allowed to call. There was no such thing as caller ID in 1979, so we had to answer the phone in case it was somebody else.

Mom once called and accused me of stealing her hair dryer. I hadn't, but she could not find it and didn't believe me. She reduced me to tears, telling me to look for it anyway. I hung up on her.

She called back. We fought, and I hung up again.

When I didn't answer the phone, the babysitter did. My mother told her to search my room. I called my new best friend, Donna Saraisky, crying. I had met her in sixth grade in my new school. She and her twin sister stood out in the cafeteria, wearing kerchiefs over their wavy, thick brown hair. Kerchiefs were not in fashion in middle school, and I later learned that Donna and her sister Lauren wore them in solidarity with a friend who had Leukemia.

The night my mother kept calling the house accusing me of stealing her hair dryer, Donna and her father came to get me. I cried to Donna about my mother, her craziness, and what a bad person I was for not loving my own mother.

As Dad and Pat were going to be at work until late, and I was still upset, the Saraiskies offered to have me sleep over. I didn't know then that one day I would call the Saraiskies *family*, and that they would be there for both my weddings and the birth of my two children; whereas, my father would not be there for any of these events.

When my Dad came to pick me up the next morning at Donna's, he was mad at me, mad that I had called Donna, mad that I had gone crying to the Saraiskies, and mad that I hadn't handled this on my own.

My father wanted me to rely on him and only him. If he wasn't available, I should get a grip.

That Thanksgiving, it was Mom's turn to have us, and I didn't want to go. Dad said I wouldn't have to go only if I got sick.

The Wednesday before Thanksgiving, I cried and cried all day at school. After school, Dad took us to the Port Authority. It was chaos with all the holiday travelers, and we had to wait for several buses before there was a bus with enough room. I worked myself into such a state that I did eventually get sick. Unfortunately, it was only after we had taken the bus to South Jersey.

Mom cooked Cornish game hens for Thanksgiving dinner. I should have been grateful that she cooked at all, but I missed the traditional turkey and I was homesick for Dad and Pat.

That weekend, Mom took us to Vermont skiing, something she and Brad loved but I was not good at. To this day, I remember the painful cold in my fingertips, the white spots that formed on my nose as I skied, inadequately dressed in jeans.

I felt guilty that I didn't want to visit my own mother.

Dad thought it would be good if Mom and I had some one-on-one time. That's all we needed, he thought. So even though it was not her turn to have me, I rode with Dad into the city one Friday after school and took the bus from the Port Authority in New York to South Jersey alone.

The first night of our mother-daughter weekend, we went to a bar/lounge to meet a friend of hers. By ten o'clock I was asking if we could *pleeeeease* go home.

"If you are tired, just lie down," Mom replied.

I didn't want to do that. I was thirteen and too old to be sleeping in restaurants.

As the night wore on and I couldn't keep my eyes open any longer, I lay my head down on the table, over my crossed arms. My eyes were closed when the cocktail waitress asked if I was all right.

My mother said, "She's fine. She's just tired."

But Mom still didn't want to go home.

After that weekend, my Dad didn't make me visit my mother again.

My mother's response was to take my Dad and me to court. Pat said, "Your mother thinks you need to see a shrink. She thinks you're crazy"... *like her.*

I had always thought there was something wrong with me. A normal daughter *loves* her mother, or at least *likes* her, and looks forward to visiting. I felt none of this.

My fear of being crazy like my mother grew worse the following year, when I learned about genes in freshman biology. I wasn't sure what my mother had, I wasn't sure what was wrong with me, and I didn't dare ask my teacher if craziness or oddness was genetic. If crazy was dominant and my mother didn't have a normal recessive gene, my prognosis was not good.

Crazy or not, I had to appear in Camden County court, again, and I had to miss school for the hearing. As my father was a famous disc jockey, Judge Minneti suggested hearing the case in his chambers to protect our privacy. When the judge asked me why I didn't want to visit my mother, I told him that my mother threw things.

The judge leaned forward in his black, billowing robe. "I don't see any scars on you."

I felt spoiled.

I tried to explain that the flying things never hit me. They simply scared me. This didn't impress the judge.

Judge Minneti finally decided that a fourteen-year-old was old enough to decide for herself if she should visit her mother or not, and declared that I didn't have to visit my mother anymore. The order insisted, though, that my father not badmouth my mother, which he really never did in those days.

Gradually, I started referring to my mother as Trish and, eventually, I stopped talking to her on the phone as well.

It was more than four years before I saw her again, during my first semester in college. She simply showed up at my dorm, unannounced.

CHAPTER 7

A Perfect Bride

DAD BROKE UP WITH Pat at some point early on when he and Trish were trying to get back together. But when that didn't work out, he went back to her. For four years, Pat drove the two and a half hours from Philadelphia to Franklin Lakes, then Oakland almost every other weekend. Dad didn't go to Philly often. How could he when he worked seven days a week?

The spring of my seventh grade, Pat insisted that she was not going to drive another winter. It was time for them to marry or for her to move on.

There was a time when Pat was my friend, and I was hers. She was pretty, she was cool, and she made my father happy. She charmed us slowly.

For my brother, who loved motorbikes and Evel Knievel, she got a signed poster when Evel stayed at the hotel she worked at. For me, I was only too happy to show her how to bake, surprised that somebody older than me didn't know how to make lemon meringue pie, my father's favorite.

So in the spring of 1978, we told Dad he should marry Pat. He never overtly responded, sometimes laughing at the suggestion, saying only, "I like her, too."

Pat would drop hints to us kids. We would drop hints to Dad.

Finally, we told Michelle to ask Dad directly if he was going to marry Pat or not. Michelle was the youngest, the cutest, and could get away with such direct questions.

There is an article in *Washingtonian* magazine from 2007 in which my father says we asked if Pat was going to be our new mom. This was one of my father's fabrications. We never thought of Pat as our mother or called her Mom. She was just Pat, a friend and a part of the family, not our mother.

Pat did not want children of her own, and she certainly never wanted to stay home with us. She was not a motherly type of person. She preferred pets to children. To be fair, her decision not to have children had much to do with wanting to keep her model's figure.

Yet, as our stepmother, there were times when Pat had to assume the duties of a parent, like when Michelle had to have eye surgery in third grade for her lazy eye; strabismus, something all three of us inherited from our father. Trish did not know Michelle was having the surgery (the cause of another fight when she found out).

Pat took Michelle for the surgery at Philadelphia Children's Hospital, in part because Pat's brother was a surgeon in Philly. After the surgery, Michelle reacted to the anesthetic, vomited and, in a haze, held her hand out to Pat to help her clean it up. Pat told us how Michelle waved her hand in the air, unable to open her eyes, moaning. I imagined her hand, something like Thing from the Adams Family. Pat was relieved when a nurse came to clean it up. I wondered, who had comforted Michelle in that moment? Did anyone stroke Michelle's forehead, tell her she was loved, that she would feel better soon?

That summer of 1978, a wedding was decided and Dad rushed to finalize the divorce from Trish. It had been five years. The divorce papers arrived only a month before the wedding date, November 17, 1978.

Pat quit her job as a sales person at Stouffers Hotel in Valley Forge a few weeks before the wedding and moved in with us. With Pat moving in, Dad let our babysitter Jane go. It felt unfair to me that, after being a part of our family for two years, Jane was so quickly discarded. But Dad assumed Pat would be home evenings with us.

Michelle and I were the bridesmaids. Gerry Hart, an Islander's hockey player, was the best man. Diane, a new friend of Pat's from the hotel was the matron of honor.

It was not a traditional service. People stood during the ceremony, which was in the same room as the reception. There were a few friends of Dad's from Philly and our neighbors from Franklin Lakes, but most of the other people were Pat's parents' friends. I can't say why nobody from Dad's family came, if they were even invited, but there were whispers that Dad's sister, Aunt Marge, did not initially approve of Pat. The only real argument over the wedding invitations was about the Gambinos Dad insisted on inviting. Pat and her mother were outraged about suspected mobsters being at the wedding, but Dad liked the Gambinos and probably thought not inviting them could have unintended consequences.

The reception was mainly finger foods that quickly ran out, but there was plenty of music and dancing. Pat, though, didn't like to dance, different from my Dad, my mother and me.

Dad and Pat held a second reception at Jimmy's Backyard in Long Island, a smaller more elegant affair, my first taste of clams casino. Most of the Islander's Hockey team and the WABC disc jockeys came to that one. After the second reception, Dad and Pat flew to Barbados for their honeymoon; while Brad, Michelle, and I went with the limousine driver back to our home where a new babysitter was waiting for us.

Years later, when I would try to figure out when exactly the relationship with my father began to crack, and Pat's influence, I would wonder about Pat's choice for matron of honor, a woman she had only recently met at work. How is it that Pat did not have a childhood friend as a maid of honor? A college friend? What kind of person doesn't need any friends?

But in eighth grade, I didn't think too much about that, because Pat was my new friend.

While we seemed like a more normal family with Dad and Pat now happily married, my friend Donna didn't like that I told Pat all my secrets and hers too. So with the eloquence of a typical eighth-grade girl, Donna dumped me as her best friend. I heard through the grapevine that she was no longer going to be my roommate on the school trip to Williamsburg. I had to find a new roommate, and a new friend.

Another girl, Kris Farnsworth was looking for a roommate, and on that single trip, we became lifelong friends. Donna and I eventually made up, too, with the same suddenness that our friendship had ended. She slipped me a note in the hallway one day, asking if I wanted to be friends again. She is someone I still call family. But in those awful few months when I was best-friendless, it was Pat who took her place. And Pat relied on me too.

Dad was obsessive about how the house was cleaned; he was even more obsessive about tracking expenses. Every time he filled the car with gas, he wrote the amount in a journal he kept on the car visor. Any stop at Grand Union, whether for milk and bread or a full week of groceries, he recorded in the journal. He instructed Pat to do the same. So when tax time approached, Dad asked Pat for her book of expenses. She came into my bedroom in a panic and showed me the blank pages of her pocket planner. "Maybe I can make them up," she whispered.

A rule follower myself, I said, "Just tell him the truth."

I did think the truth was best. No way could she make up months of expenses. But knowing there would be hell to pay, I stayed in my room when she broke the news to Dad. At least their fight that night was not because of us kids or Trish.

On career day that spring, I asked both Dad and Pat to come speak, Dad as a disc jockey, Pat as a model. Since moving in with us, Pat had not yet found another job. She had tried Ford and Elite modeling agencies, but wasn't right for them. Twenty-five was apparently old for a model.

On the weekends, she typed Dad's scripts for him for the sports segment of the news. He paid cash, since she wasn't officially employed by ABC. She looked for jobs in a new hotel being built at the Meadowlands, but she didn't get that either. It was 1979 and the country was heading into a recession.

On career day, Pat didn't have to reveal these details. The classroom was packed, her session the most interesting. I was so proud to say she was my stepmother. At twenty-five, Pat was fifteen years younger than my Dad and closer in age to Brad. I look back on some of what she had to deal with then, barely an adult herself, and know it was not an easy time for her.

My freshman year of high school, I was out sick from school for a few days. Pat took me up to school to get some books out of my locker. The hall monitor tried to stop both of us, "Girls, girls, where are your passes?" I tried to explain that Pat was my stepmother, but the teacher gave Pat, in her jeans and T-shirt, a doubtful look.

Pat certainly took on a lot joining our family as she did. She loved my father, and initially accepted us as part of the package. It wasn't long after they married, though, that Pat gave my father an ultimatum, "It's either me or the kids."

In family quarrels, Dad sided with Brad. When we got in trouble, Dad wondered if he was being too hard on us. In any fight about our mother (and there were lots), Dad told Pat to stay out of it, but she wouldn't. When I later heard Pat openly brag about the ultimatum she had given my father, I felt betrayed.

Pat is the person I can least explain in my family, except to say that she came into our family when we were all so fragile and she broke us further. And yet in 1978, I only saw the good in their marrying, thinking that Pat would make our happy four-some more complete.

CHAPTER 8

The Family Reunion

Aunt Marge, Dad, Uncle Earl at the family reunion

IT WAS EARLY MORNING and still dark outside as we waited in the living room, watching out the window for headlights of the cab to take us to the airport. Dad kept calling the cab company, and the dispatcher kept saying one was on its way, finally arriving an hour later than requested.

We missed our flight to St Louis. The best the airline could do was put us on a flight that required a connection. Events were conspiring for us to skip this family reunion, a reunion Dad probably didn't really want to go to, anyway.

Eventually we got to St. Louis at dusk. Our rooms at the motel were on the ground floor, each with a patio that opened onto a grassy area in the back of the motel. When we arrived, our aunts and cousins were sitting out back on the lawn, hanging out together.

Aunt Marge still lived in St. Louis, and never remarried after Uncle Ev died when I was in second grade. Her sons, my cousins

Rett and Steve, were teenagers. Her daughters, Mary, Chris, and Lisa were a little bit older than me. Mary and I used to be pen pals, and the summer of my fifth grade, we spent a few days together at Aunt Alice's in Queens, New York, the summer Michelle and I had stayed with Dad to avoid spoiling Mom's fun at her beach house.

When I last saw my cousin Mary, three years ago, we had dressed the same, with our jeans and poncho-style tops. Now she was wearing a leopard-skin outfit, a lot of makeup, and had gone from plump to stick thin. I wanted to rush up and hug her, but she just gave me a cool, "Hello," that told me to hang back.

Dad's oldest sister, Aunt Jane, my favorite aunt, had driven down from Illinois. She always had spunk, and even at eighty she still goes belly dancing at bonfires on the beach and cycling with friends. Even when she is upset, she smiles, trying to put a silver lining to any sucky situation. At the time of the reunion, she and her husband had recently separated, a taboo in our Catholic family particularly with four kids. Aunt Jane's children, my cousins Mike and Diane, were college age. Diane was beautiful with a Farrah Fawcett hairstyle. My cousin Paul was three years older than me, and Margaret my age. The last time I had seen any of Aunt Jane's family was when my parents were still married and I was about six. Even though it had been almost eight years, I felt an immediate ease with them. They were family.

Then someone mentioned Uncle Earl. Who was that? I turned to Brad, puzzled. "Dad has a brother?"

Brad shrugged. He didn't know, either.

Uncle Earl was seventeen when Dad was born and had served in the marines in World War II. Dad had never mentioned him. They must have been close at some point because I later learned that Uncle Earl was my sister's godfather; and when Dad finished college, he interviewed for radio jobs in California near where Uncle Earl lived. At the reunion, I met Uncle Earl's daughters, my new-found cousins Barbara and Cathy, for the first time.

When Barbara met Pat, she teased, "So. You mean you're my *Aunt!?*" Pat and Barbara were about the same age, mid-twenties.

The next morning, we drove over to Pop's house and met his

fourth wife, Aunt Vi, a tiny woman with horn-rimmed glasses. Leopard-skin pants seemed to be the fashion in St. Louis.

My stomach tightened at Pop's house, because Dad had sometimes mentioned Pop's temper, so all the cousins were on our best behavior. A pregnant pause silenced the room when someone let slip that the ceramic cardinal Dad sent for Christmas was only displayed on the coffee table for Dad's benefit; it had been tucked away the night before, when everyone else had first arrived. I watched my dad's face, but couldn't tell if it was hurt or anger he stifled in that moment.

Later that night, Brad, Margaret, Paul, Mary, and I were hanging out together back at the hotel when Paul offered Brad a beer. Brad declined, saying I would tell on him.

"No, I won't," I protested and quickly took a can of beer myself to make me just as guilty as my brother in drinking. At fourteen, it was my first time drinking. Brad complained to our cousins about what a goody two-shoes I was. I didn't want to get in trouble by drinking, but it was more important to fit in with my cousins. My cousin Paul was a rebel, a streak I strangely admired.

After a few more beers, I began jumping from one bed to the other. "Yep, just call me the flying nun!" Over the course of the evening, I had four or five beers. I was surprised I didn't feel sick or dizzy or anything. I felt free!

I figured if I didn't say good night to Dad and Pat, they might suspect something. So I went to kiss them good night, like I always did. My brother should have warned me to brush my teeth first, or maybe he was just hoping I would get in trouble. Anyway, I didn't do anything to get rid of my beer breath.

All the adults were sitting around in a circle on the lawn at the back of the hotel.

"If you're having problems with Michelle," Uncle Earl was saying, "send her to live with us over summer. We'll straighten her out."

The hair on my neck prickled. *Michelle?*

"We'll get through it," Dad answered. "Maybe Catholic school will help."

The adults stopped talking when they saw me. Michelle needed straightening out? Her room was always a mess and she couldn't keep a secret from Trish, but that was no reason to send her away from me.

I kissed Dad and Pat good night and went to bed worried. That night in the motel, my sister and I slept like spoons. I cradled her, scared that she might one day be taken away from me for reasons I didn't understand.

The next morning, Dad mentioned the beer on my breath, but I never got in trouble for it, an unusual laxness on my father's part. Did he forgive me because all the cousins had been drinking, or because laughing with his siblings quieted the voice in him that demanded perfection?

At the official reunion the next day, the sun shone brightly as we played outside at Pop's house.

I heard Dad whisper to his sisters, "Do you think she'll show?"

That started the younger cousins whispering.

"Who's he talking about?"

"Betty. The big sister," someone whispered.

"Of course, she'll come," Aunt Jane said matter-of-factly. For Aunt Jane, it was no big deal, as she kept in touch with her. Probably she was the one who had arranged for Betty and her family to come, because Aunt Jane was the forgiving type. Not like my father and Pop. Aunt Marge was just judgmental.

The whispering continued and I learned that Betty was another sister . . . a sister we didn't know my father had. This reunion was quite the eye opener!

Betty and her family did eventually show. Betty was obese; her husband was slight, and her son about my age.

We cousins weren't particularly welcoming to Betty's son. I think it was it because he was the son of the black sheep in the family. Parents don't need to openly say when they dislike someone, for the children to pick it up. Big Betty and her family didn't stay long.

It was only decades later, after I had my own children that I thought more and more about that family reunion and about Betty. Pop disowned Betty, and my father disowned me. If he repeated that part of his family cycle, what would I repeat with my own children? And if we cousins could all feel such disdain for Betty through subtle whispers, what disdain did my brother and sister later feel for me when my father forbade them to talk to me?

We drove around St. Louis later that afternoon and, oddly, Dad talked about the past. It was on this trip that we went to Federhofer's Bakery, and I discovered caramel coffee cake. I would visit the bakery thirty years later, trying to remember my father, and trying to retrace the steps that led to my disowning. How far back did that go? Was it to his own childhood, with a perfectionist mother, or even earlier, to when Pop's first wife—his true love—died in a car crash, a car that he was driving? Pop married the sister then, who later died in childbirth, so with three children to raise on his own, he married my grandmother (wife number three), a woman I never met but others have described as cold. How much had Pop steeled his heart by then, with little tenderness left for my father, the fifth baby of the family and a mama's boy? And in the Depression and postwar era, I can well imagine how Pop lauded Earl—a marine! (and the only child from his true love)—but thought little of my father, playing his silly Motown records.

Except for the awkwardness around Betty, the reunion was a happy occasion. Pop was not the scary person I imagined him. My father reminisced with his brother and sisters, and I loved hanging out with my cousins. Perhaps if there had been more of these reunions, my father could have healed. Instead, it was to be the last time I would see Pop, who died three years later. Gradually, my father drifted further from his siblings and saw them only a couple of times over the next decades. When my father was in California for a Super Bowl game, just half an hour from his brother Earl, he never bothered to visit. Should I blame that on his increasing fame or on Pat, who looked down on all of Dad's family?

Whatever rifts there may have been between my father and his siblings, Pat widened them further, just as she did between my father and me.

CHAPTER 9

The Richest Christmas

THE SUMMER OF 1979, as I was about to start high school, Dad and Pat designed their dream home. They chose a plot of land on the other side of Oakland that had a pond in the backyard, and farther behind, the Ramapo River. The most beautiful part, though, was that I would finally be in a neighborhood again, like Downs Farm and Alluvium, where I could walk out the door on any given day and find friends to play with. We would be part of a neighborhood, with spontaneous BBQs, sparklers, and roasted marshmallows in someone's backyard on Fourth of July. Or so I thought.

Dad sketched the front of the house in Tudor-style, with the stucco and arched wood pieces. Thirty years later, I saw the resemblance of this house to his childhood home on Odell Street in South Saint Louis. Our home, too, had stained-glass windows with genuine metal lattice. The bay window in the kitchen overlooked the pond. If my Dad so hated his childhood, why were there so many details like his original home? Had our recent family reunion unlocked some of the happy memories?

That fall, we shopped for light fixtures in New York, on the Bowery, walking cautiously around the homeless people sleeping on the sidewalk. For the kitchen, we chose a Tiffany lamp, and every home I've had since has had a Tiffany lamp hanging in the kitchen.

While the Oakland house was nearing completion, I started as a freshman in high school at Indian Hills, where I got a part in the school play, Miep in *The Diary of Ann Frank*.

On moving day, I stayed after school for rehearsal like I always did. I didn't think about how I was supposed to get home to our new house. Dad and Pat showed up at the school with an inexplicable fury that I was at theatre rehearsal.

They came in through the backstage entrance, and I immediately saw the anger in my Dad's face. "You were supposed to come straight home. Get in the car!"

The drama teacher, Mr. Smith, tried to talk to my father and Pat to see what was wrong. I rushed to get my jacket and homework, overhearing bits of Dad's anger. *Selfish! Moving day! Didn't know where she was!* The other students fell silent and looked away as I hurried out of the school.

Once in the car, my father continued shouting at me. "What the fuck were you thinking? We're busy moving, and you decide to stay after for goddamn theatre?"

At home, I stood in my new bedroom and stared out the window, sobbing.

Dad marched by my room and shouted at me, "Are you thinking of killing yourself? Jumping out the window?"

I shook my head no. If suicide had crossed my mind, I would have dismissed it. That's the one thing God does not forgive. I was only upset with myself for not having thought things through. Of course I shouldn't have stayed after school that day. Normally, I thought things through and I was always responsible. To have my dad so angry at me was devastating, a feeling I never wanted to have again.

Later that awful night, the front doorbell rang. It was Diane and John, two seniors from my theatre class. Mr. Smith had sent them over to help us unpack. He thought that was why my Dad was so mad at me. Mr. Smith meant well, but he was wrong. And it only embarrassed my father more.

It was one more mark against me and not the happy start I had imagined in our new home. It turns out, it was never to be a happy home. The beauty of the Tudor house was only in its façade.

A month later, Dad and Pat's first wedding anniversary was coming up on November 17, 1979. I wanted to throw them a surprise party. With Dad only getting home from work at eleven at night, it would have to be a late party.

I got one of the neighbors to buy champagne, caviar, and nice cheese, paid for with my babysitting money. I hid the champagne in the bottom of the vegetable drawer. Dad and Pat had already made friends with two of the neighbors, so I invited them and another couple, the Petroskis. Mr. Petroski owned Airbrook Limo, which often took Dad to the airport for his Islanders games. I told them all to come over at eleven P.M. Part of the gift was that Brad would babysit at the one neighbor's, and I would babysit for the other. It was a school night, but it was all part of the surprise party.

The school play was only a couple of weeks away, so rehearsals were going later after school. On that Monday, Pat picked me up just after six P.M. When I climbed into Pat's car, she turned on the radio and said, "Listen." The radio was permanently tuned to 77 WABC. I listened to the song, then to a commercial. I didn't know what she wanted me to pay attention to. Instead of Dad's voice on the air, it was just another commercial. Finally, she said, "Your father's not on the air."

I imagined the worst. "What do you mean? Was he in an accident?"

"When he didn't come on, I called the station. Dan Ingram answered the hotline. He said he was canned . . . Fired." Dan Ingram was the two-to-six-P.M. DJ.

"So where is he?"

"I don't know."

I could do the math. Dad normally got to the station by four thirty. If he knew by six, he would have been home by seven. He should have been home by now.

Brad and Michelle were both home and already knew the bad news. We worried and waited for Dad to come home. Brad and I whispered between ourselves. Should we call the neighbors to cancel the party? But that would mean telling them why, telling them Dad had been fired. I didn't want to be the one to do that.

It was nine o'clock when Dad finally walked in. We sat at the kitchen table. Dad made himself a Johnny Walker with ice. His eyes were moist as he explained.

"Brady wants to change the programming. It's all over." He took a sip of his drink. His throat was thick, his words slow. "I'll never make this kind of money again . . . New York is the biggest market."

Al Brady. What a jerk! Just a few weeks earlier, Dad had begged to have off on Saturdays to do the six o'clock sports for Channel 7. Brady, the new program director, had refused, saying he had big plans for Dad.

Disc jockeying and sportscasting were separate jobs with different bosses. Dad would still have his weekend sportscasting and the Islanders, but it wasn't enough to live on.

We were quiet for a long while. Finally, I cleared my throat. "Um, well, Brad and I have something to tell you." Brad shot me a look to shut up, but I didn't know what else to do.

"We kinda planned a surprise anniversary party for you and Pat." I handed them their anniversary card that contained a letter explaining their gift. "I'll call everyone and tell them not to come."

Dad hesitated and said, "No. No. I think it would be good to be with people. I'd like them to come around."

He suggested the friends could come over earlier though, since he was already home. Happy anniversary.

With Dad out of work and our future uncertain, that year should have been our worst Christmas, yet it remains in my mind as our happiest ever.

One night Dad took us to the mall to go Christmas shopping without Pat, so we would have time to look for something special her. We each went off in different directions looking for gift ideas. At the end of the night, Dad said he wanted to show us something and walked us over to one of those temporary kiosks. The display was full of art work of copper etchings and molds. Dad pointed to one with a male lion perched on a rock with his family nestled around him.

"I can't afford it this year, but one day, I want to get that for Pat and me." He stood for awhile, staring at the artwork.

"It's nice, Dad." I noted the price tag, close to a hundred dollars. Dad always liked lions, and in this picture, the lion was the protector, majestic and strong. The etchings seemed to radiate colors, even though it was all done in copper. I could picture the lion family, alone in the wilderness.

We walked away slowly, and I knew my father was sad for all the reasons he couldn't buy that picture. Dad was getting worried that he couldn't provide for us.

In the dark parking lot of the mall, he walked ahead, eyes downcast, not in the Christmas spirit. I was determined to find a way to buy that copper picture.

Over the coming weeks, I saved. I babysat as much as I could. When the Indian Hills drama club was asked to provide a stage crew for a church's Christmas show, I leapt at the chance to be part of it. I would get paid. Even though I was a freshman and low in rank, I begged to be allowed to work both performances, explaining to Mr. Smith what I was saving for. My job was to gently shake snowflakes over the carolers on the stage, and as the white confetti swirled softly through the air, I thought how it was bringing me one step closer to that special gift for Dad and Pat.

While I worked to earn money for that gift, Brad, Michelle, and I also planned something special for Grandma and Grandpa, Pat's parents, and decided to design a plaque for them. The inscription said something like, "While we were not born into your family, we couldn't have found more perfect grandparents than you." The plaque was signed by all three of us.

To add to my high spirits, Aunt Jane and my cousin Paul were coming for Christmas. I hadn't expected to be able to see them again so soon after the reunion.

As the weeks flew by, I finally had enough money to buy the copper lion artwork. Pat took us to the mall this time. I made an excuse as to why Michelle and I had to go off shopping on our own. As we approached the kiosk for the copper artwork, I gasped. The lion wasn't there. Somebody else had bought it!

My heart sank. I walked around hoping to find another. Nothing. I started to wander away, defeated, when Michelle spotted something with lions hanging in the lower corner. It had simply been moved! I bought it.

Once school let out for Christmas break, my days were filled with baking. Sugar cookies, pecan snow balls, candy cane, and chocolate chip. I baked all day from morning to midnight. I only too happily mopped the brown, tiled floor each night, on my hands and knees erasing any trace of spilt flour. We gave cookies to neighbors, to friends, and still had plenty on hand for all the family that would be with us.

Christmas morning finally arrived! We usually went to midnight mass, so Christmas morning was a casual, cozy start to the day. We gathered in the living room, still dressed in our nightgowns and bathrobes. Dad would have his coffee in hand. When we got hungry, we'd bring in a Danish or slice of coffee cake from the Wyckoff bakery.

We each took turns handing out gifts, opening them one at a time to savor the surprises. It was hard for me to pace myself. I didn't want to give out all the special gifts right away. We took turns opening gifts from Santa, gifts from each other, and finally we gave Grandma and Grandpa theirs. Grandma did the opening. Her eyes misted when she read the inscription, then she left the room. For a moment, I thought I had made a big mistake that it hit a nerve since we were not her blood grandchildren.

When she came back to the room, teary-eyed, she hugged each of us, with tears of joy. She said, "Nothing could be better than instant grandchildren."

I bought Paul a ski hat. He seemed uncomfortable. He and Aunt Jane had asked us not to get them gifts, saying they couldn't buy us anything in return. They didn't realize that we really did feel that their being with us was a bigger gift, the best gift.

Pat picked out a gift from the family for Aunt Jane, a toaster oven. I was concerned about how Aunt Jane would carry this back on the train. Sure enough, when they headed home, that gift got left behind. Pat took it as a slight, but I saw it differently. It seemed I often did. I thought maybe Aunt Jane didn't want the gift because it's hard to accept something when you can't give in return. And seriously, could anything be more impractical when traveling?

Finally, I couldn't wait any longer! I gave Dad and Pat their present. They sat together on the living room floor. Pat ripped the paper off and Dad eased the box open. As he glimpsed what was inside, he fought back the tears. Pat kept asking, "What? What is it?" How could he explain?

He couldn't. I couldn't. At first Dad just hugged Pat, trying not to cry. Then, he pulled me to them and hugged me. No words were needed.

The lion copper mold had a prominent place in the living room. It initially had a special place in the next house in Maryland. Years later, it was no longer hung at all. I never knew if it was because they had outgrown their taste for it—they could afford much finer things by then. Or was it that Pat never really liked it, never understood the significance of either the picture or the gift?

The rest of that Christmas week was equally special. Pat's brother, our new Uncle Dick carved the turkey. Dad, the son of a butcher, was hesitant to let anyone mess with his meat. But Dick was fast becoming a renowned surgeon and carved that turkey better than Dad ever had.

We played Uno almost every night around the kitchen table. Paul kept winning of course. Uno is a card game of chance but also of lying about what cards you have. Paul had the best poker face, the rebel who knew how to be sneaky. Dad laughed with his sister. He was full of admiration for her, saying she looked classy in a particular sweater. He was proud of the way Aunt Jane was standing on her own two feet after her divorce and running her own tobacco store. In the 1970s, tobacco was still big business and considered safe.

The only tense moment was one night when we went into New York with Dad. Dad went to the TV station where he still had his weekend job to work on a story. Paul was old enough to drive, so he drove Pat's car while Dad worked. Paul, Brad, Michelle, and I planned to go ice skating at Rockefeller Center. Aunt Jane and Pat stayed home. We parked on the street across from the ABC studios. The only problem was that we had to keep putting quarters in the parking meter. I still wonder why we didn't park in the same garage Dad did. Did it cost too much? It was not easy to estimate time for renting skates, skating, walking back to the studio, and so on, when navigating the holiday crowds took more time than we realized. So we got a parking ticket. We thought that would be that. We'd have to pay the ticket. But instead, as we were coming back to put more quarters in, a tow truck was hooking up Pat's car. As the tow truck pulled away from the curb, taking Pat's car with him, Paul ran down the street, chasing it. The truck was faster than Paul.

When we got back to the TV station and told Dad what had happened, he was livid.

After he was done with his work, we went to the compound, a creepy, dark place along the water front. We had to pay several hundred dollars—cash only—for the ticket, the towing, the impounding. At first, they wouldn't even talk to us, because Dad couldn't present the car registration. That was in the glove compartment of the car. Duh. But then the registration was to Pat Lackman, not to Pat Michael. Pat had never changed the registration to her married name, so there was no apparent association with my father.

My father threatened. He used his name, but this was double-edged. Channel 7 had recently done a news report on the city's shady towing practices. Now Mr. big-shot George Michael was asking them to help him out? Puleaaaase!

While the manager was contemplating what to do and trying to contact Pat, we all waited off to the side, silent. Brad, Michelle, and I knew to shut up when Dad was angry. Paul did not. So Paul offered, "Why don't we just jump the fence and take the car. I've got the keys."

Dad whacked Paul alongside his head. Paul never saw it coming. Paul later told me that his own father had never ever done such a thing. Dad started lecturing Paul. Ordered him to straighten up. Ordered him to get a haircut, and the list went on. I don't think Paul heard a word of it. He was shocked.

Dad didn't admire Paul's rebellious streak the way I did.

We got the car back. The night may have ended on a low note, but that week sealed my relationship with my Aunt Jane and cousin Paul. They were the only family members who dared to stay in touch with me following my disowning. That Christmas also served as a constant reminder that we were happiest, closest, when we were on the brink of being the poorest.

The way we were that Christmas 1979 kept my hope alive for decades that we could be that family again. It also gave rise to my belief that money, too much of it, was part of our family's demise.

I look back at all the events that led up to our family's crumbling: my father remarrying, my father getting fired, my father being famous, my growing up. Was there any way to prevent what would happen?

The rest of that winter, Dad worked every lead, trying to find a full-time job. He went into the TV station more often, doing special segments on athletes. There was a rumor that he was being considered for the Olympics. The Mets were considering him for play-by-play.

Pat did not like the idea of the Mets. "We'll never see him. He'll be on the road all year. Hockey, then baseball? No way."

In those days, Pat and I were close.

I didn't want Daddy traveling either, but he needed a job. He was depressed. Sometimes he'd go back into WABC anyway. Pat said it was just what Liz Kyley, a short-lived DJ at WABC, had done after she got fired. Dad had chastised Liz for moping. Now Pat said Dad was moping. Dad's agent wasn't helping matters. When a DJ gets fired from the top market, anywhere else is downhill.

Dad set his sights on full-time sportscasting. He sent demo tapes to stations around the country. Pat expressed concern to me. "I'd never kick a man when he was down, but I don't know that this is going to work." It wasn't only that Dad had lost his job. Pat complained that Dad acted more like a friend to us than a father. And then there was Trish. Pat would never be rid of Trish. Pat would wait for Dad to find a job, before leaving him, before leaving us.

Finally, a station in Washington, DC, seemed promising. It wasn't a big market, and they were last place in the ratings. But that meant there was room to turn the station around. The general manager, John Rohrbeck, had just hired a new weatherman and movie critic. Dad would be the new sports director. He would be in charge. Rohrbeck was assembling a new team at WRC, an NBC affiliate.

Warner Wolf, Dad's sports boss at Channel 7 had come from DC. Warner joked with Dad that he didn't want him going there, because it would make it harder for Warner to ever go back to DC.

I had been to DC on our sixth-grade class trip. Washington, DC, with the cherry blossoms and white buildings, was beautiful.

When the negotiations got serious, Dad told John Rohrbeck that he needed Pat with him. John said he would give her a job too, but that it had to be official. She had to join the union as a writer. Pat's father was a labor negotiator, and Pat hated unions. The only good news was that they doubled her pay over the cash Dad had been paying her. Dad and Pat became a package deal that Rohrbeck accepted. Their future was looking up.

That winter, I got the lead in the play, *Last of the Red Hot Lovers*. On opening night, Dad sat front row in the theatre in the round. I entered stage left, in my blue disco dress, feathered hair, with a big white flower comb sweeping my hair back to one side. Dad's laughter bellowed through the quiet room. Everyone turned their attention to him. It was his way of letting me know he was there. I knew what he was thinking: I looked the perfect bimbo.

Dad was even more impressed by my performance. He bragged to his new boss that I was a rising actress. This performance, he didn't describe as "boring." This performance made my dad declare, "You'll be an actress one day!"

Any child wants her parents to be proud. But with a mother who neglected us and a father whose love had to be earned, it was more than that. Imagine a dull, gray room, empty of sound and life. With Dad proud of me, that dull room would be transformed into a paradise of sunshine. I yearned to keep my place in Dad's paradise—until, eventually, I realized there was a price, and that the price was a moving target. That year, though, I was my usual responsible, overachieving self, and my father loved me.

We weren't quite sure when we would be moving to DC, because Dad and Pat had to find a house first. They started their jobs together at WRC-TV in April 1980. They told me I shouldn't try out for the spring play, because we most likely would be moving before that performance. Dad and Pat flew down to DC on Sunday evenings, and came back the following Saturday morning. Brad, Michelle, and I stayed behind in Oakland. On our own. It does shock me somewhat that they left us alone all week in a different state, but again, it was normal to me then. After all, I could cook, clean, and babysit Michelle just fine.

While Dad and Pat started their new lives in DC, I entered limbo. I broke up with my first real boyfriend, Wayne, a junior I had met through theatre. I didn't want my last few weeks in Oakland to be torn between time with him and time with friends. I needn't have broken up with Wayne, though, and I could have tried out for the play, as it was July before we would eventually move. Instead, I sat in the audience at the spring play, *Our Town*, and watched Wayne's new girlfriend give a moving performance. It seemed everyone else was living, moving on; while I waited for my new life to start, somewhere near DC.

At the end of freshman year in spring, I was allowed to play rec softball, because it wouldn't matter if I left before the season finished. Dad prearranged for the coach to drive me to practices. I didn't like to inconvenience anyone, so as soon as it was warm enough, I rode my bike the two and a half miles to Oakland Rec Fields.

One Sunday when Dad and Pat were home for the weekend, we went to brunch after church. As soon as we got home, Brad decided to call Trish. Pat got angry. Why couldn't Brad wait until after they left for the airport to call his mother? Dad tried to mediate, as usual. With all the shouting, I couldn't blame them for wanting to leave us, to get away from the fighting. I was mad at Brad. He could have waited. Brad always did what Brad wanted to do, when he wanted to. He didn't care what problems he caused.

For Mother's Day, Brad, Michelle, and I flew down to DC by ourselves. Dad and Pat were living at The Embassy Row Hotel. That weekend, we all went house-hunting in Maryland. The whole weekend was awkward. We children didn't fit in, didn't belong there.

We hadn't gotten Pat a Mother's Day present, because there had been nobody home to take us to the mall. So that Sunday morning, we lamely shopped at the drugstore down the street from the hotel and bought her a box of chocolates. It was pathetic.

On the flight home, Brad and Michelle sat together. I sat next to a woman with shoulder-length, dark brown hair and glasses, beautiful like Pat. I glimpsed an NBC peacock logo on her bag, so I started talking about how we would soon be moving to DC and that my father recently joined NBC. She said she was a journalist. She wrote her name on a scrap of paper. *Linda Ellerbee.* I saved the handwritten note for months, wanting to ask Dad if he knew her, but there never seemed to be chance.

When we got back to New York, we spotted the driver from Airbrook Limo with his sign, just like Dad told us. He drove us home, to a house that was empty and dark.

One Friday night in June, Brad decided to throw a party at the lake behind our house. Brad was known for throwing a good party, from a party he threw at our old house on Breakneck Road. During that unauthorized party, Pat, Michelle, and I had been visiting Pat's parents in Philadelphia for the weekend. So while Dad was at work, Brad threw a party the town never forgot. Lots of beer. Fists in walls. Police. In Brad's defense and technically speaking, he followed the rules this time, or at least tried to. This party was not at the house. Instead, he had it behind the house, down by the river. Even so, it was not allowed. The problem was that Friday night was the night I usually cleaned the house, to get it in perfect order for when Dad and Pat came home. I wouldn't have time Saturday morning because I had a softball game. As the night went on, the party at the river spilled over into the house. Someone needed to use the bathroom. Someone made macaroni and cheese, making a mess on the stove. Someone threw up in the bathroom. I re-cleaned once, then refused to clean again.

Brad was doing his best to keep his friends out of the house. His friends were doing their best to get me involved. If I joined in the party, I would be complicit in his guilt. Even when one of Brad's friends, a boy I had a crush on, tried talking to me in the hallway for a minute, it was a minute too long.

Brad tried to clean up the next morning. By his standard, he did a pretty good job. I spotted every mistake though, shouting at him the whole time. It's only now that I think, what a pain-in-the-ass sister I was. Then I went to my softball game.

When I got home, Dad and Pat were already home. Dad commented on the dirty stove. I said nothing. Brad said nothing. At first, it was me who got in trouble. I hadn't done a good job. I hadn't kept the house in order.

Eventually Dad cornered me in the upstairs hallway.

"What's going on?"

"Nothing," I muttered.

"Don't give me that, Cindi. Just tell me the truth. Did your brother have friends over?"

I had to think about this. Technically, he didn't. But I knew full well the rule on lies of omission. "No, he did not have friends over."

Dad kept quizzing me until I caved. "He had a party at the river. He really tried to keep them out of the house."

Dad told me how to play this. He would confront Brad at a family meeting. I was to claim that I was not going to lie for him anymore. Then I should run out of the house. The drama would surely get Brad to tell the truth.

Dad called all of us into the kitchen and did what he had said he would. By the time I ran out of the kitchen and out of the house, my tears were real. I stood at the fence along the stables up the street. I was ashamed of myself. I had betrayed my brother to save myself.

Dad would probably have started the tirade with Brad on how disappointed he was in him, how he couldn't be trusted, and the fatal blow, "why can't you be more like your sister?" It is a remark that can kill any love between siblings and one my father repeated often—at least until I fell from his grace. For all the times my father said he did not want to be like his father, he was unbelievably blind to how he was exactly like Pop, in the way Pop used to tell Dad he'd never amount to anything. Truly, what's worse: being disowned, or suffering a lifetime of my father's disappointed looks?

I have heard that it was my father's mother, who was the real cold-hearted one and who most pit one child against another in the Gimpel house. My father clearly parented the same on this count too. In this way, he taught me how *not* to raise my own children. I have taught them to protect one another, always.

The only good to come out of Brad's pseudo party was that we got a babysitter. Maybe it was the party. Maybe it was that school had let out for the summer, and Dad and Pat knew there was more free time for us to get in trouble.

The year my father lost his job was the lowest I ever saw him. He had lost his job and it seemed he might lose Pat.

A co-worker of my father's, Jim Vance, once said that the thing that terrified my father more than anything was failure. Being second best would be a failure in my father's eyes.

With hindsight, I understand why my father was relentless in his pursuit of becoming the best sportscaster in Washington and in the country. He was trying to fill a void made by Pop, who had told him he'd never be anybody.

Overachieving can be just as addictive as any drug. Maybe Dad's fans made him feel loved, in the same way that pleasing my teachers and, later, my bosses, filled the hole my father had left in me.

CHAPTER 10

The Sportscaster's Daughter

IN LATE JULY 1980, we moved from Oakland, New Jersey, to Darnestown, Maryland, a rural town just north of Washington, DC. It was one of the hottest summers on record, and we had our first taste of stifling humidity.

The house on Plainfield Lane was a new construction, but the builder had run out of money when the recession hit. So, we got it for a more affordable price compared to the luxury homes in Potomac where most of Dad's new co-workers lived.

I was happy to be with Dad and Pat again, but I missed my friends in Oakland. My friend Donna Saraisky had thrown me a going away party, and while we all promised to write each other, I knew I would no longer be part of that close-knit group at school. My other best friend, Kris, came to our house to say good-bye as the movers loaded the truck. She left with tears in her eyes, and my Dad wondered if he was doing the right thing, uprooting us, taking us way from our friends, but really, he had no choice. He had a new career in DC.

Being together with Dad and Pat also meant that we children were once again the cause of all their fights. The first week in our new home, they went off to work together, while Brad, Michelle, and I stayed home, trying to settle in but, with only a few other houses on our lone street, there was no way to make new friends.

One afternoon, the phone man came to install phone jacks. I told Brad to deal with him, while I helped Michelle organize her new bedroom.

The next morning, Brad and I both got in trouble for not checking the phone man's work. One jack didn't work at all, and the jack in the hallway was near the bottom of the floor instead of at shoulder height for a wall phone. Dad laid into Brad and me, then said the conversation was over. But Pat wouldn't drop it. So, Dad got mad at Pat. He shouted at her, and she thundered around the house. Then they went off to work together, leaving us behind to squabble about who was really at fault. I wondered if divorce was better than staying married.

On that day, I only regretted my mistake at not having followed the phone man around the house, or really, at entrusting Brad to check things. When I reread that diary entry decades later though, I could only think, *Are you freaking kidding me?* If Dad was so damn particular about where he wanted the jacks, he should have marked the wall before he and Pat went to work. But my Dad, of course, could never accept blame, and demanded perfection even from the disorganized brains of two teenagers.

Despite the screw up with the phone man, I tried to greet my new home in Maryland with optimism. I had a romantic view of our rural street. We lived on an acre of land, with our backyard buttressing a farm. Occasionally, a black cow grazed near the fence. The air was fresher in Maryland than in New Jersey; none of the chemical smell that forced me to hold my breath for stretches as we used to drive with Dad into New York. In the morning, I even heard a real live rooster crowing in the distance!

Our house on Plainfield Lane was not part of a neighborhood; a lone street with a scattering of homes that divided the wealthy neighborhood of Spring Meadows, and more rural homes near the C&O canal that only recently got running water. As a stand-alone street, the families here chose where to send their children to school. The three other teenagers on our street went to Wootton High School, considered a better school district, but their parents had to drive them. We would be going to Seneca Valley, because there was a bus.

On our first day at school, I felt car sick as the forty-five-minute bus ride meandered along the country roads. I learned the word "red neck," and heard some boys talk about how they had burned a cross in someone's yard the week before to "learn him a lesson."

Our school in Oakland had only a couple of black students, but those kids didn't seem any different from me. Seneca Valley was about 30 percent black, and there were unspoken rules between blacks and whites.

During flextime, a twenty-minute break between classes, I went down a hallway looking for the school store and instead ended up where only the black students hung out. One of the guys wrapped his hands around my waist, "Hey, baby." I hurriedly continued down the hall. The black girls glared at me. I later learned this was Eric Drain, star football player.

It seemed wiser to get to Chemistry early than risk going down another wrong hallway. It was geeky to sit alone in the empty class-room during flextime, but better than standing in the hallway talking to nobody. I picked a seat at the back of the room and was relieved when another girl, also a sophomore, eventually walked in and introduced herself. Deanna looked like a young Dolly Parton, with perfect make up and a smile that offered the hope of a new friend.

I wondered about the boy who kept staring at me during class. Deanna told me it was Bob Morse, a junior who was going out with one of her best friends. (Bob later was the best man at my first wed-ding and a lifelong friend.) My brother was in my class, too. Neither of us was happy about that, so when he walked in, we merely nodded at one another. In New Jersey, Brad had gone to a Catholic all-boys high school, Don Bosco. If Seneca Valley felt foreign to me, it must have been a bigger shock for Brad.

Besides getting used to a new school, Brad, Michelle, and I had to learn to live with Dad and Pat again. Once they started their jobs in DC, we kids had been in New Jersey without them for four months; Dad and Pat had been a childless couple, living on their own in a hotel.

Dad's new work schedule was hard for me. He left earlier for work than in New Jersey, and we didn't see him and Pat after school. Saturday was the only time we had as a family. A couple of times, they tried to come home for dinner midweek, between the six and eleven o'clock news, but it was a rush. I had to have dinner ready for a quick turn-around, and Dad and Pat struggled to switch from the frenetic pace of the newsroom to a leisurely, "How was your day at school, kids?" dinner conversation. After a few fraught dinners, they gave up on the idea.

So each day after school, Pat normally called from the news station to make sure we had gotten home okay. Whoever got to the phone first had a chance to talk, and Dad only occasionally had time to get on the phone to say hi to us. Rarely was there time for them to talk to all three of us, so the race to the phone gave my brother, sister, and me one more thing to fight about.

I missed them.

While we were starting a new life in Maryland, Trish's life was crumbling. Her car was repossessed from so many unpaid parking tickets. Then her home was foreclosed on. When Dad was out of work, he didn't have to keep paying Trish alimony. I knew none of this at the time, because Trish and I weren't on speaking terms. I only knew that she hadn't bothered to call Brad and Michelle for four months. To me, it was more proof that our mother didn't care about us at all.

One night that October, Trish showed up at the TV station out of the blue, demanding that Dad meet her in the lobby. Pat begged Dad not go, but he did. I hated picturing Pat having to beg my father. Trish insisted that Dad tell her where we lived and our new phone number. Dad refused. He only promised that he would have Brad and Michelle call her.

Pat was insistent that we not tell Trish where we lived. This was her chance to live in peace without having to wonder when Trish would call or show up unexpectedly at our new home and cause a scene.

With the hindsight of becoming a mother, this is one of those times when I wonder if my mother was naturally crazy or if my father drove her to craziness. Dad never told Trish we were moving to Maryland and, with her phone disconnected, Brad and Michelle couldn't get in touch with her. But my father knew Trish's friends. He could have contacted her if he really wanted to. If Dad and Pat didn't want Trish calling on our new phone number, it would have been easy enough to get a second phone line for Trish to call on, even in 1980.

After Trish's scene at the news station, Dad agreed to bring Michelle into work one evening so she could go out to dinner with Trish. She was supposed to be back at the TV station by nine P.M. But Trish was never on time. Sure enough, she was late. She claimed that it was because Michelle became hysterical at having to say good-bye and cried so hard.

Eventually Trish took Dad back to court, demanding to know where we lived and demanding back-alimony. The judge forced Dad to give her our new phone number.

My initial excitement at moving to Maryland soon gave way to a constant longing. My father was never home. I watched him on the five thirty and six P.M. news shows. There were times I'd want to talk to him and Pat about boyfriend problems or school or squabbles with Brad and Michelle; but there wasn't much opportunity. Other times, I held it all in, because it made missing them hurt less.

I wanted to tell them, for example, about Mike Pultro. I had met Mike the summer before, when he and a bunch of other guys rented a beach house across the street from Jill Parker's house in Brigantine. Mike was a musician and played as a percussionist in the casinos in Atlantic City, including for the Miss America Pageant. Mike was Italian and totally handsome. We had written each other letters a few times over the year. Mike was twenty-three and thought I was seventeen; Jill and I had lied about our age, knowing that a house full of good-looking guys wouldn't be interested in us if they knew we were really fifteen. To be fair, I looked older than I was, and I acted older, too.

The past summer when I was visiting Jill for the week, Mike and I went for a walk on the beach late one night. Jill and her boyfriend went for their own walk. Mike and I lay on a beach blanket and talked and talked, with the whisper of the waves and an occasional shooting star streaming across the sky.

At one point, Mike told me he had something important to say, but he wasn't sure how I would take it. I encouraged him to say what he was thinking, all the while dreading the possibilities. Would it be some criticism of me, or something I did that bugged him? I thought he was going to break off our friendship or something. I stared intently at the stars, not wanting to look at Mike, holding my breath.

"There are only two people in the world that I have ever felt comfortable talking to. You are one of them. I feel I can talk to you about anything."

I exhaled. "I do, too," I said quietly.

Then he leaned over and gently kissed me.

We both lay there for a moment, my heart thudded. A wave nipped at the edge of the blanket, and we scrambled to get up before getting wet.

Mike scooped up the blanket. We walked along the beach, wordlessly.

"Aren't you going to say anything?" he prompted.

"Um . . . that was nice?"

What was there to say when friendship becomes something more? Should I tell him I was only fifteen?

We sat in Mike's car and talked for hours, about little things and big things. How afraid I was to be going to a new school. How we would stay in touch. He told me I'd have a great time, and have lots of boyfriends. I laughed, saying I wasn't interested in lots of boyfriends. *Just one*. Finally, at two in the morning, I went inside. We parted with one last gentle kiss, not knowing when we would see each other again.

There was ten years difference between Dad and Pat. Pat often said, "When you are eighteen, you're pretty much open to dating anybody." She had dated a much older person when she was in college in London for a semester. It was my cousin, Paul, though, who once told me I was "jailbait," while wishing me happy birthday. More embarrassing was that Paul had to explain to me what it meant. One day, when I casually asked Pat about dating older boys, she assumed

I meant a senior who had asked me to homecoming, but I was think-ing about Mike.

After that single walk on the beach, Mike and I wrote each other weekly. He made me promise to have fun in my new home in Mary-land and to date other people. We vowed to stay friends, but we both knew there was something more, a seed that had to stay dormant, at least for now.

That fall, when Pat went to Philadelphia to visit her parents for a few days, I had some time alone with Dad. I almost told him about Mike, but he seemed preoccupied with work so I didn't, thinking my relationship with Mike was wrong.

What relationship? It was one kiss. There was no relationship. He lived a billion miles away. We wrote letters to each other. That's all. The age difference didn't matter.

Well, clearly it did matter, because I lied to Mike about my age. If there was nothing wrong, then why was I keeping Mike a secret from Dad?

Christmas Eve, Mike sent me a dozen red roses. When Dad and Pat asked who they were from, the lie came easily. "They're from Jill . . . and Mike."

In high school, Mike was one of the few constants in my life, and his letters were a lifeline to me. Mike was my first taste of uncondi-tional love, someone who did what was best for me, instead of for himself. So different from my father. And my mother.

Mike never took advantage of me. His letter's lifted my spirits, with a complement, a flirtation, the little details of his week at work or of running on the beach. Of course, our relationship would bring its own problems. It would have to. Because it was one of the first secrets I kept from Dad.

Some cries for help are drastic: getting drunk, cutting, anorexia. Others are as subtle as a whimper, like mine.

In my speech class the fall of my junior year, for our first speech we had to introduce ourselves by comparing ourselves to a fruit or a vegetable. I compared myself to a lemon, bright and smiling on the outside, but sour and sad on the inside. I hadn't realized how pathetic it sounded until I said it aloud. It was true, though.

Dad, Pat, and I were drifting apart. They were never home. When they were, all they did was nitpick about something. I put on some weight and Pat said I was now "two pounds past pleasantly plump." I wasn't happy with my weight, which was twenty pounds from my ideal, but it seemed like one small failing.

We came home to an empty house every day. While we didn't keep junk food in the house, it was easy to whip a bowl of frosting as a snack. And, honest to God, why did school clubs sell Hershey candy bars as a fundraiser? As I had no neighbors, I ate the majority of them.

Fortunately, by senior year, the drama club switched to light bulbs as the fundraiser! But the junk food had done its damage. Also, when in Oakland, I had ridden my bike around town to friends' houses. In Maryland, everything was more spread out so I got no exercise at all.

I thought my weight shouldn't matter, though. I was an A student, in mostly honors classes, took care of Michelle, driving her to her friend's house or to the movies whenever she wanted. I kept the house clean. I didn't do drugs. I didn't have sex. I didn't throw parties. I never had friends over when Dad and Pat weren't home, which meant I never had friends over, period. I did pretty much everything they expected. Still, it wasn't enough.

My parents were so black and white in their opinions. I was gray. I couldn't figure out what to think. We disagreed on so many things. Like, why couldn't black people and white people date? Eric Drain, the black football player, who had said hi to me the first day of school, told my brother he thought I was cute. But Dad and Pat squashed any thoughts of flirting back. Pat said, "If ever you have a baby . . . Their hair is different. Everything." I wasn't sure this was a good argument since we were talking about dating, not marriage. I didn't think it mattered.

I wasn't a trail blazer or a raging liberal and, in 1980, there weren't many interracial couples. But even then, I was open-minded about most things.

Pat suggested, with disdain, "Are you a fence sitter?"

Girls shouldn't drink beer, was another rule of Pat's. But everyone drank beer at field parties. There is nothing else to drink in the middle of a field.

Even my dad argued with Pat on this one. "My sisters drink beer."

Pat replied, eyebrow arched, "Exactly."

Dad's sisters, my aunts, were from St. Louis and had probably worked at the Busch brewery at some point. Pat was from Broomall, a rich suburb of Philadelphia, and Dad sometimes affectionately called her a blueblood or a JAP, Jewish American Princess. Pat's father was Jewish and her mother was Catholic, but Pat didn't believe much in either religion.

Then there was one Saturday night when Trish called during dinner. The phone on the wall was just behind my chair. These were the days before caller ID and voicemail.

We answered the phone whenever it rang. Trish asked for Michelle and I said she would call her back after dinner. I hung up and Pat told Michelle not to call back. I wasn't on speaking terms with Trish myself but I didn't think Pat was being fair to Michelle. I voiced my opinion, "If Michelle wants to call her back, she should be allowed to." An icy silence followed. After that, I said nothing.

So my second cry for help in speech class was about this changing relationship with my dad.

Dad and Pop had never been close, and Dad had said to me, "I don't want to make the same mistakes with you kids that my father made with me."

We had only met Pop that one time for the family reunion. Pop was diagnosed with cancer shortly before we moved to Maryland, and Dad flew back to St. Louis a few times to see him. He had seen his father more in the last year than in the previous ten.

Dad was sitting at our kitchen table in Maryland, when I heard him on the phone with Pop. "Pop, it's okay . . . All that's in the past . . . No, Pop . . . No, it wasn't that bad."

Eventually, my father said good-bye and hung up. He sat there silently for a few minutes, then rubbed his face, and choked out a comment to nobody in particular. "Why? Why does it always have to be too late?"

Pop died a few months later. He had waited until the very end to fix things with his son. I too felt like time was running out for me and my father.

In speech class, I started to tell this story. On paper, it was just the cold facts. I got partway through my speech, when my throat began to close. I bit my inner cheek to squelch the tears. Everyone stared down at their desks. Nobody looked up at me. I ended abruptly. "I just hope with my own father, it will never be too late."

I rushed back to my seat and stared at my desk, too.

My cries for help were whimpers. The crappy thing about whimpers is that there was nothing anyone could do. I once tried to tell Pat I wasn't sure Dad loved me anymore. She shifted the blame onto me.

"Your father's not an alcoholic, is he?" she answered, suggesting I had nothing to complain about.

So I thought the problem was me. I was needy, insecure.

Other times, Pat blamed Trish for my insecurity, suggesting that because my mother never loved me, I didn't trust my father's love. It was an interesting theory that subtly became a fact in my brain for decades: *my mother doesn't love me.* Certainly, my mother hadn't taken care of me, that much was clear.

Despite all the anguish in those high school years, I too got caught up in the excitement of my father's growing success. Our first Halloween in Maryland, Dad asked me to write a poem about football, because everything I wrote in those days rhymed—and he did his blooper videos to my poem, on the air, for all of Washington to hear. At Christmas, when WRC-TV decided to record a promo of the news team singing Christmas carols at Tyson's Corner mall, Dad called us kids to join him. Brad drove us to the mall in northern Virginia, so all our smiling, singing faces could be seen during the commercial breaks on TV.

Dad would ask us what we thought of his show, what our friends thought, and which news reporter seemed the best. I liked the short woman with reddish hair, Katie Couric. Dad replied, "Well, yeah, she's nice . . ." not needing to spell out that "nice" was not enough to be number one. Years later, I was surprised to see this "nice" reporter, whom my father thought would never amount to much, hosting the *Today* show. I wanted to ask her if it was really possible to be nice and successful at the same time. How did she do it? More so, I wanted to ask her daughters what was real, because it seemed to me that my father had traded us for his fame.

Even so, in those first years in DC, I filled my scrapbook with articles of my Dad's steady rise from fourth place in the ratings to number two. (I don't think my dad replaced Glenn Brenner as the number one sportscaster until Brenner passed away in 1992.) I was proud of my father, to be sure, but it seemed to me he was becoming less and less my father, and more and more the sportscaster.

CHAPTER 11

First Love

THE FALL OF MY junior year in high school, I met a boy who would change my life and the relationship with my father, forever.

A foreign exchange student from Switzerland, George looked Italian with his dark complexion and dark brown hair. He was undeniably handsome. My breath caught the first time I saw him in the hallway. He wore turtleneck sweaters, like my father. They shared more than just the same first name.

I went on a hayride in the hopes of meeting this foreigner called George. We met, and I flirted with him by throwing musty hay on him. A few weeks later, we both were servers for the dinner theater production, and we talked some more.

When George finally asked me out, he took me to dinner at Sir Walter Raleigh's, a fancy place with candles on each oak table; his brother in his host family had to drive us. Even though George was seventeen, exchange students weren't allowed to drive while in the US. His host brother was in my Honors English class, which made the chauffeur thing especially awkward. At dinner, George ordered wine, because in Switzerland you can drink at any age and he got mad when the waitress carded him. He tried to argue that because he was Swiss, he should be allowed to have wine as Swiss law should apply. The restaurant refused. My face flushed with embarrassment. I would never argue once caught trying to drink under age. At the same time, I admired how he stood up for what he wanted and talked about his plans to one day be a lawyer.

During dinner, he told me that the rugby team couldn't believe he had asked out "George Michael's daughter." I had often suspected that boys didn't ask me out because they were intimidated by my father. Other times, I thought it was that I was not pretty or skinny or fun enough. It took me awhile to learn that being the sportscaster's daughter in a town that idolizes sports even more than politics put me in the shadow of my father's aura. In New Jersey, Dad was only a voice on the radio. In Maryland, he was more than a voice. He was a face and a force that would change sportscasting across the country.

After that first date, George didn't ask me out again for weeks. I agonized that I had been too quiet on our date. Then confusingly, George would sometimes walk me to my classes, his arm possessively around my waist. Finally, he told me he wanted to go out with me, but the chauffeuring thing was embarrassing. Could I drive, he wondered. I thought this was fine, and asked Pat if it was okay.

Pat was mortified. "Girls aren't supposed to drive on a date. The boy is supposed to pick you up." I explained that he wasn't allowed, but it didn't convince her.

When Pat told my father that I had suggested driving on a date, Dad said, "I would have liked to punch your lights out for that one."

So, over Christmas break, George came over for dinner. Everyone in the family played Uno around the kitchen table, just as we had done the Christmas when Aunt Jane and Paul had visited. George told my father he planned to earn his first million by the time he was twenty-five. He declared this not as a wish but as a fact of his future. Dad laughed with gusto at George's declaration, dismissing his goal as unrealistic but admiring the boy's ambition. That Christmas, George gave me a gold necklace with a stemmed rose pendant. After Christmas, I was allowed to drive for our dates. He had won my father over, in a way that no boy had done before or since.

While I was floating in my first serious relationship, Brad was heading for trouble. He and my parents fought all the time. They fought about rules, his grades, his friends. Dad said maybe Brad wasn't college material, a cruel remark coming from someone who graduated high school 149th out of a class of 189, a detail my father had not shared with us himself; I only stumbled across it in an old newspaper article decades later.

One day when we came home from school, Brad's room had been ransacked, his dresser drawers upended, the underwear, socks, and T-shirts strewn across the rust-colored carpet. There was a note from Dad on the floor. Brad picked it up and handed it to me. "Stay out of my things," the note said.

"What did you do?"

Brad's eyes were wet. "I looked at his magazines . . . *Playboy* magazines."

I stared back at him, shocked. Trish used to leave her *Playgirl* magazines lying on her nightstand. It was no big deal. When Dad was a bachelor DJ, he left his *Joy of Sex* book on the coffee table. I couldn't see what Brad did that was so wrong.

I was grasping for any justification for my father's reaction and pictured Brad digging in my father's dresser drawers. "Where were they?"

Brad shrugged and mumbled, "In his room." There could have been any reason Brad went to Dad's room, to bum a cigarette, whatever. It's not like their room was off limits. There were times that I thought Brad was a jerk, that he purposely tried to piss our father off. But *this*? This was too much. Brad didn't deserve this. My father was the one who was not being fair. Nobody deserved this.

"I'll help you clean up."

My brother shook his head, no, holding in his pain. "Just go."

I stood there for a moment, trying to decide what was worse, helping my brother pick up his ransacked room or leaving him alone in his shame.

Finally, I walked out of his room.

Why had my father lost his temper that day? Was it the magazines, or the bigger secret, Dad's mail-order porn videos? Nobody could ever know that the famed sportscaster watched such things. I guess that would make him lose his cool.

For Brad's eighteenth birthday that October, I bought him a six-pack of beer. Technically, my father bought the beer. I stood with Dad at the cash register and handed him the money.

Brad was legally allowed to drink now, just making the cutoff before the drinking age went to twenty-one. That Saturday night, after Brad and Pat's birthday dinner (as coincidence would have it, they shared the exact same birthdate), Brad was excited to be able to take his beer over to a girl's house on the next street. He was officially an adult! He was legal!

He and this girl weren't particularly close, but she knew it was his birthday and had invited him to a small party. Brad came back a short while later. When I asked why he was home so early, he said they were doing drugs, so he left.

My birthday gift now seemed lame. I was quietly proud of Brad though. A lot of other guys would have stayed and joined in.

My father said nothing of Brad's strength in knowing to walk out of there. My father could have salvaged Brad's eighteenth birthday and made it special by taking him to a bar, father and son, but he didn't. He kept watching whatever movie was on TV. Brad went up to his bedroom, alone.

Brad's regular friends didn't do drugs, but they did stupid things. Pete, Alan, and Addy were rednecks. Alan hated blacks and called them niggers. Pete's brother was in jail for shooting someone. Addy's eyes were such pits of blackness that he plain scared me.

In Oakland, Brad had been in the cool crowd and had his pick of girlfriends. In Maryland, he hung out with the rejects, because that's who lived near us and that's who Brad met on the bus the first day of school.

During Christmas break, two months after Brad's eighteenth birthday, Pat called from work to say they would be home late, meaning after one o'clock in the morning. Brad had been arrested. Dad and Pat had to go the court house for an arraignment.

The next morning, my father was alone at the breakfast table with his coffee, when he told me what happened.

Brad and his friends had decided to break into the police compound to steal radios out of the impounded cars. Brad was accused of being the look-out. I didn't believe that. Brad probably said he wasn't going to join in, probably tried to talk his idiotic friends out of their idiotic plan, failed, and then was stuck there, forced to wait outside the fence.

Some policemen were guarding the compound from within an unmarked car outside the fence. The policemen could overhear the boys planning. Pete and Alan even peed on the unmarked car, while the police ducked down. *Idiots!* Once the boys climbed over the fence, the police let the dogs loose on them.

My father took a sip of his coffee, flicked a cigarette ash into the ashtray, and continued his story. "So there we are in court at two in the morning, and everyone's asking, 'What's George Michael doing here? What's George Michael doing here?'"

I couldn't understand how my father was thinking about his own embarrassment and reputation, while Brad was sitting in a jail cell. I was afraid and sad for Brad.

"Maybe we should go to a family counselor," I offered. In truth, I wanted this as much for myself as for Brad.

"Ain't no way in hell I'm doing that."

Dad took a drag on his cigarette, the smoke curled in the air. In his view, talking to a counselor was only for crazy or weak people.

I contemplated his answer. "Remember when you chaperoned Brad's Boy Scout trip?" Brad was nine or so and they had gone rafting. The boat tipped over, which was both a laugh and scary because one of the boys couldn't swim. "Maybe just you and he should go away for a weekend."

Dad scrunched up his face as if the thought was absurd and I was both stupid and melodramatic. Instead, my dad told Brad he could either leave home and change his name, or stay here and his home would be like prison. Brad stayed home, as if he had a choice.

Because Brad was eighteen, he was tried as an adult. He hadn't taken anything or climbed the fence, so he might get off with community service, if he was lucky.

Brad came sullenly into the kitchen, head hung low. I couldn't stop staring at the red marks around his wrists. I was surprised Brad braved the kitchen at all. I would have hidden in my room.

Dad left the table without a word. I busied myself with the dishes.

Whether there is a single moment or several that define us as parents, this was my father's moment. There was none of the self-blame a normal father would feel, no "Where did I go wrong . . . how do I save my son . . . how do I get him with the right friends?" No sir. My father took all the credit for our successes and none of the blame for our screw ups.

I could blame all the crap on Pop. My father was, after all, just falling back on what he had seen Pop do when faced with a wayward child.

I will never say that my father did the best he could. He didn't. If he pursued being a good father, like he had done in those golden years when he first got custody of us, or with the same dogged determination that he pursued being the best in sports, he would have hugged Brad that morning, told him he loved him, told him he would make time for him, and tried to listen to his son, no matter the pain and feelings of failure that might have seeped in. But my father did none of that.

Maybe Pat was right, that we were lucky our father wasn't an alcoholic. But I think it is the other way around. My father was lucky none of us was a total delinquent, lucky that Brad didn't let that hurt turn to a rage and one day, say, smash my father's windshield in.

So even though I was often mad at my brother, it was my father's treatment of Brad that widened the divide between my father and me.

I was struggling to figure things out about my dad, even about Pat. I was also trying to learn how to be someone's girlfriend. George and I were officially a couple, my first real boyfriend. He called me his sunshine. Indeed, my eyes shone more brightly now that here was someone who truly liked me.

For his birthday that April, I gave him an engraved, silver bracelet, something permanent and a reminder of me that he could take with him back to Switzerland.

When Michelle had a solo in her junior high's talent show, George and I went to see her perform. Dad and Pat were at work. My sister would be roller-skating to "Freeze Frame", having practiced every day for weeks in our garage. Some of the acts were on stage, but for Michelle's act, they cleared the back of the auditorium/gym, just to be sure she didn't skate off the stage. The night of the talent show, she skated out in her hot-pink shorts (my hand-me downs) and maroon body suit. She looked good. She skated to the rhythm of the music, skating backwards, faster, and faster in a wide circle. My breath caught when I noticed one of the students sitting on the floor, his foot jutting out slightly. In our garage, there were no students sitting around. I squeezed George's hand hard. The music ended and the audience roared with its applause. She hadn't tripped! Michelle's was the best act. Even George said, "I feel like a bloody proud father here!" Indeed, Dad should have seen Michelle that night. She was the star, and he would have been proud. Michelle repeated the act for Dad the next day, in the garage. It wasn't the same.

George and I had our perfect dates, but that spring, our differences of opinion grew into more difficult squabbles, testing my loyalties and making me question what I was willing to do to keep a boyfriend. George didn't like my best friend Deanna, and he couldn't keep his nasty comments to himself. He would make a joke about the way my friend did her makeup, likening it to peeling back the lid on a can of tuna fish. "She rolls her face on in the morning," he'd say, and begin a peeling motion along his cheek. If he didn't like her, why should I? If I really cared about him, he argued, I would choose to spend time with him rather than with Deanna. I didn't think the way George did, but I was a people-pleaser, a chameleon who wanted to keep the peace.

When I got my hair permed like Pat's, George looked me up and down as he would a vagrant and said nothing. He didn't need to. I learned to blow my hair straight.

Our final argument came in New York when the school drama club took a weekend field trip to see some Broadway shows. I knew New York. I remembered how the city worked from when we had visited my father on the weekends when I was ten. So at seventeen when we were getting on the bus in New York City, I knew you had to have exact change ready. George did not have any change and only had a single large bill. So I gathered my quarters and paid for both of us. For me, it wasn't about who paid. It was about not holding up the bus driver or the line of people behind us getting annoyed.

George's face grew dark as it always did before erupting. He was insulted. He started cursing in Swiss-German. I tried to explain that it was no big deal, that you had to have exact change for buses, and that I didn't mind paying. It was only a couple of dollars. He seethed. By the end of the day, when his tantrum still hadn't subsided, I told him I was done with his temper. Done trying to please him. Done. Done. Done. I was breaking up with him.

That night when the drama teacher, Dr. Bogar, came to check on us for curfew, he told me that George was not in his hotel room. He said he had no choice but to put him on a bus back to DC, alone. I told Dr. Bogar it was all my fault, that I shouldn't have broken up with him while we were in the city. He didn't get along with his host family, and I was all he had in America. I should have waited until we got back to Maryland before breaking things off.

Fortunately, George came back to his room soon after, before Bogar called the host family, so Bogar gave him a second chance.

The next day, my friend Donna Saraisky from Oakland, planned to meet us in the city to join us for dinner. At dinner that night, George tried to woo me back by giving Donna and me each a long-stemmed rose. I had explained to Donna about our fight. At this point, I didn't even want her to meet George. I told him I didn't want the rose. Donna, always well-mannered, accepted both roses.

The five-hour bus journey from New York to Maryland was like someone pouring salt on an open wound. On the ride up to New York, George and I had sat together. Now we sat apart, in different seats, giving the whole bus witness to our break up.

At one point, he asked the girl next to me to switch seats with him so he could talk to me. She couldn't say no. He begged me to give him another chance. I was his only joy in America, and he was going back to Switzerland in two months. Couldn't I do this for him? Couldn't I just give him two more months?

I told him I needed a break and asked him to give me time. He said okay. We agreed on a two-week hiatus. At the end of the conversation, he didn't go back to his seat and I didn't know how to tell him to go, so we rode silently, wishing the journey would end.

In the weeks that followed, we avoided each other in the hallways at school. When I saw him laughing with another girl, my heart ached. I argued with myself that I didn't love George. I didn't believe in love, because in my view love lasted forever and nothing lasted forever. Just look at Dad and Trish. They had loved each other and nearly destroyed each other. Dad and Pat didn't seem any happier, fighting constantly. I told myself that my feelings for George were nothing more than a high school crush.

Mike was a different story. My friend Deanna was the first to tell me I loved him. I presented my argument to her that *nothing* lasts forever.

When George and I had our most bitter fights, I would call Mike to vent. Mike was, first and foremost, my friend. He listened. He made me laugh. I could not sort out what I felt for Mike, or what I felt for George. Mike was the shooting stars at the beach, the soothing lull of the sound of the waves. I was not allowed to love him, though; because Dad and Pat would never approve. George was a force, like diving off the high dive at Downs Farm's swimming pool when I was eight: exhilarating and frightening that could end in a subtle splash or a painful belly flop. George and I looked good together. I was lucky he wanted someone like me to be his girlfriend, his "sunshine," as he called me.

So after the two week hiatus, George and I got back together. We didn't fight so much in those final weeks. He really did try to control his temper and rude comments. Then of course, there was the romance of prom. George showed up in the limousine donning a red cummerbund, breathtakingly handsome. Our date that night was the kind of prom every girl should have, with dancing and happiness and laughter. George's face only showed annoyance when I said I had to be in by midnight—most of the other students were driving to the beach to watch the sunrise; but I was only a junior and adhered to my parents curfew, whether they were home or not.

I still didn't believe I loved George, but I couldn't explain the void in my heart when he left for good that July. Had I only imagined the last year? How could I go from seeing a person every single day, laughing, kissing, fighting, to nothing? Not even a phone conversation.

The hole in my heart was not only from George, but from Dad. He criticized me constantly. I asked if I could go by myself to the beach, or with my friend Deanna, saying I needed time to think. The ocean soothed my soul. Dad said no.

My once-weekly letters to Mike turned into phone calls. He seemed to be the only person who understood me, and I was desperate to see him.

Dad and Pat went to Cheyenne, Wyoming, like they did every year for the rodeo. Michelle was visiting Trish, who now lived in Philly. I had the day off from work. So I drove to Ocean City, New Jersey, to see Mike for the day, a four-hour drive. I had driven almost that far before, when George and I went to King's Dominion in Williamsburg, Virginia, so I was confident that I could handle the drive.

Mike and I spent the day at the beach. He introduced me to his girlfriend, who was selling Chipwich ice creams on the boardwalk. He had told me about her, but a current of jealousy ran through me. I couldn't explain what I felt. I only knew that at the end of our day, I felt happy, I felt loved.

I was only a little disappointed that Mike didn't kiss me good-bye. We were friends, but we both knew there was something more. For the drive home, I took caffeinated diet pills to be sure I stayed awake.

Dad and Pat came home Saturday, while I was at work. Sunday morning they called me into the kitchen. I was dressed in my waitress smock, ready for work.

There was no small talk. Dad ordered me to sit down.

His voice boomed. "Where were you Tuesday?"

I hesitated, knowing the day. "Work, I guess."

I never saw his hand coming. He hit me hard across my face, almost knocking me out of the chair, which teetered with the blow.

"Don't you fucking lie to me. I'll ask you one more time. Where were you Tuesday?"

I righted myself in the chair. "I drove to the shore." I hiccupped.

He slapped me again across the face. "How do you think it feels to get a call from Grandma saying Jim and Irene passed you on the highway near Ocean City? 'What's Cindi doing in Ocean City?'"

Pat's brother from Philadelphia passed me on the highway? What were the chances? Clearly God was punishing me for lying.

My dad continued, his voice booming, "I thought there must be some mistake. Not Cindi. Cindi wouldn't be such a sneak. Not Cindi. Who'd you go see?"

I could say Jill. I could say nobody, but I didn't. "Mike. Mike Pultro."

My father slapped me again. "You think I didn't notice all these phone calls to New Jersey on the phone bill? So I called Mike Pultro. Pretended to be Brad getting blamed for mileage on the car. At least *he* didn't lie to me."

Pat drummed her fingernails on the kitchen table then asked, "Are you a slut?" Her one eyebrow was raised, that look of superiority and judgment cast down.

This stopped my crying and, in that moment, I hated her. "No."

"George has only been gone a month, and you run off to see Mike Pultro?"

I knew they would never understand about Mike. I knew they would find a way to cheapen our relationship.

"How do we know you and George really went to Kings Dominion?"

"We went there. We brought back the souvenir cups," I tried to offer as proof.

"How do we know you didn't buy them somewhere else?"

I couldn't respond. Where else would we have gone? Where else would someone buy such souvenir cups?

My father resumed his tirade. He interrogated me about my drinking. Which friends drank? He called me a liar, a sneak, inconsiderate, selfish, and fat. He gave me an ultimatum: I could leave home and never come back, or stay here and accept that life would be different. Very different.

"You're going on a diet. You're going to put your weight on the refrigerator every day. You are not allowed to go anywhere or use the car for anything except for work and to drive Michelle places."

Eventually, he dismissed me. I was late for work but grateful for a place to escape to. At work, I forced a smile to the customers at my tables. I was sorry that my cheek was only red. But even if it were blue, what could anyone have said?

I didn't dare call Mike, not when Dad was monitoring the phone bill. It was Mike who finally called me. I told him everything, and ended with the thought that that maybe they were right: I was not a good person.

Mike told me to leave and said I shouldn't stop believing in myself. He said what Dad and Pat were doing was wrong. That my father had lied to him, pretended to be my brother. *That* was wrong.

Where would I go, I sobbed? I needed them. I loved them. It was me who had to change. I had to steel myself. I had to accept their view—of me, of the world. I had to learn to stop caring.

Mike tried to talk me out of this way of thinking and said he wanted me to talk to a friend of his, a psychologist about the way my parents were acting. I told Mike I didn't think we could be friends anymore. Steeling my heart meant letting go of him too.

The next letter I got from Mike, he ended with, "The one thing I didn't tell you on the phone that I should have—I love you."

I clutched the letter in my hand and held onto his words, a thread connecting me to the part of me I was trying to let die.

I went on a diet. I wasn't told how to lose weight, only that I had to. The Dexatrim pills were not doing the trick, so I bought a diet book—the Scarsdale diet—and dropped twenty-five pounds in a month. I weighed myself every day and posted it on the refrigerator as ordered. To this day, I weigh myself every day. I can't say that my father was completely wrong in his approach. It worked, after all. But when my own children are gaining weight, I exercise alongside them and cook healthier meals. Dad, on the other hand, continued to cook the vegetables with cheese sauce, hamburgers with buttered buns, and the best darn apricot turnovers, with homemade vanilla frosting.

A few weeks after my trip to the shore, Dad asked Brad to take Michelle to get a physical as she was starting at the middle school. Brad's car broke down so he couldn't go, and Dad told me to take her. I took her to a clinic (we didn't have a regular doctor), but the clinic wouldn't see Michelle, as I was not her legal guardian and not eighteen. Dad was livid. Somehow this was my fault.

Dad called the clinic and wrote a note giving me permission to bring my sister to the doctor. When Michelle came out of the doctor's office, she hissed at me, "You are such a liar."

"What? What do you mean? What happened?" Michelle just glared at me with disgust, then looked out the car window as I drove home. I can still think back to that look of animosity and mark it as her first look of coldness that would eventually become permanent.

It was the next morning before I found out what had happened. Dad summoned me into the kitchen.

"How could you lie again?"

I wracked my brain. What had I done wrong?

"Your weight. How could you just make that up?"

"I didn't," I replied quietly. Arguing with my father was not something to be done loudly, if at all.

"There is no way that Michelle weighs more than you." So that was it. Michelle was not fat, but she was taller than me and bigger boned.

I offered to get the scale. Pat, Michelle, and Dad all stared at me, the black sheep, the fat little liar. I stood on the scale and waited for each of them to look. The scale was correct. I had not lied.

But there was no apology. From anyone. I should have known better than to hope for one. Those days were long gone.

I was losing my spirit. I tried reading religious self-help books. I tried sorting things out by writing in my journal. But I wasn't sure that was safe. I had once caught Pat reading Michelle's journal. After that, I had hid my own journal in Brad's room, under his mattress.

Even so, in the weeks that followed my trip to see Mike, Dad made a reference to a thought I had only ever expressed in my journal. It was a thought about Pat and how she was never willing to consider that she might be wrong, but that at least Dad would. I had never voiced this thought aloud to Deanna or Donna, so nothing could have been overheard on the phone. I got in trouble for having such a thought, though, that Dad said he could see in my face. So I stopped writing.

Wait. I had written about my trip to see Mike in my diary. Did that mean that Pat's brother passing me on the highway was a lie and not some divine punishment? Was it nothing more than . . . Pat was reading my diary. PAT . . . WAS . . . READING . . . MY FUCKING DIARY? The whole time, my dad was calling me a liar and a sneak? God, thirty years later, and I am still such a sucker when it comes to my father.

CHAPTER 12

A Fall from Grace

WHATEVER THE CAUSE, I can trace all the origins of my ultimate disowning to the first day of school in my senior year, 1982.

Nobody warned me that my stumbles would leave me unrescuable. Perhaps other parents pick up their children when bruised. I was alone in my mistakes. At the time, I thought my trip to the shore to see Mike would be my biggest mistake. But I was wrong.

One of my punishments for having driven to the shore to see Mike was that I had to take the bus to school the first few weeks. Seniors didn't ride the bus, so it made my punishment public and my first day as a senior in high school a disappointment. It was on that first day of school that I saw the new vice principal supervising the bus arrivals, a stranger in a crowd. I didn't know then that he would be my ultimate downfall.

While riding the bus was embarrassing, school was otherwise a welcome relief, a refuge from the tension at home. Having lost weight, I looked better on the outside—but I was withering inside.

If Dad and Pat had distrusted me before my drive to the shore, they trusted me even less after. One night, I asked permission to take our drama teacher Dr. Bogar out to dinner for his birthday with my friend Karen. She had the lead in the fall play, *Last of the Red Hot Lovers*, the same play I had starred in as a freshman in New Jersey. I was the assistant director.

Dad and Pat had said it was okay to take him out to dinner. Since Pat had hired a housekeeper (pointedly remarking that it was my inability to handle both cleaning the house and my school work), Michelle wouldn't be home alone. But when I wasn't home when Pat called that evening, I was immediately in trouble. When I got home from dinner, Michelle relayed Pat's message to me, "You have to wait up until they get home."

"But that's not until after midnight."

Michelle shrugged.

I countered, "Did you even tell them where I was?"

I waited up until after midnight. I was never one of those people who could get by without sleep, and just thinking about the six A.M. start, five hours of sleep, got me more upset. I sat alone on the sofa, waiting for the lights of their car to shine in the driveway. When I finally saw the headlights, I wasn't sure if I should stay seated in the lounge chair or if I should go greet them at the garage door. I decided to wait in the kitchen, standing.

They marched into the house. "Who gave you permission to be out on a school night?" my father accused.

"You did. Remember, I asked if Karen and I could take Dr. Bogar out to dinner . . . for his birthday?"

The realization crossed both their faces. But there was no apology.

I missed the days when my Dad and I were close.

One thing that had always made my Dad happy was baked goods. The idea of a peace offering gradually formed in my head. I couldn't handle Dad and Pat together, but maybe I could handle them one on one.

Pat was away for a couple days visiting her parents in Philadelphia, so when I got home from school, I baked Dad a cake. If I hurried, I could have it baked and frosted in time to take to the station after the six o'clock news. I baked a butter cake with fudge frosting, adding extra butter to the frosting, just the way he liked it.

When I got to the station, he was still on the air. The guard at the desk let me go to the sports room. The guys knew me from the

New Year's Eve dinners and the Father's Day segment we had shot at Oriole's stadium the previous June.

When I walked in with the cake, Stoney, one of the sports producers, asked, alarmed, "Is it his birthday?" Dad was the boss and it would have been bad if anyone had forgotten his birthday. At work, he was known for demanding perfection and unequivocal loyalty.

"No, I just wanted to bake him a cake."

When Dad walked into the sports room, he was surprised to see me, but not mad. I presented him with the cake. He gave me a light hug and suggested we go to dinner.

During dinner he declared, "You have to talk to us, Cindi."

"I know. I'm trying." I couldn't find the words for the storm inside my heart. My throat closed and I stifled tears. There were so many things I wanted to say.

"And you have to make peace with Pat. You should invite her to dinner when she gets back."

I knew he was right. I couldn't get along with my father without getting along with Pat. Still, I was more intimidated by her. When there was conflict, it seemed like he was willing to listen, and he sometimes doubted himself. But not Pat. With Pat, life's rules were black and white, never shades of gray, and she never doubted she was right.

I did as my father suggested, and Pat and I had our own dinner. For a few weeks things were better. Until the night of the dress rehearsal.

The week leading up to the final performance, we had an evening dress rehearsal. This had been the routine for the six other shows I had done in high school, and it should have come as no surprise to my dad and Pat. So I didn't get home until after nine on that school night. Michelle again relayed the message that I had to wait up for them.

When they got home, they called me a liar. They said I couldn't be trusted. Dad said he would call the school and I would be found out. I told him to call. I respectfully relayed this with the resolution of a prisoner who will be lashed no matter what.

I couldn't sleep that night. I sobbed with helplessness. Why did my dad hate me so? It was all my fault we had a housekeeper. I should have been able to handle school and the house and Michelle and my waitressing job. I was a liar. I had gone to the beach to see Mike and not told them. It was a lie of omission.

The next morning, I got dressed for school and I didn't even bother trying to hide the circles under my eyes with makeup.

When I walked into the school building that morning, Dr. Bogar was walking down the hall and greeted me cheerfully, "Good morning, Cindi."

I tried to say a simple "hello" in response but, instead, I started sobbing.

He pulled me to the side, away from the throng of students coming in. "What is it? What's wrong?"

I choked out the details, "My parents don't believe me. They don't think I was at dress rehearsal last night. They're going to call the principal."

Dr. Bogar led me to Mrs. Cage's office, my guidance counselor, while I tried to stop crying. I had never spoken to Mrs. Cage about my problems with my parents, but she always helped me with my school schedule and knew it was up to her and me alone. She knew who my father was and what he was like.

Dad had tried to joke with one of the other guidance counselors, Mr. Barrons, when we first moved to Maryland. "Put Cindi in all honor's classes because she's smart, but Brad, he's your basic dumb shit, so it doesn't matter what you put him in."

Brad had tried to laugh it off, something we all did whenever Dad made a dig that he guised in humor.

Mr. Barrons hadn't laughed. Dad again tried to be funny with another remark. Mr. Barrons set aside the papers in his hands, spread his hands flat on the desk, looked my father in the eye, and said, "Mr. Michael, if your son has a learning problem, we have special classes for remedial students."

Dad stopped joking. I had never seen someone put my father in his place. From then on, my Dad did not like Mr. Barrons. For the record, I might have gotten more As in school than my brother, but it was Brad who was the clever one, the one smart enough to figure out how to handle Dad and Pat, something I clearly never learned.

That morning, Dr. Bogar stayed with me while I tried to explain to Mrs. Cage, hiccupping through my father's accusations. "They said I couldn't be trusted, that they didn't believe me. Nobody stays at school that late." I didn't think they loved me, didn't even want me around, but to say these words aloud would be too much to admit.

Mrs. Cage paged the principal, but only the new vice principal was around. By the time the new vice principal, Dr. T., the stranger I had seen the first day of school, walked into Mrs. Cage's office, my sobs slowed to a quiver. Dr. T. introduced himself and listened to my whole story.

"Have you tried talking to them about how you feel?"

I nodded. "I baked my dad a cake . . . I invited Pat to dinner . . ." A tear slipped out as I recalled my failed attempts to make them love me. "I tried. We never see each other. It's hard for me to talk to them."

He considered this. "What about writing, writing them a letter? Sometimes, when we are upset, it's easier to write than to talk."

I nodded. I told him about a story I had written, a fictional story based on my father and me, that mirrored the scene I had tried to share in speech class last year, about Dad and Pop reconciling when it was too late. But in my fictional version, it ended with the daughter going away to college. All my stories in those days had happy endings, endings I wished would come true. In my story, the father and daughter made up before it was too late, before the girl went away to college. Real life was so very different.

"Have you shared the story with your father?"

I shook my head no.

"Don't you see how you're keeping that from him . . . not letting him know how deeply you care?"

I didn't think of it that way. I didn't share any of my stories with them anymore. They didn't have time for such things and Dad was not into my kind of stories, sentimental. He preferred Sydney Sheldon books, with power, lust, and sex.

Mrs. Cage and Dr. T. sent me back to class after I calmed down. They said they would let me know if my father called the school but suspected he wouldn't in the calm of a new day.

It was during creative writing class that Mrs. Marsh, the other vice principal, pulled me out into the hallway to let me know that my father had, indeed, called. She said my father had been very calm during the conversation. He wanted to confirm that I had been at rehearsal. Had the school known it would go on so late?

I was relieved my parents weren't home when I got back from school. It was easier not to face them. There was also not a note from them on the kitchen counter. No recognition that I had not lied. The father who had once come to my middle school to say he was sorry, who hadn't wanted the anger to last another day, no longer existed. He was gone.

Only with decades of hindsight can I see how my father's heart had hardened by this point. His getting fired, his fear of failing, and the death of his father all within two years brought my father to a place I could no longer reach. And there was Pat. She fed the seed that grew in my father, planted by his own cold-hearted father, like a weed choking the gentler parts of my dad.

On the weekend, everyone tried to pretend like nothing had happened. Dr. T.'s words bothered me, though. Maybe my dad really didn't know that I cared that much, that I was trying so hard to do everything right. Maybe my story would help him understand me.

So on Saturday, when I went to the play, I left my story on the kitchen counter with a note, explaining that it was written about us.

Dad and Pat never came to my plays in Maryland. The play wasn't important enough to them. I was only the assistant director, not even on stage.

When I got home that night, the story lay on the floor of my bedroom. No note in return, no comment. To me, it meant the story was no good. Proof my father didn't care. He didn't love me like he once had, before he was a famous sportscaster and before he married Pat.

In the months that followed, I tried to shut out all feelings. I tried to look ahead to college, that light above the clouds.

At Christmas, Mike sent me a dozen roses. I told my parents they were from him. I tried to be more honest. They didn't say anything. I got a Christmas card from George in Switzerland. It felt like last year had been a delusion.

In January, my best friend from New Jersey, Kris, returned from New Zealand after a year as an exchange student. I asked Dad if I was allowed to drive up for the weekend to visit her. I was surprised when he said yes. I figured it had more to do with my Dad liking Kris than how much he trusted me. I skipped school on Friday to go.

The drive from Germantown, Maryland, to Oakland, New Jersey, is just over four hours, and I felt confident enough driving along I-95 in the bright sunshine. But the stretch of road just before the Baltimore tunnel was nerve-wracking. Construction and concrete barriers narrowed the road, leaving no shoulder or room for error, a problem for someone with no depth perception. My heart pounded and I slowed the car to navigate the narrower lanes, but I made it through okay.

Just after lunch, I was back in Oakland, my one-time home. I had missed Kris so much. Her mom was expecting me, but for Kris, my visit was a surprise. I parked opposite her house on Route 202, a main road with double yellow lines. Their steep driveway with stone walls on either side was too dangerous to pull into. My legs were stiff from the long car ride, and I took a deep stretch as I climbed out of the car, breathing in the cold winter air, so excited to see my best friend. We had written many letters, pages and pages long, every month. I wrote about trouble with my parents and the lack of a boyfriend. She wrote about all the cute boys she was meeting, with their gorgeous accents, the fun she was having in Auckland.

I stood at the street corner, waiting to cross 202. Traffic was a little busy for midday. I wondered if I would have to cross the road in stages, first to the middle, then all the way. Finally, there was a pause in both directions. I looked left, then right again. It was clear. I started across the street, looked left one last time as I crossed. I caught a glimpse of the hood of the GMC truck as it crested the hill. I was just to the yellow dividing line when I felt my body being lifted, somersaulting through the air. Time slowed as I was airborne. I bounced on the hood before landing on the sidewalk from where I had started. I stood immediately, thinking, *My parents will kill me.*

People were beside me before I realized where they had come from. "I'm okay. I'm okay," I kept repeating. I did not cry.

I recognized the driver of the GMC truck from my old school. Billy Herndon. Why wasn't he in school? I had never liked him much when I lived here.

The police arrived quickly. I insisted I didn't need an ambulance. A police officer asked me to sit in his car, while he talked to the driver and the witnesses. They measured the skid marks on the road.

When the policeman came back to the car, I took a deep breath before forcing myself to ask the dreaded question, "Is this my fault?"

"You were crossing at a corner." He looked me over. "But your outfit blends in with the trees." I had worn my favorite brown sweater and corduroys. I had wanted to look nice for the occasion. The sweater was ruined, torn at the elbow. "You're also a minor in the state of New Jersey."

"I'll be eighteen in two weeks."

"Yeah, but right now you're a minor."

"My parents will be so mad at me. You can't tell them."

"Do they know you're here?"

"Yeah, but they'll think they shouldn't have let me come. They'll think it's my fault."

The officer encouraged me to go to the hospital to get checked out, but when I still had not shed a tear, he agreed to walk me across the street to Kris's house.

Mrs. Farnsworth opened the door. The police officer tried to make a joke to appear less intimidating. "I caught this young lady trying to run away." Mrs. Farnsworth didn't laugh. She knew how things were at home. At her deadpan stare, the policeman explained what had really happened.

Kris came up behind her mom in the doorway. Seeing her smile, I rushed to embrace her. Nothing else mattered.

We sat on the sofa and talked face-to-face for the first time in more than a year. It was only later when I tried to stand that the jarring pain forced me back down. Mrs. Farnsworth called her doctor and tried to get me an appointment, but he didn't have any free slots and thought I might need an X-ray.

So, they took me to a hospital. I didn't want to go. I was ruining Kris's homecoming. But by then, I could barely move.

At the hospital, the nurse wouldn't treat me without Dad or Pat's permission. I begged her not to call them. Mrs. Farnsworth tried to claim she was my legal guardian, agreeing that my father would be mad and knowing this would only make things worse at home. The nurse asked for proof of guardianship, which of course she didn't have, so I said forget it, I would be fine. I'd rather not have been treated than have to tell Dad and Pat about the accident. The nurse explained to me the risks of internal bleeding, insisting that I should be examined.

Finally, I relented and gave the nurse my parents' phone number at work. It was well before the five-thirty newscast, but it was still at work, a place we only called in an emergency. The nurse explained the situation, then passed the phone to me.

Pat immediately accused, "Did you even *look?*" That's when I finally burst into tears.

My father got on the phone and shouted, "Jesus H. Christ! Now I'm going to have to take off work to come get you!"

I stifled the tears and assured him, "You don't have to come. Really. They just want to be sure. I'm not that hurt. There's no blood or anything."

"Fine. But you have to get a copy of the police report," Dad ordered.

I managed to mumble, "Okay," then passed the phone back to the nurse. I couldn't talk anymore. I could keep my shit together when a car hit me, but not when my dad started shouting at me.

As it turned out, nothing was broken; just badly bruised, inside and out. They gave me some pain medicine and told me no gym for two weeks. I asked about trying out for the musical, but they said I had to wait to see how I recovered. I should have been thankful, but in a way this diagnosis was worse. It meant I had been *melodramatic.* I hadn't needed to go to the hospital.

Even though nothing was broken, I couldn't sleep that night as every time I rolled over, pain shot up my back.

I stopped by the police station when I left Oakland on Sunday morning to get a copy of the police report. It didn't have much in it. Just a drawing of the scene of the accident. I wished it said clearly who was at fault, but it didn't.

During most of the drive home, I had to lean forward in the car as it hurt to lean back against the seat. By the time I got home, I had stiffened up again. Michelle hugged me gently. Brad was at college. I asked Michelle what Dad had said about the accident.

She told me, "When I brought him his coffee in bed yesterday morning, he said, 'Your sister could be dead right now.'"

On the weekends, I usually brought Dad and Pat their coffee in bed. When Dad would wake up, he'd shout, "Is the coffee on?" I'd bring them their coffee, then Michelle and I would sit on the floor in their bedroom sharing stories of the week. When things were tense with us, though, Dad got his own coffee. It was his way of saying he didn't want me to visit.

Sunday night was when my Dad recorded his syndicated sports highlights show, *The Sports Machine*, so Dad and Pat got home around one A.M. That Sunday night, I lay in my bed, waiting for them to come check on me, to tell me they were glad I was alive. They never did.

It still hurts to think back to that night and the utter aloneness I felt, to know that my dad didn't care if I lived or died. He was too caught up on his treadmill of fame.

That night, alone in my bed, hearing Dad and Pat come home from work, getting drinks in the kitchen, and then not coming to check on me, something inside me died.

The next day, when I went to school, I left my hospital bracelet on. I needed someone to ask me what happened. I needed my friends and teachers to tell me they were glad I was okay, glad I was alive. School was the only place where anyone cared about me.

Even my eighteenth birthday was not important at home. The Redskins were in the playoffs, so we would be celebrating my birthday in March, with my dad's birthday.

It was my friends, not my family, who made me feel like I mattered. When I went to school on Monday, a new friend Mary Kay—who was trying to bridge from cheerleader to theater—and a bunch of others decorated my locker, filling it with balloons. During creative writing class, Mary Kay surprised me with a birthday cake and the whole class sang. Their kindness made it harder to steel my heart.

I wrote a poem wondering how a heart could survive when it was not loved. Dr. Bogar, also my creative writing teacher, declared it the most exceptional poem he had seen from a student in all his years of teaching. The imagery! The rhythm! The depth! He took me to the head of the English Department to share the poem.

Truthfully, I don't think the department head was quite as enthralled as Dr. Bogar, but I reveled in the praise.

For college, I wanted to apply to Temple University in Philadelphia, because they had a good theater program and I would be closer to Mike. Dad said, "No. It's in a rough part of Philly."

So, the College of William & Mary became my new first choice; it had both a good writing program and theater. I could major in both. John, my student director from my freshman year in New Jersey, was now a senior there and loved it. I had been to Williamsburg on my eighth-grade field trip and thought it was beautiful, with the gas street lamps and brick walkways. I liked the idea of a smaller college. When I told Dad the tuition, he balked; he let me apply, but both he and Pat insisted that the University of Maryland was good enough.

I didn't want to go to there. It seemed like anyone from in-state got accepted there. What was the point of my having taken such a difficult course load in high school? Brad went there and moaned about how his lectures had four hundred students, and he couldn't get the classes he needed. Maryland's application treated you like a number: no essay, no references, just GPA and SAT scores. Pat had gone to Villanova, her brother Georgetown, and my Dad St. Louis University.

As part of the admission process to William & Mary, to which I *did* apply, there is a personal interview. That I made it that far in the process seemed a positive sign, but one my father wasn't thrilled about. For the interview, I had to drive to an office building an hour away in New Carrollton. The woman interviewing me was kind. I told her, "I'm not as smart as some of my classmates, but I work hard." I wish I'd had more confidence then, but I didn't. It never occurred to me to wish that my parents had helped me prepare.

When I got the rejection letter, I was brokenhearted. Mrs. Cage was surprised too, because a classmate, a football player with lower SAT scores and no honor classes, got in. Mrs. Cage and I thought it was because I had undersold myself in the interview. There was no place for humility in the college-admission process. So, I wrote to the dean and requested a personal meeting. In my letter, I tried to make the case why William & Mary was my first choice and why they would want me. I listed all my achievements, things I hadn't wanted to brag about. I never said how little parental support I had gotten.

The dean agreed to meet with me. From where we lived in Darnestown, it was a three-hour drive to Williamsburg, Virginia. My math teacher, Mrs. Shuma, offered to drive to the campus with me, another person who believed in me. Dad and Pat did not offer. I thanked Mrs. Shuma, but said I would be okay. I was never good at accepting help.

On the day of my interview, it was a sunny day, a good omen. The campus was as I remembered it from my eighth-grade field trip: tree-lined sidewalks, brick buildings. Quaint, just like the town of Williamsburg. I could *feel* myself going there.

Sitting down with the dean, I didn't feel so much nervous as determined. I thanked him for meeting with me and greeted him with a firm handshake, like my father had taught me.

"I don't think I explained myself well in the personal interview," I started. "I told my interviewer that I wasn't as smart as my classmates, my AP classmates. I'm not dumb. I just meant to make a point that doing well in school is something I work at, harder than the others have to. Some of the people in my classes are geniuses. School comes easier for them."

He looked through my file. "Actually, you scored well in the personal interview. Your essay had high marks. Your references are excellent. Your grades look good, course work challenging. Your SAT could have been higher." At 1160, with no prep classes, I was above average in those days, but not in the same league as my classmates who were in the 1300s at least.

"Then why did you reject me?" While I couldn't be confident with my parents, I had to be with the dean. He held my future in his hands.

He set the folder down. "We look at a number of factors."

"You accepted a boy from my school, whose grades are lower than mine. Is it because he plays football?"

"Well, we get more high quality applications from females than males," he explained. "We need to maintain a mix in the student body."

I had only one chance to make my case. I took a deep breath. "So are you saying that because I'm a girl, I was rejected?"

"Basically, yes." He paused. "Cindi, I can offer you a late admittance. It would mean you'd be starting in January. However, it's not that easy to start later than the rest of the incoming freshman."

I was shaking my head *no* even as he was talking. I pictured being home all fall, doing what? Waitressing? Waiting for my adult life to start? Trying not to listen to Dad and Pat criticize my every move? I couldn't take it. "I can't wait that long. Wherever I go to school, it will be in August."

"You don't have to decide now. You can talk it over with your parents."

Wasn't it obvious enough what my parents thought? My parents who were not with me today. I made one last plea. "I believe that William & Mary is the best school for me. I would like to attend here in the fall. If that's not possible, I will make the most out of going to University of Maryland."

"I can't make you that offer."

I had given it my best. I thanked him for his time and walked out.

I had planned to meet my old student director, John, for lunch, but I was too upset. I called him from a campus phone to let him know how the interview went. I didn't even bother to stay for lunch. It wasn't my school. It never would be.

My father was relieved.

At the time, not getting into William & Mary felt like one more stumble, one more painful disappointment. Yet, what I didn't know then, if I had gotten in on regular admittance, I would have dropped out a few months later—when my father disowned me.

In the grand scheme of things, I view the Dean's rejection as one of God's little blessings, His plan to send me to a school where I had a fighting chance of being able to pay my own way.

Then there was the letter from Mike that arrived shortly after, in which he told me about a girl he had met, a dancer in one of the casinos. There was something different about the way he described her, and I just knew another dream had slipped away from me.

Shortly after my rejection from William & Mary, I was named student of the month by the Jaycees. Was it some kind of cosmic consolation prize? The head of the English Department and another English teacher I worked with on the literary magazine had nominated me. Dr. Bogar complained that nobody had consulted him. He would have nominated me too, he said. But would he have? Bogar did what was best for him, like with the fall play. He told me I had the better audition, but that he needed an assistant director, so that's the role I got, even though that wasn't what *I* wanted.

Dad didn't come to my plays, but he said he would come to the Jaycees' award ceremony since it was a small group in a private setting. He didn't like being recognized in public. The award was one small step back to Dad's approval.

A few months later, I was picked to be one of three students for an award by the local CBS station, Channel 9, for the Best of the Class of 1983. We got to have lunch with President Reagan, and we could have appeared in a promo spot on TV, but it was a hot humid day and waiting to be videotaped just to be on TV wasn't that big of a deal to me, so I left early.

Things got better with my dad, but worse with Bogar. He demanded more and more from me: better costumes for the play, more participation in writing class. How could I do it all?

Then there was Karen, a girl who had moved to Seneca Valley from Texas. We were best friends for a few months, then it was like she flipped a switch. For months, we were laughing together, eating lunch together, sharing secrets. Then we weren't.

That spring, she was supposed to be assistant directing the musical. Then she landed the role of Rizzo, the lead in *Grease*. How could she direct and act at the same time? If Bogar let Karen do that for the musical, why couldn't he have let me do the same for the fall play? He was beginning to piss me off.

So during Easter break, I worked extra hard on the costumes, sewing poodle skirts for some of the cast and white satin pants for the dance DJ, Vince Fontaine. I went to the school to drop off receipts for the fabric and other sewing supplies for Bogar to approve for reimbursement. I was big into Hallmark cards that year, for teachers and friends alike, and even though Bogar irritated me, I gave him an Easter card. I stopped by the front office to give a card to Dr. T, too. He wasn't in, so his secretary said she'd leave it in his mailbox.

Dr. T called me a few days later, at home. He had never called my house before, so I was surprised. "Cindi, is there some place we can talk?"

I hesitated, not sure what was up. "Well, um, I wasn't planning on being back at school this week."

"No, not at school. Is there some place quieter? Someplace where we can go for a walk?"

"A walk?"

"Yes, I need to talk to you."

I wasn't sure if this was about my parents, or if Bogar had complained to him about my grumpy attitude.

"I walk at the canal sometimes," I said. The C&O canal is a historic canal alongside the Potomac River, a peaceful place a few miles from my house.

Dr. T. agreed to meet me there in a couple of hours. I thought Dr. T.'s call was odd but not alarming. I had been to Bogar's house a couple times, once to write voter cards and another time after a fight with my parents. Teachers were not taboo friends back then; and, for me, they were the adults who propped me up when it seemed my parents didn't care.

At the canal, Dr. T. and I walked along the footpath, which was quiet at midday. The sun shimmered across the Potomac River, white water bubbling across the rocks where the river bends. We talked about everyday things: what I knew about the canal, the play, how things were at home. I was walking ahead.

"Just slow down a minute."

I paused and turned. That's when he kissed me.

I pulled away. "Aren't you married?" I blurted.

"I am." He was quiet.

My brain was both frozen and racing. "What . . . what are you doing then?"

Dr. T. was not the first teacher to try to kiss me. The basketball coach had tried to kiss me once. One of the players had warned me about this coach. I hadn't believed him, of course. Adults didn't do such things! Then Dad and Pat didn't believe me. Now Dr. T, a full-blown kiss!

We stood amidst the trees. "I see you in the hallway at school," he said, "and something inside me lights up. It's a sea of faces, and then, then . . . there's just you."

I didn't know what to say. I hadn't seen this coming. He was the vice principal!

Yet, he liked me. I meant something to someone.

Take an insecure girl . . . Did I stand a chance?

Eventually, I said I needed to get home. He asked if we could meet later.

"I don't know. I have to check." I needed permission to go out.

"I'll call you later then," he said.

I called Pat at work to see if I was allowed to go out. She didn't ask for details.

Dr. T. called later, and I agreed to meet at a parking lot at a grocery store. I felt nervous and excited at the same time.

In the parking lot, I climbed into his car. He headed north on 270 and eventually pulled into a busy parking lot. The restaurant was busy.

He asked me to wait in the car for a minute while he went in. He came back to the car and said everything was fine. I started to the right toward the restaurant, but he went left. Toward a hotel connected to the restaurant. I wondered if that was simply what adults did rather than parking: they went to a hotel to make out rather than park in the woods.

I still mourn the girl I had been then, my naivety, and how quickly one man destroyed it.

I stood awkwardly inside the hotel room, and talked. He kissed me. I kissed back. He pushed me onto the bed. It was all happening so fast. With George, we had barely gone to second base.

He went for the zipper on my pants. I pushed him away. "I've never done this before."

He hesitated, then said, "I believe you."

I believe you? What an odd response.

At least he stopped, and I stood up, upset. He drove me back to the parking lot to my car.

I thought we were going out to dinner.

Over the weeks, Dr. T. left me notes in my locker: how beautiful I looked, a poem about a rose. Still, it bothered me. It was *my* locker, my space.

At the same time, it felt nice that someone wanted me, even though he was older than me.

By the time he left a gold chain with a heart pendant dangling on the hook in my locker, I no longer complained.

Dr. T. started calling me most days after school. A few times, we went for a walk along the canal. We talked a lot, about his inevitable divorce, about age differences, about life.

He was fortyish. I told myself twenty years wasn't so different. Dad was older than Pat. When Dr. T. told me he had three children, I thought I could be a good friend to them, because I was a child of divorce myself. I would treat them better than Pat treated me.

I was falling in love, and I was happy.

During one of our walks, it started to rain. We ran back to our cars. We sat together and eventually kissed. I wondered about the van that was in the parking lot. Who else was out here in the rain?

I found out the next day.

Dr. T. phoned me at home to tell me the Principal had summoned him to the office. Someone had seen us.

"What did you tell him?"

"That I was counseling you."

Counseling me? Why did he lie? "You should have told him."

"It's not that straightforward."

"But I'm eighteen. What's the problem?"

"You are still a student."

I thought it didn't matter as long as I was eighteen. Bogar, who had gone out with other students, came to mind. Graduation was only a few weeks away.

We decided to wait until after graduation before meeting again— but the damage was already done.

In the morning before school, my friends and I were hanging out in the auditorium. Elizabeth, a freckle-faced junior I drove to school most mornings, was animatedly telling a story. As I approached, she smiled nervously and lowered her eyes, and the conversation stopped. *Was she talking about me?*

Dr. T. continued to leave notes in my locker. During one of our phone calls, he told me the costumes in *Grease* were wonderful, and he mentioned that his wife had come with him to the show and had gotten irritated when she saw my name in the program. She knew me as the girl he was seen walking with along the canal path.

I was puzzled about their going to the play together, if they were in the process of getting a divorce, but at the time, I didn't think too much about these inconsistencies. If only. If only I hadn't been so starved for love. If only I hadn't been so naïve. If only anyone had been home at night to ask me what was happening at school, perhaps things would have turned out so very differently. But what excuse, then, would my Dad have used eventually to disown me?

As graduation neared, the graduation committee wanted my father to be the keynote speaker for our commencement. I had mixed feelings about this. I wanted my *father* at graduation, not the famous *sportscaster*.

Seneca Valley held its graduation at the University of Maryland to accommodate all the family members who wanted to attend. My classmates and I lined up outside the basketball stadium in our yellow caps and gowns, trying not to perspire in the sunshine and humidity. The superintendent, principal, and three vice principals were also in the lineup, including Dr. T. As the guest speaker, my dad was part of the procession. Waiting outside with everyone, my father seemed unsure of himself. Should he talk to the adults or to us teenagers? In that moment, it struck me that he was not comfortable around his peers. He was nervous. He bantered with me until it was finally time for the procession. I was relieved to walk in. This was not the way I wanted my father and Dr. T. to meet, and thankfully, they didn't.

When the top ten percent of the class were asked to stand, I was happy to stand amidst the applause. When the Honor Society members were asked to stand, I stood again. What I dreaded was walking across the stage in front of my dad and Dr. T. What if someone called out, "Cindi Michael is having an affair with the vice principal!" What then?

As I crossed the stage, my father stood—and I hugged him fiercely, "Thank you! I love you."

Nobody shouted anything bad.

Now that I had graduated, it seemed safe to officially date Dr. T. He had also moved into his own apartment.

Lying in my own bed one night, I again listened to Dad and Pat shouting. Another fight with Brad. I set myself an ultimatum. I would not see Dr. T. again until I told them. Finally, there was an afternoon when it was just the three of us. Pat was lying near the pool. Dad was mowing the grass.

I was terrified. I sat at the table by the pool. Pat opened her eyes, squinting.

I came straight out with it. "I met someone. I think I'm in love."

"Really?"

For weeks, I had avoided calling Dr. T. anything. "His name's Michael."

"You mean Mike? Mike Pultro?"

"No." I swallowed hard. I forced myself to continue. It was like jumping off a cliff. "He's forty and he's the vice principal of the school. He and his wife are separated."

She arched her eyebrow. "How long have you been seeing him?"

"Well, we were trying to wait until I graduated. We haven't had a real date, but we've gone for some walks and talked on the phone." I didn't tell her about the hotel.

"Does he have children?"

"Three."

"Are you sure you're ready for this?"

"I want to try."

She shouted to my father who was working in the yard. "George, can you come over here?"

She had to call him over again. I waited for him, then relayed the whole story.

He reached for a cigarette, looking away. "Well, I'm not going to tell you I'm happy about it, but with the lifestyle you've had, I'm not going to tell you 'no.'" I was quiet. He looked out at the rolling hills. He ran his hand over his face. "Christ. I wish to hell you were going to William & Mary now."

I gave a nervous laugh.

Pat jumped in. "We have to meet him."

I nodded enthusiastically. "Yeah, yeah." The positive reaction was unexpected.

Popular opinion soon changed my father's mind.

We four met for dinner a few weeks later in DC, after the six o'clock news. Michael (Dr. T.) and I waited outside on the sidewalk to be sure we were in the right place: an upscale burger place.

When Dad and Pat walked up, they didn't greet us. Instead, they breezed straight into the restaurant.

It was only after we sat that I introduced everyone. It wasn't pleasant, but it was an attempt at acceptance.

"Shit," Dad said. "Last year Cindi wouldn't tell us anything. This year she tells us *this!*"

Everyone gave a nervous chuckle. After our meeting, though, I felt relieved. I didn't have to sneak.

A few weeks later, Michael and I went to Annapolis for the day. He bought coffee mugs for Dad and Pat. I thought it was a nice gesture. Soon they were in the trash.

A few weeks into summer, Pat's parents came to visit. Her mother— Grandma to me— tried to talk me out of the relationship.

"You haven't lived yet," she said. "You haven't even started college." She waved her hand to encompass our home. "*This* isn't normal."

We were at an impasse.

By midsummer, it didn't matter whether I was in love or not. I had become an embarrassment.

I was at work, as a waitress in a country club, when I had a personal call from a lady at the school, my boss said. I went to the back office, wondering if there was some issue with my high school transcript.

The registrar at the high school got straight to the point. "Michael is here in the office with me."

It was her tone of voice. "What's wrong?"

Michael came on the phone, his voice thick. "It's over. It's all over." I could barely hear him.

"Your father called the Board of Ed. I'm out of a job.'"

I shook my head. Dad said it was okay. "But I've graduated. I don't understand." My throat closed.

My boss knew about Michael and me. She was happy that I was happy. It didn't matter to her.

The road blurred as I drove the few miles home. I was in disbelief.

Dad's car was in the garage. I went into the kitchen.

My father stormed downstairs, dressed for work and laid into me. "You Cindi Michael are a homewrecker. Our neighbor is head of the PTO, and *you* are the topic of conversation at the next meeting! What to do about George Michael's daughter?"

He barely paused before launching into the next attack. "I hear you went to the prom with Dr. T."

"I didn't," I whispered.

"I called the principal."

"We went for some walks. I didn't go to the prom with him. I was at the movies that night." *Flashdance*, with some friends. "You can check with anyone."

Dad's accusation bore down on me. Would he hit me, like last summer? "Then what's all the talk going around about a student going to the prom with a teacher?"

I racked my brain. "It wasn't me."

"You were seen in his office with your shirt off."

My face grew hot with shame. "I've never even been in his office. Never."

"I'm telling you that man is a pervert," my dad said finally and left for work.

I turned to the one place I thought would have answers: God. I drove to a church, the only Catholic Church I knew of in the area, St. Mary's in Rockville. I had sometimes passed it on the way to the mall. But the doors were locked. A sign that God, too, was ashamed of me.

I told Michael that my father had called me a homewrecker. He started to criticize my father, but I cut him off. I would not allow him to say anything bad about my father.

Then Dad put the word out to my aunts and uncle that I was threatening his own career. The newspapers would pick up on my affair with the vice principal, and his career would be ruined.

My father's words left me with a permanent sense of shame. Decades passed, and I never went to a high-school reunion. It didn't matter what the truth was.

The rest of the summer I waitressed during the day shift and weekends as much as I could, trying not to bump into Dad.

Michael had his own apartment, so we met there. I was too scared to go out in public, thinking the whole town must be talking about us. Although he lost his job at the high school, the county couldn't technically fire him so they transferred him to an elementary school.

At home, I prepared for college on my own. I didn't ask Dad for money. I shopped on my own and paid for my own dorm things with my waitressing money.

Just before college started, we were supposed to take our family vacation in Wildwood Crest, New Jersey, as we did most summers. I drove my own car. Brad didn't come at all. Family vacations were no longer fun. I stayed for a few days and left early for the start of college, a milestone my father overlooked in planning the vacation.

When I got to campus, I watched all the other families bringing their sons and daughters to college for the first time. I was alone. I pushed this thought away. I was perfectly capable of doing this on my own.

I was assigned to St. Mary's dorm, a beautiful but old building in the middle of the campus. Brad was across campus in one of the newer high rises. The first month of college, I flourished, carried by a light heartedness I had never felt at home. People liked me! Boys liked me! There was nobody constantly criticizing me. I even was awarded another honor: Student of the Year. I didn't tell my dad. Shouldn't he love the whole me?

Dad found out about the award and called, irritated. "When were you going to tell me about this award?" he spat.

I stood in the dorm hallway, clutching the pay phone. "How did you find out?"

"Your brother told me. If this is your way of saying 'Fuck you, I don't need you,' then fuck you, too! You don't ever need to come home. Ever! You can pay for your own goddamn tuition! Do whatever the hell you want, Cindi. I don't give a damn." He hung up.

I held the dead phone in my hand and pressed my head against the dorm wall, tears running down my face.

I swallowed the lump in my throat. I would not let this beat me. I would not let him break me.

I called my childhood friend from Alluvium, Jill Parker, the only person I knew who would be strong enough to handle this. Jill had a confidence to her, a fight, that I lacked. More than once in our summers together, my dad admired her brazenness, preferring her personality to my timid one.

I fumbled with the quarters, desperate to hear Jill's voice. Mrs. Parker answered. Jill wasn't home.

"I just want to know if she still grabs the bull the by the horns?'" It was an expression Mrs. Parker had often used to describe Jill.

She laughed. "Yes, she does."

I told her then. "My dad told me never to come home again."

She gave a half laugh. "Well, sometimes your dad is full of shit."

But it wasn't only my dad who was angry. I was too. And I would show him that I didn't need him, that he had no right to treat me this way.

CHAPTER 13

My Fight to Survive

I HAD TO FIND a way to support myself and stay in college. I thought becoming a resident assistant (RA) would be the best solution. An RA lives in the dorm and acts as a supervisor, so I wouldn't have to pay for my room and board, just tuition. With my good grades, experience waitressing, and having taken care of sister, my brother, and myself I thought I was well qualified.

I made it to the final round of interviews. I'm not sure why I didn't get the job: if it was because I was a freshman, or because I sounded desperate.

So I went to the financial aid office to see how I could pay for my second semester tuition.

The lady handed me the forms. "You'll need to report your parents' income."

"Why, if my Dad is not willing to pay anything?"

"You mean he can't pay?"

"No, I mean he *won't.*"

"He's supposed to."

I stared stone-faced back at the financial-aid advisor. I didn't want to explain the whole painful mess.

After a long silence, she said, "Why don't you put down his income, and we'll see what you qualify for with it."

I whispered, "The last newspaper article listed his income at $300,000 a year."

She paused. "I don't think we can help you then."

I sat, waiting for her to offer me an alternative. I was okay as long as I had alternatives. I slowly pushed the blank forms back across to her and left.

One of my dorm-mates and I interviewed for modeling jobs at a photography school off campus. We had to indicate if we were willing to do "glamour" shots, which they explained meant "partial nudity." We both said no. Neither of us got that job either.

I applied for a job at the bar just off campus where Brad was a bouncer. The Cellar was a beer hall and sports bar; The Attic upstairs was a disco with a live band most nights. The Attic was popular, and the line to get in often snaked down the street. I was eighteen, just missing the cutoff when the drinking age went to twenty-one. Technically, I was allowed to waitress in a bar, but I wasn't allowed to drink. Since the job was nights, it worked out well with school.

They were willing to try me out, mainly because I was Brad's sister. My three years of waitressing in a posh country club didn't seem relevant.

Michael hated my being a cocktail waitress. He warned me that working in a bar was not the same as waitressing in a country club. So he called his friend Steve to see if they were hiring at the video store. They were.

I got the job. The difference was that Video Village paid only four dollars an hour; but with waitressing, I could make fifteen dollars. I took both jobs.

The dress code for The Attic was black pants and a white blouse, nothing skimpy or anything. I could see that the more I flirted, the better the tips, but I hated it. Watching other people get drunk while you are sober is not fun. Having to lock up toilet paper rolls so drunk girls didn't shove them in the toilet seemed stupid, too. My first night, I heard a crash in my section and turned in time to see my brother lifting someone over his head and throwing him out the back door. After a few weeks, I complained to my boss. "Flirting for better tips seems only one step above prostituting." Was I a snob or just naïve?

My senior year in college, I learned in a sociology class that if a cocktail waitress is raped, her job can be used as a mark against her character; that maybe she got what she deserved. The general thinking at the time was that cocktail waitresses lacked morals. It pissed me off. I was just trying not to be homeless.

Thanksgiving 1983 was the first year the University of Maryland decided to keep the campus open over the long weekend. So I would have a place to stay for the long weekend, a blessing. Michael had his kids for Thanksgiving, and he wasn't yet ready for them to meet me. My friend Donna from Oakland offered to have me at her house, but that was a four-hour drive. I knew the only way to get through the day was to steel myself by working. I bought a frozen turkey TV dinner and told The Attic I would happily waitress Thanksgiving night—seven to two A.M. Brad surprised me by telling me he too would be working that night. It made some sense. Dad usually worked Thanksgiving so the number-two sportscaster could have the day off. I didn't ask Brad what the plans were. It would hurt to know.

Not many people stayed on campus that weekend. It was eerily quiet. I tried to use the time to study. My friend Deanna, the only friend from high school I had told about Michael, was home for the weekend from Virginia Tech. I had written her about my plan for the day, and she had told me she'd come see me late morning.

The Resident Assistant let her in. I hugged Deanna fiercely.

She smiled brightly, "Hey, we're kidnapping you."

Her dad walked in behind her.

"What?" I was dismayed, confused to see her father.

"You can't stay here by yourself. It's Thanksgiving. We're kidnapping you. Let's go." For a five-foot, blue-eyed blonde, Deanna was bossy.

"It's fine. Really. I'm studying. I'm working tonight." I put on my most convincing smile.

"So you can have dinner with us," Mr. Gregory joined in, "and we'll bring you back tonight."

And so I had dinner at the Gregory's, less than five miles from my family's home.

Deanna and her family never realized what that dinner meant to me. It was hard to be there, surrounded by their family that was so close to one another while mine was anything but. And yet it was these unexpected acts of kindness that sustained me in the years I was disowned, like droplets of water on a flower struggling to stay alive.

My dorm-mates looked forward to winter break. Christmas was a bigger problem for me, because the campus closed and I didn't know where I would stay. Also, tuition was due in early January, and I hadn't saved enough money. I regretted buying my own bedding for the dorm. I could have used that money now. Plus, the muffler on my car died, then the exhaust pipe. Life was conspiring against me.

My roommate Shannon saved me. She and two other girls were moving off campus. Did I want to join them? Two bedrooms for the four of us was $135 a person, affordable. My only condition was that I could not join in any group grocery bills. I knew I wouldn't have the same food budget they would have.

A week before we were due to move, Shannon and I were studying at our desks when she said she needed to talk to me.

"You know those rumors about our roommates?" We had all heard that someone spotted them kissing outside last year. "Um, well, it's true." She paused. "Are you okay with that?"

I didn't have a strong opinion, me the fence sitter as Pat had called me. I shrugged. "I guess."

The matter seemed settled. Then a few days later, Shannon asked, "You know my friend Jane?" I nodded. "We're, um, more than friends."

I tried to follow her. "You mean like cousins?"

"No, I mean like Lori and Stephanie," our soon-to-be roommates. "Oh."

God, I was slow. My fear was that Shannon wanted Jane to move in and I would be homeless.

"I just thought you should know before you move in."

I tried to picture sharing a bedroom with Shannon and Jane in the next bed. "Does that mean she'll be like sleeping over?"

"I hadn't thought about that."

"I don't get it. You said you had a boyfriend."

"I did. It just sort of happened."

So I was moving in with three women who were either bi-sexual or homosexual. I didn't think too much about whether I approved or disapproved. I just needed a home.

Michael helped me move my few belongings over Christmas break. We spent Christmas day together, and I was grateful for his gift of a warm down coat, lavender, my favorite color.

But it was an otherwise cheerless holiday. My tuition payment loomed large.

I wrote my tuition check and had two dollars left. Waitressing tips afforded me a packet of hot dogs and a box of pasta. It would have to do. Luckily, in 1984, college students didn't yet get inundated with credit card offers.

I was managing financially, barely. Emotionally, I was sinking. I hadn't seen or spoken to my dad in months. Nobody had called me at Thanksgiving or Christmas. Michelle stopped taking my calls. Apparently, she didn't love me the way I loved her.

One night, Brad and I were setting up the tables and chairs at The Attic, when he told me that the registration on my car was about to expire. The car was still registered in Pat's name, even though I had bought it from her the summer before my senior year in high school for $900. The deal was that I could have the car as long as I got a paint job and new hubcaps. The maroon 1975 Chevy Nova was my first big investment. I hand-waxed it to keep it shiny. A neighbor driving by thought I had painted it white, I had used so much wax.

Pat was not willing to give me the title to renew the registration. "Why can't she just sign it over? It's my car," I said to Brad as I set up the tables in my section of the bar.

He shrugged.

"What if I don't do anything about the registration? What happens then?"

"They'll ticket you."

"And if the registration is in Pat's name, she gets the ticket?"

"Probably."

"So I'll run up some parking tickets and let her pay for them! Then she'll give me the damn title!"

I slammed the last chair down. I was working two jobs. I needed the car to get to work. I needed the title. Why was she doing this?

A few days later, I wrote Pat a note asking for the title and enclosed an envelope for her to send back to me. All she had to do was sign it. Problem was I didn't have any stamps. So the letter sat on my dresser for a week.

When I came out of the video store after work one night, there was a note tucked under my windshield wiper.

> *Cindi, after having sent many messages to you, I am taking my license plates which have to be returned by Wednesday. Insurance on you as well as the car is terminated as of Wednesday. Please arrange to get the title from me within 24 hours or I will have the car towed at my own expense. Pat.*

Fear ran down my back like a nest of spiders. I looked around the parking lot to see if Pat was still around. Was she watching me? I wondered about her phrasing "sent many messages." Was the conversation with Brad a message?

The next morning, I went to school and straight to work after classes. I was at work at Video Village when Brad came in. "I need the keys to the car."

One of his co-workers from the gas station where he used to work was with him, wearing a jumpsuit with a tag: TOW TRUCK DRIVER.

No! They couldn't do this to me!

I tried to ignore Brad and proceeded to check out videos for a customer.

Brad hovered. "Cindi, you've got to give me the keys. Otherwise, it will be towed."

"You can't do this. How will I get home? How will I get to work? How will I *LIVE?*"

My voice got louder. In that moment, I despised my brother for his spinelessness. Yet, I knew that saying no to Pat would be his own death sentence in the family. I stared at my brother's own defeated face. I went to the back office and tried to calm down.

The store was busy. My meltdown would have to wait. When I came out of the back office, Brad and the tow truck driver were gone—with my car.

A little while later, I heard another sales clerk on the phone. "May I take a message? Yes, sir, Mr. Michael."

I spun around, just as he hung up.

"Cindi, your Dad called."

I hadn't heard from my father in four months.

Personal phone calls weren't allowed, but I asked my boss. I dialed my Dad's work number. His familiar voice lured me like a siren, even though his words offered no comfort.

"You and Pat need to sit down and talk about the car. You need to come out to the house."

I couldn't believe what I was hearing. "How am I supposed to get to the house when I don't have a car anymore?"

"So you are never going to come home again?"

"This WAS . . . NOT . . . MY . . . CHOICE! You're the one that told me not to come home again. Ever!"

"I am hurt. You've hurt me."

"*You're* hurt? What about *me?*" Here I was, one step away from being homeless and dropping out of school, and my father was the one who was hurt?

My boss stuck his head into the office. The line of waiting customers extended out the door. I couldn't think. Tears trickled down my cheeks. "I can't talk now," I told my dad. "I need my car."

The store closed at 10:00 P.M., but with cashing out the registers and vacuuming by the time I walked out into the black night, it was 10:30. I looked over to where my car had been parked. The spot was empty. I wandered to the bus stop. The last bus had left at 10:10 P.M.

I walked along Beltway Road and Route 1, an hour's walk to the apartment. The winter wind stung my face. A side street provided a short cut but was eerily absent of cars. I wondered if this was where the girl had been raped a few weeks earlier. Would Dad even care if something happened to me?

I slunked along, wishing something bad would happen. It would be Dad's fault. Then the story would come out how he had abandoned me. He was always so worried about his image. What would they think of him then?

My heart beat fast as the street grew darker and emptier. I didn't wipe my tears. I didn't want to take my cold hands out of my coat pocket.

Before Pat came along, my father and I were so close. She was the one poisoning everything.

Finally, I reached the busier Route 1. The whiz of the cars was a comfort. I pushed the dark thoughts away.

But I couldn't sleep that night.

My father's voice played over and over in my head. *I am hurt. You've hurt me.* I didn't understand him. Why was he the one hurting? I decided to write him a letter. I rewrote it over several days. He needed to know this was about survival. Basically, I told him:

February 29, 1984
. . . I have a lot of mixed feelings inside. . . . By the tone of your voice, you apparently seem to think I am entirely responsible for our present relationship. If you recall, you were the one who called me and told me not to bother coming back. Perhaps it was a decision or phone call that was out of anger or impulse and you maybe later regretted it. But you never called. . . . I was faced with having to drop out of school, not have a home, and not be able to eat. You were dealing with "being hurt" while I was left with trying to survive. Can you even imagine what a lonely and scary feeling that is? I will say that I'm thankful that you weren't there when I lived at home because it taught me not to need you. . . . God forbid if I did need you. . . . I work full-time and go to school full-time. . . . It's all work and no play. I pay my own rent, my own tuition, my own food bills, and

my own car repairs. . . . I'd rather deal with that than deal with your backstabbing. So why did you take my car? . . . I do need it. . . . I was working on getting back to liking you when you again antagonize. How do you expect things to ever work out when you keep treating me like this? . . . Even though I think you've been an asshole, I haven't stopped loving you. Cindi

I went back and forth on whether to send the letter, it all hurt too much. But he needed to know that what he was doing was wrong, and I needed my car, so I sent it.

I had been talking to a priest at a church in Rockville, ironically, at the same church whose doors had been locked to me the day my father called me a home wrecker. I wanted to talk to Father Hughes about this, too, so I photocopied the whole letter for him to read.

He once again wore a sweater, sitting quietly in a large arm chair as he read it. Finally he looked up. "This is pretty harsh."

"Yeah, but it's all true."

"'You taught me to never need you.'" he read. "How do you think your father would take that?"

I could see his point, but it seemed everyone was more concerned about my father's feelings than mine.

It wasn't entirely true that I didn't need my father. Desperately, I needed his love and approval. My entire life I had tried so hard to be good, yet it was never enough. This was about my not wanting to crawl back on the ground, beaten.

My father never responded.

CHAPTER 14

Broken Hearts

THE TOWING OF MY car led to my first serious step away from Michael.

Most of the staff at Video Village were going to a special preview of a new horror movie *Children of the Corn* after closing. Our new assistant manager, John, tried to convince me to join them, but fun was not in my schedule.

Things were not perfect with Michael. Bogar, my old drama teacher, told me Michael was involved with another student, and I didn't know who to believe. Michael kept complaining I didn't make time for him. I didn't have time! What did he expect between school and two jobs?

Then there was the night I showed up unannounced at his apartment, just in time to see a woman, blonde and not his ex-wife, walking out. He explained it away. I didn't know how to breakup with someone. I couldn't walk away from love, even if it was the bad kind of love. Until I met John.

We were working at the front counter when a customer, a heavy-set black man, said to John, "You need to give that girl a raise. She's the best. Always smiling. Always helpful."

It was true. While my heart was fracturing from my father, I loved my job and the ease of making a customer happy.

John, six-feet tall with reddish hair and green eyes that twinkled with mischief, handed the man his video tapes and replied, "Only when she marries me." John knew I was within earshot. I chuckled but didn't meet his eyes.

The night of the movie preview, it was snowing outside. The store was especially busy, with people stocking up on video rentals for a snow day. John worked the counter alongside me.

"Come on. It's just a movie." He moved around me to grab some video tapes.

"No. It's too late . . . Besides, I don't have a car and don't want to walk home that late." I stepped away, avoiding eye contact with his piercing green eyes, not sure why my heart was fluttering.

"I'll give you a ride home . . . Just say yes." He walked off before I could refuse him again.

I told myself it wasn't a date. It was just a bunch of coworkers hanging out.

I called my roommate to let her know I would be late. While I vacuumed the store, I told myself not to be nervous, it was nothing. But still. *Only when she marries me?*

During the movie, John and I sat next to each other. *Children of the Corn* is a really scary movie and, at one point, I grabbed John's hand in fear. His hand was big and warm. Even after the evil thing disappeared beneath the corn fields, John never let go of my hand, and I didn't let go of his. I admitted to myself I had a crush on John.

After the movie, he walked me to his car, a lone Ford pickup truck in the otherwise empty lot. Snowflakes stung my cheeks, and I tried to dodge the slushy puddles in my sneakers.

We sat in John's truck while it warmed up, talking and laughing, the snow dotting the windshield. He turned on the radio to country music.

"My stepmother told him to tow it," I said bluntly about my car. Everyone at the video store knew.

He shook his head. "How've you been getting to work?"

"Taking the bus . . . walking."

"You *walk?*" He drew out the word.

"Well, only sometimes." I knew it wasn't entirely safe. "It depends if I have to close up."

"Dammit, girl, ask someone for help. Dolby could take you home, or I could. Anyone." Dolby was the head manager.

"I don't like to bother people. It's fine."

"No. It's not fine. Don't let me hear about you walking home again."

I tried to soften his mood, responding coyly, "Is this my boss ordering me?"

His frown spread into a slow smile as he shook his head, no.

I gazed back at him, my face flushed. He leaned forward, hesitating. His lips brushed mine ever so lightly. His beard tickled my lips. We kissed gently. Then the hunger between us grew. I ran my fingers through his soft reddish-brown hair.

When we came up for air, the windows had fogged, and we chuckled, glancing at each other nervously. We had done that?

John asked if I wanted to go back to his place for a beer.

My naivety had gotten me into trouble the first night with Michael, at the hotel, so this time I wanted to be clear. "I don't do that kind of thing."

"You don't drink beer?"

"Well, no, I don't drink beer, either, but . . . " Pat's rules still echoed in my head, *Ladies don't drink beer.* She probably wouldn't have approved of anyone with a pickup truck either. "I mean, going back to your place . . . you know what I mean." I couldn't bring myself to say the words, *one-night stand.* I had no idea the unwritten rules of the adult world.

"Coke, then. Wine, whatever!"

His smile was reassuring. I laughed.

The thought of Michael, on the other hand, made me feel ashamed.

"John, you know I have a boyfriend. My roommate will be worried." This last part was not at all true. I added quietly, "I don't want to lead you on."

I drew a happy face on the foggy part of the windshield and avoided his gaze.

"You're not leading me on. Nothing will happen." We studied each other for a while. "Just for a while, then I'll bring you home."

I didn't want the night to end, but I couldn't imagine going. Finally, I nodded and reached for his hand. His thigh pressed to mine.

The snow fell heavier as we headed half an hour south on the Beltway. The highway was empty. He pulled up in front of a trailer home with a large deck. I was surprised by how big it was inside, as big as my apartment. The kitchen was positioned at the end of the living room.

True to his word, John poured me a glass of white wine while he grabbed a beer. We sat on the floor, against his sofa, our feet touching in an L-shape, talking and laughing. He listened as I revealed fragments of my story and my father and how he had told me never to come home again. I didn't elaborate on Michael, except to say that he was older and my dad didn't like him.

John flirted, "What about me? Maybe your parents would like me better?"

"Uh, hate to tell you, they wouldn't get past the tattoo."

John had a big eagle on his right arm. I traced the edges of it with my finger, the gray-green wing arching over his bicep. I was not allowed to date people with tattoos.

"Oh, I was thinking of getting another one . . . Guess I'll have to put that on the back burner."

I wondered what my parents would think of John's beard. My brother Brad was never allowed to have one.

John and I talked and talked, about all the normal things one should on a first date, his family, why he had left the police force, the kind of music he liked.

It was getting late, past time for me to go. I looked out the window, worried about the snow. The roads were slick just getting here.

"Stay," he said simply.

I shook my head. "I can't."

"You take the bed. I'll take the sofa."

It took a few more rounds of debating. Then I called my roommate to let her know I was not coming home.

John and I kissed a while on his bed. His body and mine tangled together like limbs of a vine twisting toward the sunlight. His kisses, hesitant yet with a hunger, tapped a yearning in me I hadn't realized was there. I wanted more, so I pushed him away. "John, we have to stop."

He started to leave. "Shall I go?"

I pulled him back to me.

He stroked my forehead. "Have you never just slept with someone without sex?"

I laughed nervously. "No, John. I'm only nineteen. And I've only ever slept with one person. So no, I don't know how any of this works."

He wrapped his arms around me protectively and we slept in his bed, fully clothed. I slept more deeply than I had in months.

In the morning, John drove me back to my apartment. On the way, I insisted I would be fine taking the bus to work that afternoon. He shook his head. "I'm working anyway. I'll pick you up, and I won't take no for an answer."

"No, really. I can get a bus." I added firmly. "And people will talk."

My reputation had been trashed at my high school. I couldn't handle it being trashed at work, too.

"Well, I'll be at your apartment at two. If you walk past my truck and take the bus, that's your decision."

So I rode with John to work, but he let me walk into the store well ahead of him. I blushed anyway when he eventually came in.

He drove me home again that night after the store closed. I was excited about the quiet time with him—but this all seemed reckless.

"John, you'll get hurt. I can't handle this. I'm not breaking up with Michael."

"I can take care of myself."

He invited me for dinner at his place the following week, the one night I had off from work. John, it seemed, was quite the cook.

During dinner I told him I was thinking about leaving Video Village. I had a job interview for a sales position that paid more. It was all commission, but I could earn more in less time. It would be better with my school schedule. If things worked out, I could quit waitressing at The Attic.

John reached into his pocket and threw down a wad of bills. "You short on money? Here, take it. Just take it."

I gasped. At least several hundred dollars lay there. "Are you crazy? Don't you have a bank account? What if you lost that?"

"Nah, don't trust 'em. I'm making more money than I ever made as a cop."

I didn't understand this world, where someone renting videos could make more money than someone who reckoned with guns and drugs and bad guys. I would never accept John's offer, but that he had made it so unconditionally stirred something deep in me.

"Thanks, but no. I have to do this on my own."

Michael and John were from such different worlds. The pickup truck, tattoo, trailer home. Did these things matter?

I was used to thinking about what my parents thought. I didn't know what was important to *me*.

John had gotten his associate's degree, which I thought was good enough. I suspected it wouldn't pass muster with my dad and certainly not Pat.

Despite these differences, I was falling for him. John listened to country music, something I didn't like. But years later, I listened to it whenever I needed to feel the comfort John had once given me.

Once, a customer came into the store asking for The Eurythmics video and John looked back at him blankly. "The Ewww what?"

The customer tried to explain. "You know—Annie Lenox?"

I interrupted him, teasing. "Some people have no taste in music, do they?" and showed the customer where to find the box.

A few weeks passed and no raise. So I took the job selling Cutco knives. Their only condition was I had to have a car.

One of my customers at Video Village said he could get me a good deal on a new Subaru; financing was not available for a used car. I had no credit, and the financing person said I needed someone to cosign. Michael offered. It felt wrong. I wanted to breakup with Michael, but this was one more thing that would make me feel like I owed him.

When the banker asked about our relationship, Michael said, "I'm just a friend."

I accepted the sales job and gave notice at Video Village. Dolby, my boss, was disappointed, saying he didn't realize how important the raise was. He could have gotten me the raise but was waiting for the right time to ask the owner. In those days, speaking up for myself was not one of my strong points.

The Subaru was a manual clutch, something I had never driven before. When I picked up the car from the dealer, Michael had to drive it out of the lot for me. He tried to teach me, but I popped the clutch on the slightest hill and each time I slowed, the engine stalled.

I was falling in love with John and I didn't know how to breakup with Michael. I had never broken up with anyone before. What kind of person did it make me to breakup with Michael after all he had done for me?

Michael bought a set of cutlery from me. John too. John bought the full set, and I tried to talk him out of it.

"You're just trying to help me. Don't do that. Just buy what you need." These knives sold for hundreds of dollars, and I was shocked anyone would pay that much money for knives. But they did.

Despite my protests, John bought the full set.

As winter rolled into spring, my roommate Shannon asked me to stay away for the weekend so she and her girlfriend could have privacy. I had stayed at Michael's a couple of times, but not regularly. Now it was too awkward. I packed a bag anyway, not sure how things would unfold. John was working Friday night, so I stayed at Michael's. I drank enough wine to numb myself to the reality that I had nowhere else to go.

John was free Saturday and we went back to his place. When I stared into his eyes, we both knew the night would not end.

He kissed me deeply, and whispered, "I wish I had been your first."

I stroked his hair, burying my face in his neck. "Why?"

"You never forget your first. You always go back to your first."

I didn't believe him, didn't want it to be so. I was trying to get away from my first.

In the morning, I went to my car to get a change of clothes. When I came back into the trailer, John barked, "Do you always keep a bag with you?"

His words stung. How could I explain? "Do you really want me to answer that?" I replied sarcastically.

He pressed for details about where I had been the night before, about Michael. I didn't want to lie to him, but I didn't understand myself why I couldn't just break up with Michael. Hurt packed our angry exchange. I walked out of the trailer and started my car. It was easier to run away than to talk things through. He came out. "You're leaving?"

I leaned my head on the steering wheel. "I don't want to fight with you." My voice shook.

John drew me to him. "You're gonna love me, girl," he declared fiercely.

"What about you? Are you gonna love me, too?"

"Can't you tell? I already do."

I could not talk through the lump in my throat. I couldn't see why anyone would love me.

I could not say those words in return. I would never just say them, unless I was sure.

One day that spring I had a sales call in Darnestown with my former singing teacher, who was also my friend Bob's mother. As I was driving along Route 28, I passed a Jaguar with the license plate Sports4. I had heard my father just bought a Jaguar. I believed God had crossed our paths on purpose. I thought about all the things Father Hughes had said to me, how harsh the letter was, how I needed to let go of my anger. So I figured God was telling me to talk to my father. I turned my car around and drove until I spotted the Jaguar in the parking lot of the local garden center. I walked halfway across the parking lot and spotted Dad just getting out of his car.

When he saw me, his body physically jerked. "What the hell do you want?"

I hesitated. "I . . . I don't know."

"Are you still going out with that Mr. Tarantula?" My father couldn't bring himself to say the vice principal's name.

"No." It was only a half lie.

"Well if you're hoping for a hug, you're shit out of luck."

He walked away. I stood there, not wanting to believe he still didn't care.

I climbed back in my car. I had a sales call, so I couldn't let myself fall apart. Not yet. Mrs. Morse was waiting for me.

I cannot remember if she bought any knives.

After that, I climbed into my car and I broke into sobs. I needed John. But he was more than an hour away. So I headed somewhere closer, Michael's.

He wasn't home but he had given me a key. I went inside. I called John, on the kitchen wall phone, pulling the cord to me on the floor, where I crouched like a beaten puppy. I sobbed into the phone, telling John I had just seen my father.

"Are you there? Cindi? Are you there? Damn it, girl, don't do this to me."

"I'm here."

"The phone keeps cutting out. Where are you? I'll come get you."

Was the phone cutting out a warning?

"No." I didn't want him to know I was at Michael's.

I thought I heard someone climbing the stairs in the hallway. "I'll call you later." I hung up just before Michael walked in.

I told Michael what had happened and cut him off at, "That guy—"

Hearing anyone bash my father was not a way to comfort me.

After I calmed down, I went back to my apartment and called John to let him know I had made it back okay but needed to be alone.

Something broke in me that day.

The next time I saw John, he told me to forget my father, to put him out of my mind, but I couldn't. My heart wasn't wired with an off switch. Besides, it's not so easy to forget a famous father when his face popped up in commercials. Anyone who loved sports, which in DC was the whole town, wanted to talk to me about my father. He was larger than life, which made me only smaller and more worthless.

So, hardening my heart to my father meant hardening my heart to John, whether I wanted to or not.

We went out for pizza in College Park, along Route 1. He ordered a beer, and I again felt uncomfortable being underage. As we walked out, he asked me, "Are you embarrassed to be seen with me?"

"No. Why would I be?" I couldn't admit I was embarrassed that I was too young to drink.

I buried myself in school and work. Good grades and sales awards were my solace. I wondered if that was why my father became a workaholic. What pain was he shutting out? What void was he filling with success?

I met with Father Hughes and told him what had happened with my dad. He was surprised, shocked even, without any further suggestion of how to reconcile or be at peace.

He turned the conversation to Michael, saying simply, "You know you can't have a physical relationship with him." I sat there too ashamed to tell him that his advice had come too late. If I had told him about John, probably he'd tell me I was going straight to hell.

I couldn't be perfect enough, good enough, for God or my father it seemed.

I was less concerned with my soul, though, than with my next paycheck. Cutco hadn't warned me that the first few weeks of selling are easy, because friends want to buy from you. After that, the sales only trickle in. I had to work harder and scheduled more calls than originally planned.

One night after I got home, I asked my roommate if John had called. I was too insecure to call him. She said a guy had called a couple times, but never left a message.

"He asked if you still lived here."

So I got up the courage to call John. A girl answered. I recognized her voice—Chris, from the video store. John had stepped out to get some beer, she said, not bothering even to ask who was calling.

I didn't know the rules of dating in the adult world. I called my brother Brad. Did he think I should drive over there? Brad wasn't sure.

Just when I had finally trusted John, let him in, fallen for him completely, he did this. But I argued with myself that I was not being fair to John. I had not fully broken up with Michael—so why shouldn't John go out with someone else?

I wrote John a note trying to let him know everything I was juggling and how I felt about him. I drove over to his home. It was dark, no lights on.

He came to the screen door. "Didn't I tell you not to come over without calling first?"

"No, you never mentioned that."

John came out onto the deck. I leaned on the banister. We argued.

"I just hope you don't break Chris's heart the way you broke mine." I handed him the note and walked away. I didn't cry. There were no more tears. But I shook as I drove home. This proved Michael was the only person I could trust.

John called a few weeks later. My final paycheck was at the store. I suggested he mail it to me. He said no, I should come to the store.

I had hoped to see him when I went in. Instead, Chris was working the counter.

She hissed, "What do you want?" When I told her, she quickly went into the back office and got my check. I lingered, hoping to catch a glimpse of John, hoping he would realize I was there, but I withered under his new girlfriend's glare and left.

While things were falling apart with me, my three roommates were fighting with their own partners. One had started going out with a guy, so I guess she wasn't really gay. Eventually, my roommates announced they were moving out. I had thirty days to find another place to live. Michael offered his spare bedroom, saying I could come and go as I pleased. I didn't want to. He reassured me, said that I could pay him rent. My thirty days dwindled, so I told myself it was okay, just for summer. I would move back near campus in the fall, when people would be looking for roommates.

Later, my sister Michelle told me Pat routinely went through my bank statement that was still being mailed to their house. Pat had tsked smugly when she saw this rent check. I guess a woman who reads people's diaries would have no qualms about reading other people's mail.

At Michael's, I set up my bed and books in the spare bedroom. What I hadn't bargained on, was that while my furniture was in my own room, Michael assumed I would sleep in his room.

And my heart still yearned for John. John had told me he loved me. Yet, here was Michael. Seemingly loving and supportive. What was wrong with me? Why didn't I trust his love that seemed so much safer?

By midsummer my sales at Cutco were nonexistent, and I only had a few weeks to save up for fall tuition. I met with my old manager at Video Village, who said he would hire me back with higher pay. John had been promoted to manager at the Prince George's store, so I wouldn't have to face him on a daily basis. I would only have to deal with Chris.

Chris was polite enough, but hinted she and John were having problems. She even asked my advice about him, as if I understood him. Then in the next moment, she would play the movie *Staying Alive* on the big-screen TV in the store and would recite the words—"everybody uses everybody"— as if a warning to me that it never would work between John and me.

Video Village had grown to five stores, and the owners were hosting a big pool party. There would be a BBQ. I didn't want to face John and Chris together, so I didn't go.

One evening, John called the store to check if we had a movie that was out of stock at his own. Hearing his voice filled me with longing.

I kept replaying phrases in my head, things John had said. *You're going to love me . . . don't you know I already do . . .* I got it in my head that John had hooked up with Chris because he thought he didn't matter to me. I had to tell him, whether he still felt the same or not.

So one evening after work, I drove over to his store at Prince George's. I spotted John's brown pickup truck in the parking lot.

Terri, the woman who had originally hired me at Beltway Plaza, was now working as an assistant manager under John. She was at the counter. We chatted for a few minutes. I asked her if John was working. She went into the back office to get him.

My heart pounded as I waited. Maybe he would tell me to get lost.

Finally, he came and his green eyes pierced my soul.

My face burned. "Can we talk?"

We walked a few doors down. He ordered a beer. I ordered iced tea.

"How come you didn't come to the pool party?" he said.

"I couldn't."

"I was going to call you, but I heard you moved."

I took a deep breath. "I need to tell you something."

He waited.

My throat was closing. I couldn't do this. I was just a fling to him. It didn't matter. Then I blurted it out. "I wanted you to know . . . that . . . that I love you."

He was quick to respond. "No you don't. You just want what you can't have."

What?! I just bared my soul to this man and that was his take on it? I shook my head. "No. That's not what it's about." My voice was more firm this time. "I love you. It doesn't matter if you love me back, but you need to know I love you."

He changed the subject. I had summoned those words, and John belittled them.

Still, it felt like a boulder had been lifted off me. I resigned myself to the idea that it was too late for John and me.

Then he said, "How 'bout if I see if Terri can close up tonight and we go out?"

We went somewhere to listen to music, a country bar. I called Michael to say I would be late.

I couldn't seem to walk away from Michael. I kept telling myself he was a roommate, for the summer only.

After the bar, I went back to John's place. He and Chris were no longer going out, really, he said.

Before, I had always been honest with John about Michael. But now that I had told him I loved him, there was no way I could explain how I was living with Michael. So I made up a story that I was living with a friend.

John and I went out only one more time after that, and again, it was I who had called him. He drove with angry words. "You never lied to me before."

I could hear the pain in his voice, but how could I explain?

In the months that followed, I heard that John started dating Terri, my first boss at Video Village. Perhaps I should have seen the clues, like when Terri asked me out for drinks one night and asked how I felt about John. I told her that I didn't think he cared anymore about me, that even though I loved him, we weren't right for each other. She told me the night I showed up at the store to talk to him, he had seemed really happy. *If only.*

Two years later, they were married. Through John, I learned that, in love, timing matters. I would remember this lesson years later when I would meet the right person at the wrong time.

CHAPTER 15

Dying

SUMMER FELL INTO FALL and I was still living with Michael. I tried to picture my future with him. There were weeks when we got along fine and periods I thought I could one day marry him. But, always, the tension would surface. Michael wanted more than what I could give, and at times I felt suffocated.

In moving off campus, one thing I hadn't figured was how much time I would waste commuting to school. Traffic on 270, two lanes in each direction in 1984, was gridlock most mornings, making me habitually miss half my eight A.M. economics class. Then there was the gap between classes, because it was impossible to schedule consecutive classes on the same days.

One morning while driving to school, my tire blew out with a bang while I was on the Beltway. I pulled over to the shoulder. Cars whizzed past as I studied the shredded tire. A truck driver pulled over and offered to help me change it. I was scared, though. Wasn't that how young girls got abducted? So I declined. I walked along the highway to an exit ramp, found a gas station and called Brad, my go-to person for all things practical, despite our differences. So Brad came and changed the tire for me. I had missed my class by then, so I drove back to Michael's apartment. The blow out pushed me over the edge. I wanted to sleep. Forever. I was so tired, so very tired of everything.

The only sign of stress was that I bled every time I went to the bathroom. A doctor ordered a colon cancer test. I hoped it was positive. Maybe if I were dying my father would want to see me. The

results were negative. I later learned stressors can cause diarrhea, usually ten days after the event, and if severe enough, can cause bleeding.
Every day was a stressor for me, so every day I was bleeding.

That fall, I was taking my first journalism class, and the professor asked us to describe a street scene and write what we saw. Longing for my sister, who wouldn't speak to me and whom I hadn't seen
in a year, Michelle's face came to my mind. I saw her the way she used
to wait outside for our father to come get us on weekends, before he
got custody of us. Also, how she'd stayed outside when Dad and Trish
fought and the emptiness on her face when Dad drove away, knowing it would be two weeks before we'd see him again. There were the
details that, as a mother now, I can barely handle recalling. Details
like when she went to the bus stop in her pajamas. Details like the
hand-me-downs she wore (from me, which came from a thrift store
before that) that were too short with holes in the knees, and how the
other children made fun of them.

The next day, the professor read my essay aloud as an example of
writing that made him feel something. *Powerful stuff,* he wrote. *This
hurts, and that's what your job is.* He said the scene made him angry,
because the father drives off at the end, leaving the little girl alone.
I wanted to defend my father. *Must not be writing clearly enough,* I
thought. Dad had to drive off, because he no longer lived with us.
But I wonder now, did the professor see something different my
father could have done?

The praise from this professor kept my flicker of a dream to be
a writer alive. When so much was stacked against me—the risk of
being homeless, the risk of not finishing school—his words encouraged me.

But Michael thought sending a thank you card was a bad idea. Of
course, he wouldn't want me to do that, because that was what started
our own relationship—my Easter card to him my last year of high
school. This pissed me off. I should be allowed to give a card to anyone I wanted. I didn't like the rope Michael was tethering around me.

Michael also complained about my still waitressing at The Attic.
He'd rather I not pay him rent than waitress there. I refused to quit

the job. It was bad enough that I needed Michael as a constant in my life. I didn't want to need him financially, too.

I told Trish about Michael. She said I should stay with him. It took me a while to realize my mother gave a higher importance to being financially secure rather than if that someone was good for me or not. It was just one more time in my life when she was not someone I could depend on.

During semester break that winter, Michael and I took a trip to Jamaica, a romantic getaway. As we climbed the Dunn's River Falls, I believed in his love, believed in our future. At the end of the day, in the hotel's minivan, with stifling humidity and reggae music blaring, we sped through the narrow streets and swerved when someone threw a burning tire into the road. It was only when we were safely back at the hotel that we learned that riots had broken out.

We were due to leave the next day, but the airport was shut down. At first, we relished the extra day, but as one day turned into two and three, I worried. I called a friend at Video Village. She said the news reports were horrific. Riots were breaking out across the country, riots we couldn't see or hear from our hotel. The phone cut out as I talked.

Michael and I sat by the pool, the sun beating down, the blue Montego Bay calm. An American news crew was interviewing a group of stranded tourists at the next table. The group laughed, raised their cocktails, and said in a Bob Marley accent, "No problem. No worries."

I shook my head, frustrated, "I should walk over and offer a different view."

Michael got mad. "I can't give you *that*." He flipped his hand at the camera crew.

"What do you mean?"

"The fame, the glory. That's your father's world."

"This doesn't have anything to do with my father. This is about being stuck here. Who's paying for the extra nights' hotel? What about my job?"

The hotel manager said a few flights might get out the next day.

So, we camped at the airport until we could get home. On the floor of the airport, I no longer felt the closeness we had shared on the falls. I wanted to get home. I needed the paycheck and resented Michael's happiness at our being trapped.

Michael lied about little things, so I wondered if there were big lies I didn't know about. I had been living with him for six months and by accident learned he had a toupee. He was in the shower. I knocked first, shouted that I just needed my curling iron, and reached into the steamy bathroom for it. There was a strange blob of something on the counter. I grabbed my curling iron and went and sat on the bed. What had I just seen? Hair? How could I not have known? He had never liked me to run my fingers through his hair.

Then, one Sunday evening, I went to the video store after closing time to study, because it was closer than the campus library. I found it hard to study when Michael was home, like he resented my study time.

When I got home, he accused me of driving by the apartment, checking up on him. I had to wonder, why had he been looking out the bedroom window so often during the evening?

Shortly after the trip to Jamaica, my childhood friend Jill Parker was getting married. Her elegant invitation sat on my desk. I put off replying. It would be a big, fancy wedding, and I had no money for a gift or a nice dress. More than anything, I didn't want to take Michael. I couldn't face the story of how we met. So I took the coward's way out. I never replied to Jill's wedding invite. My first best friend, my soul sister. I never even sent a congratulations card, me the eternal card-giver. I chalk this up as the first sign that I was losing my soul.

The final blow up with Michael came the night of Bubs's, a new manager at Video Village, surprise birthday party. Steve, the owner of Video Village, was an ex-cop, like John. We all parked our cars far down the street so Bubs wouldn't notice when he arrived. I felt pretty in my white two-piece jumpsuit, cinched at the waist. We hid in Steve's finished basement, ready to surprise Bubs, about twenty managers and assistant managers. We jumped out in unison as he descended the steps.

"Surprise! Happy Birthday!"

A mystery visitor, a "present," arrived shortly. Several of us climbed onto the trundle sofa bed to watch the show: a professional striptease. I closed my eyes, embarrassed to look, as she brought Bubs's face to her cleavage, asking if he was hot yet. She stripped down to a sexy, white corset.

John's presence at the party made me more nervous than the stripper. I sat on the steps talking to Terri, and she asked John to get me a glass of white wine. My breath caught at how he responded to her every request. He handed me the wine, in a clear plastic cup. Our fingers touched.

Terri said, "She likes it with ice."

"It's fine, thank you, John." Saying his name hurt.

"Don't push it," he said to Terri with a grin, but he took my plastic cup back to put ice in it.

The music thumped, the chatter buzzed, my head swam. I had forgotten to eat earlier in the day. I felt the need to put my head down. I sat on the sofa bed trying to focus on the conversation. Other managers sat around me. The room seemed to tilt.

I heard a voice say, "Somebody should call Michael."

I couldn't open my eyes or say anything. I was aware of John and Terri looking at me. The room grew quieter. Someone was leaning over me, kissing me. It wasn't someone I wanted to be kissing. All I could do was turn my head away.

In the middle of the night, I came to, fully clothed, but there was someone lying next to me on the sofa, wearing a dark-brown robe, the hairs of his chest peeking out. Steve. The video store owner and Michael's friend. The room was dark. I saw a shadow of a person on the floor stand up, Jim, a store manager, making his way to the stairs.

I had to get out of there. I slunk off the sofa and tried to follow Jim up the stairs, but I couldn't stand. He tried to help me, but I fell and crawled instead, a dim light in the kitchen guiding us up.

At the top, I sat on the kitchen floor. "I can't drive. I can't even walk."

"You want me to take you home?"

"You shouldn't be driving either! I need to call Michael." I struggled to dial the number.

Michael was asleep.

"Um, sorry to wake you, but I had too much to drink. I can't drive."

He was mad and hung up on me. He knew where I was, probably guessed John was at the party.

So I went back downstairs and passed out. The next morning, Steve was still next to me and he made it clear what he wanted. He was incredulous that I didn't want the same. "What about how you kissed me last night?" he said.

"I was asleep!" I hissed.

Somehow, he convinced me to give him what he wanted, and when he was done, he said, "Nobody needs to know. And don't go acting all weird at the manager's meeting."

The only way I could cope then and in the weeks and years that followed was to pretend it never happened. I hated Steve for weeks, but set the anger aside because he was my boss and an adult and a father. That one night was my wake-up call: my soul was dying.

That morning, I drove back home to Michael's. I showered and climbed into bed. Numb. I slept for a couple hours then called Michael at work.

He was mad that I hadn't come home in the night. "What did you want me to do?" I asked.

"You could have asked me to come get you!" He shouted.

"In the middle of the night?"

"I don't trust that guy."

"Which guy?" *Does he mean John?*

"I don't trust Steve. I hear he's just—"

"He's your friend! You introduced me to Steve! You told me to go to work for him, that the video store was better, safer than the bar."

My brain buzzed like a hornet's nest. All the people I should have been able to trust were the least trustworthy people of all. Michael, the vice principal. Steve, my boss. *My father.*

I pulled out my suitcase and packed all my belongings. I called Brad to ask to stay at his place for a few days. I sat in the living room, waiting for Michael to come home from work to tell him to his face that I was leaving. I waited for hours, then couldn't wait any longer, afraid I'd lose my courage. I went to Brad's and slept on his sofa.

After a few weeks on Brad's couch, Alicia, another video store manager, and I moved into an apartment.

Even though I had moved out of Michael's, I couldn't break it off with him entirely. We still saw each other occasionally, and he helped me decorate my new bedroom. We put up a rose-colored border and pink sheers, perfect colors for the little girl I wished I still was.

One evening we were sitting on my new balcony when he simply stood up, declared every time he got too close, I put the brakes on, and walked out of my life for good. I didn't cry. By then, I felt nothing . . . about everything.

I was still determined to graduate in four years, thinking I wouldn't have the stamina to go longer. I had gone from a sales clerk to an assistant manager to manager, so I was earning enough money to more easily pay rent and tuition. Yet, I was losing myself, the nice Cindi who believed people were good. Who believed love conquered all.

I sat with Alicia on the sidewalk in front of our apartment late one night, locusts chirping in the muggy Maryland air, and said, "I don't feel anything. Nothing."

"What do you think you need to be happy?" she asked.

I stared up at the green trees, silhouettes in the moonlit sky. I couldn't have what I wanted: My father's love.

I started writing in my journal again, something I hadn't done since high school. All the entries were addressed to my father. It was the only way I knew to talk to him.

The store I managed was in Cabin John, a corner of Potomac, Maryland, where a number of my father's co-workers at the news station lived. Some of them rented videos at my store. One day, the wife of Dad's boss and Pat's best friend, Joan Rohrbeck came in. There was an awkward recognition between us. When I handed her the videos, she said, "I don't know how anyone can pretend their daughter doesn't exist."

"I don't know either," I whispered. Then I asked hesitantly, "How are they?"

She didn't know. They weren't speaking to her, either. She explained how her husband had left her and their son for another woman and moved to Los Angeles. Dad and Pat were "siding" with Mr. Rohrbeck.

Jim Vance, the lead anchor and Dad's best friend, came in once. I wasn't working that day. One of my employees excitedly told me he had been to the store. If I had been working, what would I have said to Vance? "Tell my father his daughter says hello"? Perhaps Vance could have helped me . . . helped us?

During fall registration, again, I could only get nine of the credits I needed. Another semester of full tuition without a full course load. I just couldn't bring myself to write the check. I reasoned it wasn't worth it financially and decided to take the semester off.

Like a stone that bounces into an already fractured windshield, that was the final loss that shattered me.

Despite a growing despair, my career at Video Village continued to climb. Steve offered me a job as a manager in the busiest store in the chain. My commission would be higher, and I'd be making close to $30,000, a fantastic salary for a twenty year old. While Wheaton was busy, the employees were disgruntled and customer service was poor. In managing the Cabin John store, those things had become my hallmark. At first, I declined, saying I wouldn't be able to handle it with school.

Steve stared at me. "You know, I feel as close to you now as I did that night."

I cut him off, my gaze steadfast, saying, "Nothing happened."

Steve said, "John really wants you to do this."

John was now the assistant operations manager, overseeing all the locations.

John? "What do you mean?"

Steve shrugged. "That I had to convince you. That you'd be the best one to take over. Both John and Bubs think so."

So I accepted.

I was working seventy hours a week. The Wheaton store was gradually improving. I was writing in my journal. I was going to church. I even had a new boyfriend, Bryce, a manager at another location in the chain.

But nothing could fill the void my family had left, so I never slowed down. But I was so very tired.

One day, Brad's roommate Studley told me he had seen my sister Michelle. "She misses you so much."

I was immediately alert. I missed Michelle, but it felt like she didn't care. "Did she say so?"

"She always asks me about you. You should call her."

"She's never once written back to me."

"Call her." He shook his head then. "When you ran into your Dad at the garden center, he went off on Brad."

"What do you mean?"

"It was messed up. Like he thought Brad had arranged it."

I tried to piece together what he was suggesting. "I passed him on the road. Brad had nothing to do with it."

"I know. That's what I mean. It's messed up." He repeated again, "Call Michelle."

I was scared, but I did call her, my now fifteen-year-old sister who still lived at home.

Finally, she answered and sounded happy to hear from me. We talked for a while, and eventually, I worked up the courage to ask if she wanted to get together.

"Yes. I mean, you *are* my sister. But you know, I won't get any brownie points if Dad and Pat know."

Michelle was alone every day after school until Dad and Pat got home after midnight. I pictured her coming home to that empty house. It had been lonely when Brad and I were there too.

I went one night the following week.

My heart raced as I pulled onto Plainfield Lane, both from fear in case Pat was unexpectedly home, as well as excitement to see my sister. Our dog Teddy, a white Poodle-Spitz Terrier greeted me at the driveway. At first he barked at me, a stranger. He didn't know me anymore. I stooped down and called his name. He kept barking as I slowly held out my hand so he could smell me. Finally, he grabbed onto my hand with his teeth, the way he showed affection, and whimpered. It had been almost two years.

I didn't go inside. Michelle came out to meet me. She had grown so much and was now taller than me. She was tan, and her blue eyes sparkled. I was self-conscious about how pale and tired looking I was.

We went to the mall and had a portrait taken. We walked and talked. A sophomore in high school, she told me about which teachers she had, which ones I knew. She said Bogar, my old drama teacher, would sometimes bump into her in the hallway, she thought on purpose.

It was so good to see her. We agreed I had to be careful about when to call. Dad and Pat couldn't know or she would get in trouble. We decided she couldn't call me, couldn't risk Dad seeing it on the phone bill.

Michelle and I resumed a fragile relationship, but it didn't replace the longing I had for my father.

I was okay as long as I was working, but whenever I slowed down, the pain slowly crept in, twisting my heart like tourniquet, squeezing out any beats of joy.

I missed school, that beacon had been my hope. I started to think I would never graduate.

John was assigned to work at my store alongside me to help make sure operations were improving. He and Terri were engaged. Being around him was raw, a constant reminder of a love I had lost. I was working eighty hours a week, just like my father.

The pain crept in most often at night, as I lie in bed in the quiet of the blackened room. I would say my prayers and change the words, "Now I lay me down to sleep, let me die before I wake, I pray the Lord my soul to take." The only reason I didn't take my life was that I was taught it was the one sin God would never forgive. He would forgive me for Michael, for the night with Steve, but never for killing myself. But if it just happened that I would die of natural causes, get hit by a car or something, I would have been eternally grateful.

Steve called me at home Saturday morning with some question about the store. I didn't feel like getting out of bed. I stared at my pink curtains. I told him I was beginning not to care anymore, about school, about anything.

I look back on this time as my life's albatross: being disowned is a lifelong pain that nags on birthdays, in unexpected moments, or at places I have been with my family. To cope, I can either numb myself to that pain or I can slow down, reflect, and let the pain seep in, the price for sometimes feeling joy or love. The price for keeping my soul. I never want to go back to how I felt that fall of 1985, when there was nothing left of Cindi except an emptiness, a ghost of a person who no longer believed in dreams and happiness, who no longer had any hope.

Throughout my twenty years of being disowned, people have said to me, "Forget your father! You are better off without him." They don't realize that forgetting is dangerous. Forgetting has its own consequences. *Look what forgetting did to my Dad.*

So I keep their memories alive, in photos on the wall, in my wallet.

But on that Saturday morning in October 1985, I understood none of these things and simply stopped caring about everything. Steve told me to get some rest, to go have fun with friends.

Donna, my one-time best friend from New Jersey, and her twin sister Lauren just happened to be in DC for the weekend. We agreed to meet for lunch. As the day wore on, they decided they'd rather sleep over at my apartment than party at the dorms at American University with another old friend. When we got back to my apartment, the red light blinked on the answering machine, a message from Steve.

"I spoke to your father. Call me back."

Steve had taken it upon himself to call my dad. Perhaps it was his redemption for the night at Bubs' party.

"Your dad said it would be good if you went out to the house tonight. Everyone's there for a birthday dinner." Pat and Brad's.

"I'm not going out there. I'm not *welcome* there." I pictured the last meeting with my father outside the garden center.

"You both need to stop this bullshit and talk. Claire and I will drive you." Claire, Steve's on-again, off-again second wife, had moved back in with Steve.

I hung up, nauseous. I was supposed to be having fun with my best friend. I wanted her to meet my new boyfriend Bryce who was coming over later. Donna and Lauren told me I should go and offered to go with me, but I declined knowing this would irritate my father and not wanting to further ruin Donna and Lauren's night.

Steve and Claire drove me. As we got closer, my mouth tasted bitter. *Fear.*

Brad answered the door. As I set foot into the tiled entryway, my heart raced. Perhaps I should have been filled with hope, but I was not. I followed my brother to the right into the family room, noting new white carpeting, new beige furniture. Dad had dozed off in a new chair and ottoman. Pat was upstairs. Michelle and I shyly said hello, pretending we hadn't seen each other in years. Teddy gnawed my hand. Dinner was already finished. The TV was on.

Claire gently shook my dad awake. "George. George, look who's here! It's your daughter. It's Cindi." I hung back. Claire didn't know my dad. This was not a joyous reunion.

He startled awake. She pushed me toward him. *Awkward.* We had no choice but to touch each other. It was not an embrace. I stepped back.

"Let me wake up," he said gruffly. Steve and Claire's presence prevented him from saying anything crass, like, "Get the hell off me."

Eventually my father introduced himself to Claire and Steve and suggested we talk around the table in the kitchen. Pat had come downstairs and our eyes met but we didn't speak. Dad began his inquisition.

He puffed on his Marlboro cigarette. "Are you still seeing Dr. T?"

"No."

"Why'd you go live with him?"

"I couldn't find a roommate."

He puffed, blew out, and let the smoke curl into the air like a verdict. "Why'd you leave him?"

I tried to find words. "He wasn't good for me."

Dad was quiet a moment, reflecting. He blew another circle of smoke in the air.

"I can see how some of the things I did pushed you more to him."

It was unusual for my dad to admit such a thing. My brain tried to work this out. I tried not to show surprise.

If he had realized this, why hadn't he told me? Why would he cut me out of his life?

The kitchen was quiet as Dad took a long drag on the cigarette. "I hear you dropped out of school."

"No. I couldn't get the classes I needed."

"So you dropped out," he stated as if I were a failure.

"No, I just wasn't willing to pay full tuition for only nine credits."

Brad jumped in, attesting to how hard it was to get the correct courses.

"What about Trish? Why did you get back with her?"

"She showed up at my dorm one night. I felt like I should try to forgive her."

"Well, you're sure as shit on your own with that one," Dad quipped.

"Are you a lesbian?" Dad asked.

"What?" I looked bewildered. Where was this coming from?

Dad laughed, trying to sound hip. "I heard you were living with a bunch of dikes. I'll accept you if you're a lesbian, Cindi. I just want to know." In reality, he would only accept such a situation up until the point when others started whispering and judging.

"I don't think my roommates were *all* lesbians," I added, "I think they were just . . . experimenting."

He weighed my answer.

"I have a boyfriend," I said. What kind of proof did he want?

The questions went on, with Brad mediating. At one point, I thought, *Brad is good. He knows how to handle them now.* In the two years since I was banished, Brad's status in the family had improved.

The conversation eased. We laughed about some things. I didn't feel immediately accepted or forgiven. But the door, once firmly shut, had been cracked open.

I would have to prove myself, to earn their love again.

Brad drove me home. "Aren't you glad you came?"

I was thankful for the darkness. "Sort of . . . it just seems you were all happy enough without me," it was a fear that would never fully go away.

CHAPTER 16

Tip Toeing Perfectly

BRAD BROUGHT DAD AND Pat to the video store a few weeks later to see where I worked. We were in a new location by then and the store looked impressive, with its freshly painted walls in gray and red, charcoal laminate shelves, and new plush gray carpet. What caught Dad's eye was the plaque on the wall: for Sales Person of the Month, "Cindi Michael" was listed repeatedly, an award from the days before I was a manager.

"You are a winner," Dad declared.

He was proud. I changed the subject. "Did Brad show you how he wired the whole store with surround sound?"

I tossed Brad the key. "Here, show him what you did." Brad had taught himself how to wire audio. I didn't want Dad's pride if Brad didn't get it, too.

A few more weeks later, Dad and Pat met my boyfriend Bryce. I was nervous. I wasn't on sure footing with my family. Would they approve? Bryce was unusually quiet. I warned him to cover his tattoo, a cute tiger on his arm.

The conversation flowed smoothly enough until Bryce reached across the table for the salt, and a tiger paw peered out under his short-sleeved shirt. My dad glanced at it, then became intent on his food.

Bryce drank another beer and another, and was relieved when Michelle offered him yet another.

I later asked Dad what he thought of Bryce. He tried to say the right thing. "Nice guy." But he wouldn't make eye contact with me, and he changed the subject.

Pat's mom was more direct. "He sounds like a boar, and I don't mean B-O-R-E." She laughed at her own joke, "Although he sounded like that, too!"

Her words stung, but I knew that he was not their type. He was nice, honest, and hard-working. That was enough for me.

At Christmas that year, I was excited to be with my family again. I splurged and got everyone special gifts. Bryce's family invited me to celebrate with them, but Bryce was not invited to mine. His family gave me nice, meaningful gifts—a chocolate gateau because I loved chocolate, a toiletry bag for when I stayed overnight. We had a laugh at that one, though. Bryce still lived with his parents, so I never stayed over.

Bryce didn't get a gift from my parents. Dad had asked me to pick up his gift for Pat, a replica Egyptian Tutankhamun necklace, from White Flint Mall since I often drove past there. Dad's check was for over $6000, and I was terrified of being responsible for the necklace, even for an hour. Dad and Pat gave me a coral necklace and matching earrings, pale apricot in color, my favorite color then. I still keep the necklace in my jewelry box, periodically fingering the polished beads, wondering if they ever even think of me. I don't wear it anymore, though. I will say it's too young looking for me, but really, it's just too painful.

Despite having two families in my life that year, I went to Christmas Eve mass alone, worried Dad might skip midnight mass at the last minute. I had much to be thankful for, and I wanted to be sure God heard me.

Dad never explicitly apologized for things that happened during my two-year shunning, but he tried to make amends. The bearings on my Subaru melted, stranding me on the highway, and then, the steering started acting up. So Dad told me to go to the Nissan dealership, the same place he had bought Pat's new car, and recommended a Nissan 200 SX. Although my salary at Video Village was good, I was worried this was beyond my budget. My new car payment would be double that of the Subaru's, but the salesman told me my father was handling the down payment of several thousand dollars. Dad never explained this to me or gave me a budget; it was all through the Nissan dealer. I took this as Dad's way of saying sorry for what happened with the towing of the Chevy Nova. And I loved this new car—maroon-colored with a dashboard that reminded me of KITT, the car from *Knight Rider*.

I was excited too when Dad and Pat asked for my help. Super Bowl XX was in New Orleans, and Dad and Pat didn't want to leave Michelle alone all week. Would I mind staying with her? I was thrilled. I still had to work at the video store, but I would stay with Michelle overnight and get to hang out with my sister after work.

The awkward thing was Bryce. It didn't matter that I was twenty-one now. Friends were not allowed over at our house when Dad and Pat weren't home, and certainly not a boyfriend they didn't like.

Bryce didn't like the idea that he wouldn't see me for a whole week, so he offered to drive to Darnestown one afternoon. What was I supposed to do, tell him no? I made it clear that he could not stay over. He brought some videos, picking ones Michelle might like, and the three of us watched a movie. He had a couple of beers, and because it was late, I told him to stay over. We slept on the floor in our clothes. I still felt guilty. Would I get disowned again? Michelle, at least, liked Bryce.

I had to work Super Bowl Sunday. When I called from the store to check on Michelle, I heard voices in the background.

"Are you having a party?"

"No, not really. I just invited a few friends over."

"Is that okay with Dad and Pat?" Michelle was quiet.

I told her, "Just make sure they aren't there when I get home." If I didn't see anything, it was not my fault.

The drive from Wheaton to Darnestown would normally only take forty-five minutes, but snow was falling heavily. When I got home, the party was still going on. It was a small group of friends, six or seven, but one girl was throwing up in the bathroom.

I told Michelle, "Either their parents come get them, or I'm driving them home. Now!"

We cleaned the house the best we could, but Dad and Pat still found out. I don't know how. Pat called me, accusing, "Did you plan it with her?" She didn't believe me when I said no. The thing that really bothered me was how Pat tried to divide us. She chastised Michelle for putting me in a difficult spot and ruining my chance to prove my worth to her and Dad. I dreaded that Bryce would get thrown into this. I would have to tell them the truth.

It was Michelle who told me they asked her if he had come over. She said yes but that he had left early in the evening. She lied for me.

That spring, I decided to leave Video Village. Steve told me there was a cash flow problem. The chain had grown too fast, all commissions would be cut, and some assistant managers would be laid off. He told me that if I quit, somebody else would keep their job.

Without the commission, my pay would be less than if I waitressed. I talked it over with Dad and Pat and decided to resign. I figured I could get enough hours at The Attic, or I would find a nicer place to work. Then Bryce broke up with me. Maybe the end was in the works when I went back to being the "sportscaster's daughter."

Dad gave me tuition money for the spring semester, so I was back in school! I only needed to pay my living expenses, so things were not as tight as before.

This was the first time I was not working full time while in school. With all my attention on school, I developed a plan. If I went to summer school, increased my credits to twenty-two in the fall and eighteen the following spring, I could still graduate on time. The problem was, I could not do this while working at all.

I gently presented the plan to Dad and Pat. I stayed over one night and brought them coffee in bed the next morning.

I made small talk, described my idea, then finally asked, "So what do you think? Would you be willing to pay both tuition and living expenses for a year?"

He balked. "We can't afford that. We just don't have the money." The irritation was clear in his voice.

"It's fine. It's fine." I was in danger of angering my father, so quickly changed the subject. "Did Michelle tell you she got a letter from George Steinmann?" George Steinmann, the foreign exchange student who was my boyfriend in high school. I hadn't heard from him in years.

Dad took a drag of his cigarette. Still perturbed, he said. "Oh, yeah?"

"Apparently he's been sending letters to me all this time to St. Mary's Hall at Maryland. I never got any of them. He wanted to know why I had not written back."

"You gonna write back?"

"I think so."

The conversation eased as long as I didn't bring up money or school again. I squelched my disappointment, admonishing myself for wanting too much. The newspapers said my dad made over $300,000. He had an expensive car, he bought Pat gifts that cost thousands of dollars, and Pat and her mom were taking a trip to Egypt. But they had just bought the house next door so that they could use the land for a new horse and burros.

I told myself I was being selfish expecting them to pay for school and board, that I should consider myself lucky to be back in the family at all. Asking for more was greedy.

Eventually, my father changed his mind and said he would pay for my last year of tuition and board. So I did my two sessions of summer school, fifty-eight credits in that last year. It was a heavy course load, but easier than the schedule I had been keeping the first three years of college. So much easier that I scored eighteen As and only one B that last year.

It was the first day of midterm exams in October. I didn't sleep well the night before, studying late and unable to turn my brain off. Then in the middle of the night, a cricket chirping in my bedroom taunted me. I told myself that lone cricket would never hurt me. In those days, I read books by Stephen King, and in the black of night, that cricket turned into something evil and supersized. So I did what any bug-fearing girl would do. I got the vacuum with the very long nozzle and sucked it up from a safe distance.

That seemed a good idea at two in the morning, but as the night wore on, I pictured that poor Jiminy Cricket suffocating to death, maybe even its babies suffocating in that vacuum cleaner bag, making me the meanest person in the world. Worse, didn't killing a cricket bring seven year's bad luck?

So on that sunny morning in October, I wanted to be sure I was early to campus for my first exam in eighteenth century English literature. I crossed the hump on the rail road tracks on Contee Road, leading to Route 1. I was less than a mile from my apartment in Laurel, Maryland. Traffic was often heavy at this time of day and backed up from the traffic light where Contee Road ended in a T junction at Route 1. But this morning, a policeman had pulled somebody over on the other side of the road and was writing the driver a ticket, making traffic even slower than usual with rubberneckers.

I waited at the red light and glanced in the rear view mirror. I could see a car coming fast over the hump for the rail road tracks and she wasn't slowing. There was nowhere for me to go. She swerved at the last second as I fleetingly thought I would be okay.

When I opened my eyes, two people were standing in front of my car. The woman was the driver of the car that had hit me. The man was the driver of the car in front of me, whose car I crashed into when I got hit from behind.

I tried to focus on them, but their bodies were blurry. My head was throbbing. I could not figure out what I had hit the back of my head on. I grabbed my headrest, pulling at the padded fabric.

"Thank God she's wearing a seat belt," a voice muffled through my closed window.

Someone whistled to the policeman to come over. He asked me if I was okay. Could I stand? I tried to get out of the car. Why was my head hurting? "I need to get to school. I have my first exam."

Someone pulled my car to the side of the road for me. The police officer handed us forms to fill in to exchange insurance information. I started to fill it in, but couldn't make out the words, so I handed it to someone else to do for me.

I told the policeman I wasn't sure what to do. I didn't want to miss my exam, but I wasn't feeling good. He thought the car was drivable.

I waited for the shaking to stop and for my vision to refocus, then drove the fifteen minutes to campus. All I could think about was my exam. I parked my car but when I stood to get out, a searing pain ran up my spine. I tried to close the car door but it wouldn't shut. The car's frame had been bent.

I walked over to the health center and burst into tears. They thought I should go to a hospital. The nurse wanted to call an ambulance, but I begged her not to. I would be fine. I just needed to calm down. They suggested I call my parents.

Dad thought I should get checked out and asked me to call him to let him know what was happening. I didn't have money for a taxi to the hospital, so the health center covered it.

At the hospital, the pain spread from my head to my neck. I lay on a cold table for an X-ray of my neck and spine. When I tried to sit up, daggers of pain knocked me back down, until the X-ray technician gently helped me up.

I called Dad from the emergency room. "They took an X-ray, so I don't know yet what's going on."

"Hold on. I'm expecting a call from Vance." Just like that, the line went quiet. Jim Vance, the lead news anchor and Dad's best friend, was recovering from drug rehab.

I tried to tell myself Vance needed my Dad more, that my feelings should not be hurt by being put on hold. I wanted to hang up.

When Dad came back on the line, I masked my hurt. "I'll call you later, when I know more."

I was given pain killers and a neck brace and released. The problem was, I didn't have a way home. I tried calling Brad but he wasn't home. The hospital organized a taxi to take me back to campus. The cab driver first stopped at a bank for me to get money for the cab fare. Once on campus, I found a friend to take me home.

The full pain didn't hit me until the next day. A friend was taking me back to campus to get things out of my car. As he accelerated, I yelped from a pain in the front of my neck.

So began months of problems and years of intermittent neck issues. In the immediate days that followed, I had debilitating headaches.

The insurance company of the driver who hit me, Geico, called me the next day, confusing me with their policy holder. "Miss, this is your third accident within a year."

It took more than a month, but Geico insisted the car could be repaired by straightening the frame, and they refused to pay for the loss in value of my car. After the accident, my sporty new Nissan 200 SX shimmied whenever it went over thirty-five miles an hour. This car accident ruined a symbolic peace offering from Dad and Pat.

The aggravation of the car accident was overshadowed by the excitement of a profile the *Washington Post* wanted to do on my father. The reporter, Stephanie Mansfield, had come to the house for the interview, and the photographer took some nice pictures of Dad with his burros. Dad even made Stephanie and the photographer his legendary hamburgers. It was all very exciting. Until the article came out.

"She crucified me," Dad said. It revealed his birth name, George Michael Gimpel, a name he hated and had legally changed fifteen years before. The profile painted him as an ego-centric embellisher who got caught in multiple lies. One person described Dad as "the highest paid fourteen year old in Washington, DC" and talked about him "shoveling bull." Well, duh, he was cleaning the burros' stable during the interview.

Dad was furious and demanded a retraction. The editor refused. While Mansfield had some incorrect details (she spoke of him wearing a Gucci belt; really it was just a nice belt from Cheyenne, Wyoming), the *Post* stood behind the substance of the story. The reporter had interviewed one of Dad's oldest friends from St. Louis. The friend didn't say anything bad about my father, but Dad never spoke to him again. Revealing my father's birth name was a betrayal.

Up until this point, anything I had ever read or heard about my Dad had been positive, glowing even. Except for Trish, nobody else had dared to criticize my father.

Pat expressed her own fears to me. "Can you imagine if Mansfield got a hold of Trish . . . or of Brad?"

I understood the concern about the reporter talking to Trish, but why Brad? I thought it curious they had no concern over what I might have said, having been disowned for two years. The part of the article that described Dad as a good father nagged at me. Did whoever had described him as a good father know I had been disowned? Did they think Dad was right to do that to me? That I deserved what I got? On this point, the article was one more proof that I was the one who did not appreciate my father enough. If the *Post* printed it, mustn't it be true?

Eventually, this reporter became the bully in my mind. She had hurt my father, tainted him in a way he didn't deserve. Besides, she wrote he had two sons and one daughter. If she got a fact like that wrong, the whole article was questionable.

Oddly, it was this article, decades later, that reminded me about this other side of my father, and that I was not the only person he had cut out of his life. He had lied about when his mother died, saying she died when he was a teen, when in fact she worked to put him through a private university and died when he was thirty. If he would lie about something as profound as that, what story, then, did he tell about me the whole time I was disowned?

So, was I the problem or was my father? At twenty-one, my loyalty was still with my father, and I was shocked that anyone dared to cross him. The last person to do that had paid dearly for her mistake, losing her husband, her home, her children, her credit, and her sanity: my mother.

The car accident happened just a few weeks before George Stein-mann was coming to visit. It was the first time in four years we would see each other. Ever since he had written to my sister, we resumed our letter writing. We both longed for an in-person visit, and finally, with a break in his army service, he planned to come to the US for a week. He sent a telegram saying he was arriving DC in two weeks, on Friday. There were no more details about whether he'd be staying with me or with our friend, Bob, or even which of the three airports in DC.

I called his mom to get the airport details, but was too shy to ask where he would be staying. I asked Michelle to come with me to the airport, to make our reunion less awkward.

The three of us went out to dinner, and it was only during din-ner that I was sure he was staying with me for the week. I made the mistake of ordering spaghetti, far too messy to eat in front of a boy I was still trying to impress.

During that week, George and I went to campus together. He studied on his own in the library, while I went to my classes. We met up with old high school friends, and did tequila slammers at a bar in College Park. I took him to DC, and we strolled around the Washington Monument and the Lincoln Memorial, catching each other up on the last four years of our lives. I didn't immediately tell him why my dad had disowned me for two years—that came later. He told me how none of the girlfriends he had had compared to me, and that he still wore the ID bracelet I had given him in high school.

We had dinner at my parents' house, and George brought them a bottle of fine red wine. My dad and he laughed together, as George talked about his military career, now a sergeant, and laid out his ambitious plans to be a lawyer.

Later, Dad said to me, "I've always liked him. He's a man's man."

On his last night, we sat by candle light on my sofa. George's eyes filled with tears, and he declared in his rusty English, "I can never call you my own again."

At twenty-one, I thought his word choice was more because of his German language, and I was flattered that someone like him wanted someone like me (*tainted*). We decided that our old high school crush could be something more, but neither of us could commit beyond that. I believed we had to live in the same country to see if our relationship would work. George had a few more years of university and military service, so it made sense for me to try to live in Switzerland for a period after I graduated.

I began applying for jobs there and found books on how to work abroad. I could au pair for someone. I could teach English. I was willing to do anything as long as it gave George and me a chance to see how deep our relationship was. Could we be something more than just high school sweethearts?

I would not be discouraged until I had written at least a hundred letters; that was my finish line. Thinking a senator could help get me a work permit abroad, I sent a picture of George and me to our state senator. Pat's parents wrote to one of their political connections, too. Ours was a true love story: American girl falls for Swiss exchange student, separated by silly international laws!

I was so certain of my eventual move to Switzerland that when the lease was up on my apartment a few weeks before I was due to graduate, I moved back home to Darnestown. Dad and Pat agreed there was no point in renewing my lease for a year when I was destined to move to Switzerland within a few months.

I planned to go to Switzerland in June for George's university ball and lined up some interviews, mainly at schools to teach English and a few with some recruiters. Some prospects were with US companies with offices in Switzerland. All warned me that without a work permit, they could not hire me.

Nothing swayed my determination to be with George, and it is only with hindsight that I can see how the need for my father's approval further motivated me. George had my father's approval, unlike all my recent boyfriends. When I showed Pat a picture of George in his sergeant's uniform, her breath caught. His brown hair, brown eyes, and olive complexion made him look like a younger version of George Clooney.

Pat and her parents wanted to go with me to Switzerland, a combination vacation and opportunity to meet George's parents. Dad planned to come too, and I even applied for his passport when I applying for my own. Pat handed me the application with Dad's birthdate, 1939, and warned, "Don't tell anyone." I had never known my dad's real age. That's also when I learned that my birth name was not Michael, but Gimpel. Dad and Trish had it changed legally when I was five.

As our trip drew near, Dad changed his mind about coming to Switzerland, saying he had too much work to take off for a week. He looked at coming over on the Concorde for a couple days. I suspected it wasn't just his schedule that held him back. In Switzerland, he wouldn't be the famous sportscaster. He would only be there as my father, a nobody.

I was to stay in Switzerland three weeks, a few days at the Steinmann's home near Lucerne, then some time at George's school apartment in St. Gallen, near the Austrian border. The first week I would stay with Pat and her parents at the Monopol-Metropole in Lucerne.

The day we arrived was sunny, a good omen that this was a place I could live. The Lake of Lucerne was picturesque with its blue-green water and snow-capped mountains in the distance. George drove me up a hill to a café where we shared a glass of wine in the early afternoon, sitting on a patio that overlooked the lake. It had been eight long months since we had seen each other, phoning and writing as often as we could. Jet lag pulled at me, but George's smile and joy at my finally being physically next to him kept me going.

When I had left Washington, DC, it had been hot and humid, and I hadn't been prepared for the cooler days in Switzerland. By day two, it was drizzly. Mrs. Steinmann took us sightseeing during the day while George studied. In the evening, we all ate at an Italian restaurant in the old part of the city. Between the jet lag and the change in weather, I could feel a cold coming on. Mrs. Steinmann noticed I wasn't feeling well and suggested an early night. George wanted to go out to a disco after. At first I said yes, but as we stood to go, I agreed it was better for me to go back to the hotel with Pat. I needed some sleep.

The next morning, we met George and his mom for a boat ride on Lake Lucerne. George would not meet my eyes. He had begun a cold-shoulder treatment. I sat next to him on the boat, trying to bring him out of his bad mood, but he was unrelenting. He joked with Pat or her parents, but he was distant with me.

As Pat and I walked back to the hotel, she commented on George's coldness. "Gee, Cindi, I'm not so sure I should be leaving you here if he's going to treat you like that."

"He's just mad that I didn't want to go out last night."

George was the same way the following day. When we had a moment alone, I confronted him. "If you are going to treat me like this the entire time, I'll go back home with Pat. You can't just ignore me."

"You come all this way and you go to bed early? It's boring! *Muesam!*" He cursed in Swiss German, words I didn't understand, but the anger and disgust were painfully clear.

Our fight went on until both of us were in tears. He was sorry. I was sorry. We would be okay.

Mrs. Steinmann invited us to their home for dinner, a penthouse apartment that overlooked the Lake of Lucerne. George's father and sister welcomed me into their home, and it was so nice for everyone to meet.

We had aperitifs on the balcony, and Pat shared her story of how she and Dad had met.

Mrs. Steinmann commented, "How brave of you to take on three children like that."

Pat replied. "Well, it hasn't always been easy. Early on, I told him it's me or the kids."

Her remark reverberated like an echo in the Grand Canyon, repeating in my head while the rest of the conversation fogged into a dull buzz. *It's me or the kids. She made him choose. Me or the kids.*

As we sat down for dinner, the conversation moved to a safer topic of the burros that Dad and Pat had recently adopted. One was pregnant and due in August. Pat promised the Steinmanns that she would send pictures of the burros, but she never did. She never wrote a thank you note, either, for all the guided tours and hospitality.

Pat and her parents left after a week, and I got down to the business of job interviews. Some were three hours away from St.

Gallen in the French part of the country in Montreaux. One was atop a mountain in the ski resort of Crans Montana. George got in a bad mood driving away from that one, down narrow windy roads, ravines on either side, imagining the drive he would have to do to visit me on the weekends.

Toward the end of my three-week trip, George showed me off at his university ball. I wore a white dress with a glittery mesh as the V-neck. The back was open to the small of my back. One of his friends declared we were the best looking couple at the whole dance. I didn't need a glass slipper to reinforce the dream that we belonged together.

On my last weekend in Switzerland, we went hiking in the Alps. We started in lush greenery at the base, then climbed to snow-laced tops. After three weeks of drizzling rain, the sky was now clear blue, the views of the mountains and emerald river roaring far below breath taking. Each person we passed said "*Grueizi*," Swiss German for "hello" or "greetings." George's dog Terri, a sweet Cocker Spaniel, came with us. We laughed at how Terri seemed to do the hike twice. She would run ahead and then run back to make sure she hadn't left us behind. Half-way through the hike, we picnicked by a lake. George made a camp fire with two sticks, something he learned in the army, and grilled sausages.

After lunch, we continued hiking, but the trail we had intended to take was washed away from the heavy rains of the past month. We were forced to go further and higher than we had planned. I trusted George, though, to guide me, to know the way. As we rounded the mountainside, we faced a waterfall, the water pooling to an unknown depth, then continuing over the mountain. Some other hikers had turned back, but a few had not. George suggested the hike was longer if we turned back. It might turn dark, and we weren't prepared to hike that long. He worried that the water was normally just a trickle here. He shouted above the roar of the falls that he would see how deep it was first, then come get me. At the middle, it was up to his thighs. George came back and first carried a trembling Terri across, then came back to guide me. He held my hand firmly as the force of the water dared to push me closer to the edge. Once all three of us were firmly on dry rock on the other side, we hugged each other, my legs shaking from fatigue and fear. The kind of person George was that day was the person I fell in love with; the person I saw less of after we married.

After three weeks in his country, our good-bye at the airport was tearful, but I was determined and hopeful. A few of the interviews were promising. The two schools would let me know in August, based on their fall enrollment. So I told George, "Don't worry! I will see you in August!"

At home, I told Dad about the trip and the interviews. "Crans Montana seems the best chance, but it's really remote. George got in such a bad mood driving back from there." I giggled, recalling his moodiness, all because he wanted to be closer to me!

Dad was sitting at the kitchen table, post dinner, while I rinsed the dishes. "So you'd go there, by yourself, even though you don't speak German?"

I had studied French for five years and was fluent in that but had only taken a semester of German since George and I reconnected. "I'd see George on the weekends, and I'd be teaching English. How else can we be together?"

Dad blurted, "Well, you know you'd end up getting divorced."

I stopped washing and just stared at him. *No, I didn't know that.* What was that supposed to mean? That the more George got to know me, the less he'd like?

There was nothing I could say in response, so I bit the inside of my cheek to keep the hurt in. I have bit this part of my cheek so many times that it is scarred from the inside.

At the time, I thought the remark was only about my own short-comings, about how undesirable a wife I was for someone as ambi-tious, smart, and handsome as George. I never considered then that my father's words might have been more about him and his lack of faith in love, than about me. I had to prove my father wrong. I would never ever get divorced, no matter what George did to me.

The summer of 1987 was an anxious one of waiting for news

from Switzerland, but it was also a summer of seeing my family in the glare of a light newly shining after my two-year shunning. Pat's comment about Brad and the Mansfield article ("Can you imagine if she had gotten a hold of your brother?") bothered me in a way I could not articulate. When my father ordered everyone in the sports department, Michelle, and me red corduroy Sports Machine jackets, I promptly asked, "Where is Brad's?"

"He wouldn't want one," my father said dismissively.

"Did you ask him?" I asked hesitantly. I still worried that if I irritated my father enough, I would lose his love again.

"I can't get any more anyway."

I fingered my name, embroidered in white against the red jacket. I could pull the stitching out. Brad deserved the jacket more than I did. "I could give him mine."

"Oh, for Chrissake, I'll order him one." I don't know if my father ever did order Brad a jacket, but it was a slight against my brother that I thought was just plain mean.

And then there was Pat, who kept declaring, "I don't think Cathy likes you. Did you see the way she looked at you during dinner?" Cathy was Brad's live-in girlfriend. I liked Cathy, but I was willing to bet that Cathy could see more clearly than I how Brad's place in the family had shifted since my return.

"We get along fine," I replied.

And then when we got pictures back from that same dinner, Pat showed me a picture of Cathy looking at me sideways. "See, look at that. Look how she is looking at you."

I glanced at the picture and refused to comment. Anyone can have an odd expression at just the wrong moment.

But then there was the night that my father tried to tell me Brad suggested I had been a hooker during the time I was disowned. I refused to believe my father.

Dad turned to Pat, "Isn't that what he suggested? You were turning tricks or something."

Pat nodded, "Yep. Even mentioned your friend Frank."

I gasped, incredulous. "Frank, my *friend* Frank? The bar tender?"

They both nodded. "He's my friend. And only my friend!" Frank was one of those people I met while working at The Attic, who probably could have taken advantage of me and didn't.

"So . . . what? Am I supposed to confront Brad about this or what?"

Brad was coming to dinner that night, so I had time to think. I didn't believe my father, or Pat. For some reason that I didn't understand, they were trying to divide us, just like the time in Oakland when Dad cornered me in the hallway about the party at the lake behind our house.

I would not let them do that. I had been out of the family dynamics for two years, and, like a girl with bad eyes getting her first glasses, I could see things about my family now that I had once viewed as normal. It was not beyond reason that Brad was flailing his arms, as any son whose father's love has to be fought for would do, because my return had pushed Brad further from the family. Then again, Brad was never good with money, so maybe he just couldn't figure out how I had survived on so little for so long.

So that night, after dinner and a video in the family room, Brad got up to leave. I jumped up from the sofa and said, "I'll walk you out." As I followed him up the driveway, I thought it probably pissed him off too that in my summer stay at the house, I had moved into Brad's old room (Michelle had taken my bedroom the first year I was in college).

Brad walked ahead of me. Walking him out to his car was not our normal routine. The night was black. There were no streetlights on Plainfield Lane. There was just the glow of the lamp from the family room. Brad and I could see in, but they could not see out. "So, um, Dad said something that I need to ask you about."

He got to his car and turned to face me, "What's that?"

"Something about me turning tricks."

Brad avoided my gaze.

It wasn't anger that ran through me then so much as it was disbelief . . . and pity. "Why would you do that? I worked two jobs, sometimes three at time."

He had no answer. His eyes still refused to meet mine, which said everything. I walked away then, back into the house, a house where only Brad no longer lived.

My father called from the family room, "What did he say?"

I hesitated. Was my father goading me? In past times, I would have rejoined my family in the living room, acknowledged what Brad had said or not said, then basked in my father's glow. But now, I vowed not to get sucked into those old ways. I shouted from the hallway. "Nothing, he didn't say anything." I raced up the stairs to my bedroom, Brad's old room, and buried my face in my pillow, alone in the dark.

While I was uncertain of my place with my father that summer, I was sure of my sister. Michelle was waitressing in an Italian restaurant, and most evenings we were on our own in the house. I imagined how lonely it had been for her the years she had come home from school to an empty house.

One day she was lying on my bed, telling me about boy who had broken her heart. Finally, she said, "I wish I could be more like Pat. At work, everyone calls her the ice princess."

I thought then, *I've been away too long.* An ice princess was the exact opposite of who I wanted to be and who Michelle was.

Another day, she was hanging out in my room, and I praised her honey-tanned legs, so different from my pale, dimpled thighs.

She sat bolt upright and said, "What? You mean because they're so fat?"

I stared back at her, dumbfounded.

She glared. "You're surprised I don't have dimples because I'm so fat."

"No, Michelle. You're not fat! Look at my thighs! Why are mine all dimpled, and yours are so smooth?" Her remark shouldn't have surprised me, though. In my years of being disowned, I had kept my weight off, while Michelle had grown taller than me and was a little plump but still not as heavy as I had once been. But I never once heard Dad criticize my sister's weight the way he had criticized me in high school.

When Michelle came home one day and declared she would be getting her hair colored, I replied with sadness, "Don't do it! People *pay* to have highlights like yours put in!" But Michelle didn't like her sun-streaked highlights, so she dyed her hair anyway. I understood her insecurities. I had felt them too, still did in fact. But I had a boyfriend now, and Michelle was at that stage where boys stayed away from her, the sportscaster's daughter. Also, her long-time best friend had recently dumped her, and in the middle of the night someone had smashed eggs on the dashboard of her unlocked car. High school sucked.

Michelle needed cheering up, so I took her to the one place that has always soothed my soul: the beach.

Michelle and I each brought a girlfriend, and we drove to Ocean City, Maryland, for the day. The four of us laughed in the sun, dove the waves, threw a Frisbee, and tanned ourselves on the beach. At the end of the day, my sister thanked me and said, "It's just what I needed."

It never occurred to me, then, that my sister had always been the taker and I the giver. I only realized that later, when she took what little I had left.

CHAPTER 17

Spilt Sugar

Dad with his first horse, Cheyenne

Dad with the first of many paint horses that he and Pat bred

THE SUMMER OF 1987, I worked temp jobs while I waited to hear about getting a permit in Switzerland. I entered data at a real-estate firm and typed proposals at Birch & Davis, a small consulting firm in Bethesda. I had heard back from a few Swiss companies but no work permit. So by August, my only remaining hope was the school in Crans Montana. We had corresponded over the summer, and the director asked me to call him before dawn, afternoon in Switzerland. While the rest of the house was asleep, I sat alone in my father's study in the back of the house, so I wouldn't wake anyone. I took a deep breath and said a silent prayer.

The director was sorry; I was too inexperienced. He hired a teacher with experience teaching abroad. I hung up and cried. I couldn't call George, who was back in the army for the summer.

I would have to let him know by letter. So I went to my temp job that day, and when Birch & Davis offered me a permanent position, I accepted.

Dad and Pat were disappointed for me, but they didn't have any suggestions. Since I wasn't moving to Switzerland, I said I would start to look for an apartment.

"You don't have to move out," Dad said.

"Well, this, this was only temporary until I learned about the work permit." I was doing the dishes as we spoke. It was rare that we ever just sat and talked. "You guys are moving to Comus, anyway. What am I supposed to do, commute from there?" Dad and Pat had just bought a horse farm farther north of Washington, DC.

"Yes," Dad replied matter-of-factly. "If I can drive it, so can you."

"You don't drive in rush hour. Even from here, it takes me an hour to get to work with all the traffic." River Road into Bethesda was such a parking lot that I could actually leave my coffee cup on the car's dashboard and drink it leisurely. "Besides, what about when George has leave from the army next March. Are you going to let him stay with us?"

"Hell, no!"

Dad laughed, but he was serious. No boyfriends or fiancés or anything in-between would ever be allowed overnight, even in a bedroom down the hall. Brad and his girlfriend Cathy had been living together for three years, and never once had they stayed over together at Dad and Pat's house.

"Well, then," I replied.

Here was the thing about my father: if you hurt him, he would hurt you back. You just may not know when or how.

So a few weeks later we were talking about the planned trip to Wildwood Crest, New Jersey, the place where Michelle had once won all those Little Miss Admiral contests. I hadn't been there in four years but said I would join them this summer. The pregnant burro, though, changed our vacation plans. What if the burro gave birth while we were at the shore? Pat in particular did not want to miss the birth, so we all agreed to cancel the trip.

Dad complained. "But will everyone still take time off?"

I said I wasn't sure, to which Dad reached over to Michelle in the kitchen chair next to him and pulled her close, saying, "Well, Michelle anyway. She's always been my favorite."

Pat tisked, "Geoooorge," in a voice that relayed, *you shouldn't say such things even if that is how you really feel.*

He looked at me triumphantly, voice booming. "What?" suggesting I had nothing to complain about: he had merely spoken the truth. Get over it!

If I got teary eyed over one of my father's zings, he'd call me a candy ass, too. Best just to do the dishes and not think too hard about such remarks. Michelle might have been Dad's favorite most of the time, because she was the cutest, but there were years that I was his favorite, because I made him the most proud.

While Dad hinted he wanted me to keep on living with them at home, Pat did not. Our deepest conflict started over spilt sugar. Literally.

One Saturday night, Pat had spilt sugar on the floor while baking. The next day, as I walked across the kitchen in my high heels, my father grimaced at the gritting sound. He complained about Pat not cleaning up. I used the dustpan to sweep up what I could and replied nonchalantly, "It's no big deal. I'll mop when I get home from church."

Dad grumbled, still annoyed that Pat left the mess in the first place.

"You know cleaning is not one of Pat's strong points," I said.

It was Dad who had taught me how to clean, to tilt my head to catch the sunlight to check for dust, to run my fingers along the floor, the dresser, the counter, for any spots I might have missed. My remark seemed to me a simple fact, not intended as a slight.

When I got home from church, Dad and Pat had already left for work. Michelle told me I was not to touch any of Pat's laundry or go near her room. When I had moved back home that spring, after their house cleaner/babysitter had quit and they hadn't found a replacement, I had offered to clean to help out.

So, I asked Michelle what had happened, why Pat would say such a thing, but she didn't know. To this day, I still don't know what exactly my father said to Pat. With his tendency to embellish and how pissed off he was about the sugar anyway, it couldn't have been pretty.

Pat's instructions for me not to touch her stuff presented a major dilemma. How could I do Dad's, Michelle's, and my laundry, but leave Pat's out? What if Michelle misheard and then I got in trouble for not cleaning?

"So I'm supposed to clean Dad's bathroom sink, but not Pat's?" Michelle shrugged in reply. It seemed safer to me just to clean as I had been doing the last few months.

Monday through Friday we didn't see each other, as I worked a regular office schedule. Friday and Saturday were Pat's days off. All that week we didn't speak, which was not so unusual. When I got home from work Friday evening, though, Pat was in her room with the door shut. Michelle was at work. Pat ate her dinner in her bedroom, watching TV up there. It was not something she had ever done before.

I ate alone at the table, waiting for some clue as to what I had done wrong and some opening to fix it. I sat alone in the den and watched *Beauty and the Beast,* anxiously listening for her bedroom door to creak open. I went to bed before Dad got home.

Saturday night, it was just Dad, Pat, and me for dinner, burgers and chips. Pat still wouldn't talk to me, leaving Dad in the middle. I wondered if he knew that Pat had avoided me all of Friday evening.

Dad must have felt the tension, because when Pat made a joke, he didn't laugh. Then she added lightly, "How about if I pour this bag of chips over your head?"

"You do that and I'll break your fucking face." Dad never talked to Pat this way.

Pat normally wouldn't stand for it. "I was only joking," she replied, looking at him icily.

He backed off a bit, muttering, "It's just the sort of thing Trish would pull."

I knew tonight was not a night for joking. And besides, if either of them started throwing bags of potato chips at one another, I would have been the one to have to clean their mess up.

Pat and I never recovered from the spilt sugar incident, and things went downhill from there, over just about everything.

Dad offered to pay me for the months of cleaning house, but Pat complained, "Why do we have to pay everyone?" I returned the check to Dad, saying I had offered to clean the house to be helpful not for the money. Cash the check, and I piss Pat off. Don't cash the check, and I piss my father off. I was trying not to piss *anyone* off, so the check remained on the counter for weeks, further pissing all three of us off.

Then, our dog Teddy kept peeing on the carpet. He was not healthy. Dad would shout at Teddy and rub his nose in it, but really, Teddy couldn't help it as the vet said he had developed a tumor. Teddy couldn't wait very long before going outside. He was really good about standing at the front door and barking to go out, but it could be hours between when Michelle and I left in the morning and when Dad and Pat woke up. After one-too-many accidents, I was informed that Teddy would be put to sleep. I didn't think it was right. When I had moved home that summer, I could see the worms coming out of his butt, and yet Pat only took him to the vet when he started dragging his bottom on the carpet. Now that Teddy was sick, it seemed all-too-easy to just put him to sleep. In my view, if he had gone to the vet more regularly, instead of only when the worms were apparent, Teddy might not have gotten so sick. Perhaps the tumor could have been treated. Granted, if my parents didn't take such good care of us children, I shouldn't have expected much with the dog. But Pat loved animals so I thought she would have taken better care of him.

When I told Dad and Pat that I didn't think it was fair the way they were so quickly putting Teddy to sleep, Pat told me I was being immature, that even the vet declared I must have some issue for not wanting Teddy's life to be ended humanely. There was no room for discussion or grief, just the resurfaced criticism of how insensitive and selfish I was being.

Eventually, I found an apartment in Silver Spring that was almost within my budget. Of the dozens I had looked at, they were the nicest, bordering a beautiful park and only a block from the police station, making me think it was safe. I could afford a small car payment but certainly not the $285 I was currently paying for the Nissan SX. I made it a point to call Pat at work to tell her about this apartment, and that I thought I would have to trade in my car to afford the rent. I wanted to talk to my father, but that's not how things worked with them. I had to go through Pat.

I waited a few days to see if Dad would leave a note on the kitchen counter or at least call me back, but he didn't.

Here was another thing about my father: if he thought he was being used, he got angry. I was getting worried that my conversation about the lower car payment would be interpreted as asking him for money. As the days went by, I assumed he was angry. I also knew from my past apartments that a high car payment on my apartment application would mean my application would be denied. I had to make it clear to my father that I was not asking him for money. So I traded in my car. This backfired. He left a note on the counter.

> ~~Cindy~~
> *Cindi, we have been down this road before. You have been mad at me/Pat all week for reasons known only to you. You don't really have any reason to be angry other than the fact I made "a face" or something. You know what your attitude has been and you know how you have played your games this week—i.e., buy a car, no discussion—no help or thought needed from us—it's your privilege—you are your own person—you have every right! But when it comes to attitudes, you MUST think in terms of "risk-benefits"—"cause-effect"—"action-reaction." My feelings are directly the result of your attitudes—and you know how easily you can change everything with simple conversation. Try it!*
> *The check is yours—you earned it. Dad*

Dad's note was the first hint I got that Pat had not told Dad about any of our conversations. She was the gate-keeper to him, and she had intentionally not told him I was thinking about selling the car. Her revenge for the sugar incident. I studied Dad's note. He interpreted my fear of pissing them off as being mad at them. And what was the deal with his spelling my name wrong, when he was probably the one who had taught me to spell it with an "i" at the end?

If I wanted to piss Dad and Pat off, I would have ripped the note and the check to shreds, then sprinkled some sugar to drive home the point. But in those days, I lacked any such anger or courage.

Instead, I wrote a loving note in return and graciously returned the check.

Through yet another note on the counter, I asked Dad if I could go visit George at Christmas in Switzerland. I explained that I would be working an extra job at a bookstore to earn money for my flight. I explained—carefully and tactfully—that for the cheapest airfare, I would have to fly on Christmas night, but at least I would be able to spend Christmas morning and early afternoon at home with the family. Yay!

I tried to communicate more clearly, as my father had instructed me to. It felt awkward leaving all this in a note, but I had learned that going through Pat did not guarantee my father would get my message. If I called the station, Pat answered. The talent—father or not—never answered the phone directly, and rarely had time to talk to his children. So, Dad wrote back that it was okay to go to Switzerland, again told me to cash the check, and I finally did.

I wrote another note about the date I would be moving into my apartment. Nobody offered to help, but that wasn't too surprising. They hadn't helped me move back home (or move to college or move the four other times the last four years), so I didn't expect them to help me now. Instead, it was my friends who helped me make my new apartment a home, hanging drapes, putting up shelves, and hanging pictures—pictures of my family.

My parents were moving to a new house shortly after, but they never gave me the actual moving date. (So much for Dad's stellar communication skills!) Instead, I had to ask Michelle when they were moving. I drove out to Comus after work that night to help unpack, and again, Pat avoided me. Pat's parents were there to help, and they too seemed distant toward me. Dad was away on a business trip, but I hadn't known this. It was clear I was not wanted there. I unpacked in a room by myself for several hours then left. I have long wondered if Pat ever told my father I had at least tried to help or even that I had driven out.

Christmas day morning, I drove out to Comus, suitcase ready for my trip to Switzerland later that night. Dad and Pat, her parents, Brad, and Michelle all seemed in good spirits. I still have the music box my sister gave me with the dancing clown, and remember my father saying what a great gift it was. The music doesn't play anymore, but I cannot part with this gift, a gift from the last Christmas I ever spent with my family.

Michelle drove me to the airport that afternoon for my trip to Switzerland. The Steinmanns had waited to have their Christmas dinner until I arrived, eating Christmas dinner at a special restaurant. I preferred dinner at home, not in a fancy restaurant, but I felt honored that they had waited for me. An informal dinner at home with homemade turkey and mashed potatoes and two kinds of stuffing is more the way I like to celebrate. The Swiss Christmas tree, with real candles, scared me. Electric bulbs in red and yellow and blue, while superficial, seemed safer. I had baked chocolate chip cookies and brought them over. For the three-year old daughter of George's closest friends, Corrine, I hand carried a big, white, fluffy Kringle Bear, with a red bow, a special from J. C. Penney that year.

George and I rented a hotel room at the *Pilatus am See* for New Year's Eve. We didn't need to go out dancing, and instead shared champagne in the room, relishing some alone time. He floated the idea that if all went well in March, when he planned to come to the US for two months, perhaps we should marry.

People say you should listen to your gut. My gut reaction to George's idea was hesitation. I wasn't sure I was ready for marriage. I wasn't sure we had had enough time together. I argued with myself. I didn't want to be apart from George, but marriage was *forever*. I kept my worry to myself. After all, he had simply floated a thought.

Michelle picked me up from the airport, and on the drive home, I told her everything. I called Dad and Pat to let them know I was back safely. They didn't ask about the trip. I could trace the growing distance between Dad and Pat and me to the spilt sugar, then to the car, then to my moving out, but I didn't know how to fix things.

On my twenty-third birthday that January, I waited to see if anyone in my family would remember. It was a stupid test of love.

My friend Donna Saraisky from New Jersey came down for the weekend. We went to see *Empire of the Sun* (big mistake—we didn't know it was a World War II movie and cried our eyes out). She bought me a birthday cake from a bakery, loaded with thick white frosting that I love.

When we returned to my apartment, there was a message on the answering machine from my father. Better than nothing. Super Bowl was a busy time, so we usually celebrated my birthday in March, with my father's, one more subtle way of saying my father mattered and I did not. I sulked. I watched my Dad on TV, missing him.

When George asked me to come to Switzerland for the weekend for an army officer's ball, I wasn't sure of the protocol. Should I ask my parents for permission or simply inform them I was going? Mr. Steinmann was willing to pay for my ticket, and George would fly back with me during his army leave to stay in the US for a few months as we had long planned. I argued with myself that it was only for a weekend. It's not like Dad and Pat ever knew where I was on a daily basis anyway, and the only way I knew where *they* were was by watching the news. So, I took the coward's way and told Michelle what I was doing, knowing she'd tell Dad. I explained to Michelle that it was even more important that I go: George had just had an accident with a grenade. During a training exercise, the grenade had detonated early and George had been hit in the face. I needed to see him!

I was literally in Switzerland for a weekend, arriving Friday morning for the ball that evening, and then returned to the US on Sunday with George. Mr. Steinmann met me at the airport and gave graphic details about how much blood the face had. But by now, his scars were mainly a swollen lip and a line from the stitches.

George and I had so looked forward to these few months when we would be together. No more letters. No more late night phone calls. Finally, a real relationship! We drove out to my parents' new house and ranch in Comus for my father's and my birthday dinner. Whatever tension there was between my parents and me that evening was overshadowed by everyone's excitement to have George visiting.

I only saw the joy from that dinner. I had not been there for the preparation, as my sister had. I was not privy to the dread that she later said preceded my arrival, nor the anger that followed.

Instead, when my sister was graduating high school a few months later, she asked me not to come to her graduation ceremony. "It would be too tense," she said. "Dad's birthday was bad enough." *Really?*

But I had known things were not right between my parents and me since the spilt sugar. They moved house without even telling me when! No birthday card. And I should have asked for permission to go to Switzerland for the ball. Twenty-three or not, if I wanted Dad's love I had to do things his way, and more specifically, I needed to appease Pat. My sister knew this better than me, so by shunning me from her graduation, she gained brownie points with Pat, and ultimately, with Dad.

I cried on George's shoulder. I had more of a right to be at Michelle's graduation than they did. I had looked after her more than they did—for most of her life. I was the one at her talent show, not them. I was the one to dry her tears when a boy used her, not them. I was the one to rub cream on her scalp when she was going bald from nerves, not them. Until college, I was the one home after school with her at night, not them.

My sister had made her choice, and she chose our father.

CHAPTER 18

Engaged

GEORGE ASKED ME TO marry him in early June, 1988, after we had gone to see an Orioles baseball game. We had fought that spring, with a fierceness that scared me. Just like the summer before, George could go days without speaking to me when he was angry. But he promised me he would work on the "cold shoulder treatment," and I trusted him. I believed love could conquer all, and said yes.

"Are you going to ask my dad for permission?" I said.

"No," he replied in that tone that said, *don't be ridiculous*. While I was old fashioned, George was not, and like my father, George liked to be his own boss.

After he proposed, we ran out late at night and bought a bottle of champagne. We called his parents, filled glasses in hand, the middle of their night in Switzerland. They were thrilled. The next morning, I called Dad and Pat to ask if we could meet up for dinner.

Dad suggested we come into the station and go out to dinner between news broadcasts. With Michelle banning me from her graduation and her remark about how tense Dad's birthday dinner had been, I was nervous.

When George and I got to the station, I was told they had already left for dinner and no one knew where they went. They suspected Quigley's, their usual, but didn't know where it was. One of the producers *thought* Dad knew I was coming, but he wasn't positive. Michelle was with them, he said. Trying to guess what my Dad was thinking, what his actions signaled, was maddening.

George assured me there must have been a misunderstanding of where to meet. We should try to find the restaurant. We went to Quigleys. It was packed, laughter, and conversation, and glasses clinking at various tables. Dad, Pat, and Michelle were seated in the raised portion in the middle of the restaurant, already eating dinner. Dinner between news shows was always on a tight schedule.

George and I sat down and hurriedly ordered something that wouldn't take long to prepare. I apologized for being late, saying I thought we were to meet at the station.

George made small talk then announced he had some news, "I asked Cindi to marry me." He chuckled in his warm manner, "and she said yes."

My father responded, glibly, "Good for you."

I hesitantly talked about wedding plans, our options to marry in the US or in Switzerland. "So we can either get married in the US next February when George has a longer break from school and the army . . . or we can get married in Switzerland in October, when he has a weekend leave from the army."

Dad declared, "I don't give a shit where you get married, I'm not coming to your wedding, no matter when or where."

My face tingled with the months of bottled up anxiety.

My father's temper was legendary. He'd thrown a carousel of music tapes across a room and broken a foot while kicking a chair in the studio. At dinner that night, Dad accused me of not behaving as an active member of the family. I was selfish and inconsiderate. The way I sold my car with no discussion, the way I took off to Switzerland for the weekend without permission. The list went on.

My father's litany of complaints continued, and tears spilled down my face. I didn't have any tissues and nobody offered one, not even George. I wiped the snot with the clean white linen napkin.

The waiter interrupted, serving George and me our dinners.

Pat added to the criticism, "And when you moved home last summer, all you ever did was put down your sister. I would have thought as the big sister, you'd want to build her up."

I whispered to Michelle an incredulous "How?" This was my

sister, the same person who had told me how grateful she was I was home again, the sister whom I rushed to the dentist last spring when a burro knocked her tooth loose—an accident I tended to because our parents refused to open their bedroom door, in the middle of the freaking afternoon.

Michelle smugly described how I had criticized her for dying her hair. Technically speaking, I had been critical, since I had told her that people would pay for the beautiful highlights that she had naturally, that she shouldn't dye them away. But even then, I knew her explanation didn't matter. She had chosen her allegiance before her graduation. She needed my father more than she needed me. And to keep his love, she needed Pat.

My father concluded, "I don't know you, Cindi."

"No, you don't." It was the only time my voice was strong.

Selfish and inconsiderate were two things I was sure I was not, the only two things I knew for sure about myself. Insecure, stubborn, and clueless about how to handle my father and my stepmother, yes. Maybe unworthy of love, theirs or George's, yes.

It was George who finally decided the dinner should end. He had little to say—and he didn't defend me.

As we stood to leave, my father asked, "Don't I get a hug?"

I was staggered.

I could not understand him. In so many words and in so many ways, he had told me he did not love me. He wouldn't come to my wedding, yet, here he was, asking for a hug.

I buried my face in his chest, breathing in his cologne, his blazer scratching my cheek. I held him tight, not knowing that hug would have to last me a lifetime.

I did not hug my sister good-bye. I have not seen her since that night, twenty-four years ago.

After that night, George and I tried to make plans for our wedding and for my life in Switzerland. It was not the happy time it should have been. I agonized over every decision. Should the engagement announcement have both our parents' names? George decided no, pointedly reminding me that my father said he wanted nothing to do with our wedding. Do we even send them the announcement? George wanted to send them the announcement out of spite. I wanted to send it in the hope my father would change his mind.

We planned for a small wedding in Switzerland. If my family wanted nothing to do with it, then we should at least make it easy for George's family, and marrying in Switzerland meant I could get a work permit sooner. In July, George returned to Switzerland to the military, leaving me alone to plan a life-changing move: quotes from movers, what to take, what to sell, what job interviews to line up, again.

I shopped alone for a wedding dress. I went to the only wedding dress shop I knew of where the storekeeper told me I had to buy off the rack; there wasn't time to custom order a new dress. I tried on gowns, alone on the stool in the dressing room, trying not to cry. Another bride-to-be was laughing with her friend.

Michelle should be here with me, I thought. But all I could picture was the smug look in her eyes at dinner. I shook off my moment of pity. I had to get a grip. My to-do-list was long and time was tight. I slipped into the puffy dress, posed for the mirror, and tried to focus on the dress's iridescent hue, the pretty lace around the bodice, rather than the sad face that stared back at me.

I gave two months' notice at work at Birch and Davis, agreeing to work through the busy proposal season.

A few weeks before I was due to leave for Switzerland, I called home. *"Communicate!"* my father had written in his note.

I sat alone in my kitchen, at the cream-colored table I had decided to keep, to bring to Switzerland. I had sold my bed and had been sleeping on the sofa that I would move overseas. My apartment looked like a shell of the home it had been the past year. I was frazzled by so many decisions, and I didn't want another lashing. But I forced myself to call.

I bit the inside of my cheek. Thank God Dad answered and not Pat.

"So, um, I wanted to let you know, um, that I am going in a few weeks." Dad didn't respond. I continued. "I fly out on Thursday, September first."

"What did you do with all your things?"

"I sold some things, and the rest goes over in a container."

"What about your car?"

"I've been trying to sell it but if I haven't by then, the dealer has agreed to buy it back."

"We got your engagement announcement but nothing about the wedding."

"It will be the weekend in October when George has leave from the army. We'll figure out where when I get over there."

My father didn't offer to take me to the airport, and I knew by then not to ask.

CHAPTER 19

Fairy Tales

I ARRIVED IN SWITZERLAND on a sunny day. George embraced me as I came through the airport gate, making me feel like this was where I belonged. "We're your family now," his mother assured me.

In Switzerland, we settled on the details of the church, a quaint seventeenth-century chapel along the lake. During the week, George was in the army, and from Saturday morning to Sunday afternoon, he had leave. One afternoon, we handwrote the dozen or so wedding invitations on cards that showed the Chagall window from a cathedral in Zurich.

My father didn't reply. Pat's parents replied with a simple remark, "A wedding should be where the bride lives." It was the only clue that my father had not told anyone what he had said to me that night in the restaurant.

Fair or not, I did not invite Trish. I still had hope of my father coming and that meant excluding her.

I wondered if I should send Brad his own personal invitation; I had addressed the invitation to the Michael Family but that didn't guarantee my father would necessarily tell Brad anything.

"You think he's going to come if your father doesn't?" George looked at me like I was a simpleton. "We didn't buy extra cards."

"Well, I can go back by myself to buy one."

I could manage the train myself to the stationery store, but I knew George was right. Brad would only come if everyone else came. And it's not like Brad was sorry to see me go.

During the week, while George was in the army, I spent my time looking for a job and an apartment. One weekend, I drove to the army base in Andermatt to visit George. The roads leading up to Andermatt were narrow and winding, with sharp drop offs at each curve as the mountain climbs. By the time I got to the base, I was a wreck. I complained about the difficult drive, and how hard it was to find an apartment in St. Gallen. We were sitting in his room, a simple barrack. "I know how to ask how much it costs in German (*Wie viel kostet die Wohnung?*), and how many rooms (*Wie viele Zimmer?*), but then when they answer, I don't understand."

George replied, "This is all a big mistake."

It was as if he dropped a concrete slab on me. I blinked. And blinked again. "What?"

"It's a big mistake. You don't know the language. It'll be too hard."

I was looking for comfort, for support. What I got in return was the realization that I was truly alone. What did he want me to do? Call the movers and tell them to turn the boat around?

I drove back alone to the Steinmanns' apartment and cried to them. Mr. Steinmann was angry. "This is nonsense. I will talk to George. He has to support you better." Mr. Steinmann had been through this before. He had met Mrs. Steinmann in South Africa, so he knew my move would not be trouble-free.

Our next fight was over our wedding night. I thought it was bad luck for George to see me the morning of our wedding, but the Swiss have no such superstition. I had planned to stay with Donna, my maid of honor at her hotel. I told George this, but he disagreed and assumed I would change my mind. When I didn't, George was furious with me. It was easy for him not to talk to me, to give me the "cold shoulder," and for me to pretend everything would be fine, as each Sunday he returned to base for the week. These are the lies that are most dangerous, the ones we tell ourselves that we are not even aware of.

As the wedding day neared, Mr. Saraisky offered to walk me down the aisle. I declined. I didn't want anyone occupying my father's place next to me. It was his place and his alone. Either my dad would be next to me, or nobody would.

The day before the church wedding, everyone arrived from the US. Bob, our friend from high school, would be the best man. Donna came, and Mr. and Mrs. Saraisky. Donna, Bob, George and I went to the town hall for the civil wedding, the equivalent in the US of picking up the marriage certificate.

When we got back to the Steinmann's, George's sister, Sharon told me my father had called.

My heart raced with hope.

Sharon continued in her broken English. "I tried to tell him you went to get married but not to the church . . . *Zivil verheiratet* . . . but I didn't know how to say."

I tried to work out what time it was in the US. It was early enough for him to have caught a flight. "Did he ask me to call him back?" Sharon just shrugged. "Maybe I should call him back," I said to George.

George's face grew dark. "Why? So he can ruin our day?"

"But what if he's changed his mind?"

"And what?" he hissed. "What about Bob? What about the Saraiskies? . . . what about *my* parents? He's had four months!" George muttered some German curse words.

Mrs. Steinmann came cheerily into the hallway, not knowing what was transpiring. "Come on you two. Come on to the balcony and have some champagne with everyone."

I didn't call my father back that evening, procrastinating until a few days later.

Years later, I pictured my dad and his phone call. He would have called from the kitchen table, midmorning his time zone, a coffee and cigarette in hand. I pictured a father who wanted to be at my wedding, sitting alone at the kitchen table, shocked, and hurt things had not gone his way. Was it only that he hadn't wanted me to move to Switzerland? Had that been the real crux of his anger with me?

But on the evening before my wedding, I didn't allow myself to dwell, and instead, I drank champagne and prepared for my fairy-tale wedding.

My wedding day was a bright sunny morning in October. I had my hair done in a Russian braid at a beauty parlor near the hotel, my nails and make up I did myself. Donna snuck me a Reese's Peanut Butter Cup for breakfast, my antidote for stress. Mr. Steinmann organized for everyone to drive a Mercedes, a kind of procession along the private road that led to the chapel. I rode in Mr. Steinmann's car, with Donna helping stuff my puffy gown into the back seat of the Mercedes.

I waited outside the church with Donna and Corinne, our four-year old flower girl. At first Corinne didn't want to say hello to me, not recognizing me in the poofy dress and veil. The church attendant opened the heavy wooden doors for Corinne first, who so precisely let each rose petal float to the floor as she walked ahead of me. It was Donna who had told me to walk slowly, to remember each moment, a word of advice passed onto her from one of our other Oakland friends.

I walked down the aisle alone, smiling to Mrs. Saraisky, to George's friends, his mother, and finally to George as he turned around, his smile of praise drawing me to him, the chords of the old organ carrying me forward. When I got to the alter, I heard the church door bang. I turned, hoping to see my father rushing in. It wasn't. It was the door being closed.

Our honeymoon was a quick weekend in Locarno, the Italian part of Switzerland. We only had a weekend because George had to be back in the army on Monday.

So, in a way, my honeymoon was mostly spent with Donna, touring Austria. She and I took a train to Salzburg and then onto Vienna. Donna had been to Europe throughout high school, skiing with her family in the Alps, and then in college, she and some friends had toured Europe for a few weeks, staying in youth hostels in different countries. For me, though, this was all new—the adventure of riding a train, figuring out tram routes, and spontaneously searching for a reasonable place to sleep in whatever city we decided to stop in.

I knew at some point, I would have to call my father. Anxiety gnawed at me. Nobody had sent so much as a congratulations card.

If I called with a hurt or angry tone in my voice, it would only drive the wedge further between us. Yet, he had called.

In Vienna, Donna and I went to the PTT, the post office, the main place people went to make long distance calls. You didn't put money in; rather, made a call from a private booth and then paid your bill. I stood alone in the booth while Donna waited outside. I took a deep breath before dialing. I tried to pick a time as convenient as possible for Dad, not at work, not too early in the morning.

Pat answered. She didn't say hello or ask how the wedding had gone. "I'll get your father."

I forced myself to sound cheerful and told Dad George was back in the army for the week, so I was in Austria with Donna for a few days. I couldn't bring myself to mention the wedding, the pain of his absence, and he didn't ask.

The conversation was terse. It cost me thirty dollars, my budget for one night at a youth hostel. Phone calls to my father were clearly not worth the cost. I vowed then to stick more to writing, so I didn't have to hear the silence in his voice.

Donna and Bob went back to America, and I began my job at Dow Chemical. There was a comfort in working for an American company, where everyone at work spoke English. I lived with the Steinmanns the first two months until George and I could take over the apartment in St. Gallen.

I caught the 6:10 train from St. Gallen to Zurich each morning, arriving two hours later. It was a long commute, but I hadn't found any English-speaking jobs in St. Gallen. Some days I would skip lunch to catch the 5:25 train to get home at 7:30 in the evening, but more often I got home after eight at night.

There were times that George and I could get along beautifully, basking in the romance of our new life together. He was my Swiss prince charming, and I was his sunshine.

But there was his temper and our differences. I had not brought my kitchen plates from the US, thinking the weight to transport them made it too costly. So George met me in Zurich one day after work to shop for kitchen plates, Thursday evening (*Abend Verkauf*), the only evening stores stayed open. We went to a high-end depart-ment store, Globus. Each plate was more than twenty dollars, what I had once paid for my entire set of dishes at J. C. Penney.

I expressed my doubt, whispering to George, "They seem expen-sive. Isn't there another store to look in?" *A mall? An Ikea?*

I wanted a boxed set. I knew what my salary was to support both of us, and I had no savings. How could we possibly pay this much for every individual plate?

George grew angrier. "We are not in America anymore," he hissed. "There's no such thing as a boxed set."

The sales clerk heard my concern. She suggested we look in Migros, a super market chain. While she intended to be helpful, her suggestion insulted George. He stormed out of the store and didn't wait for me.

I had high heels on from work and couldn't catch up. I have bun-ions, inherited from both my mother and father, so walking in high heels is painful. When I took the train, I wore sneakers to the office, and changed to heels once at work. But in shopping with George, I had kept my heels on to look presentable to him.

I trotted along the dark street trying to catch up. He crossed the street well ahead of me, and I stepped into the crosswalk without looking, just as a car nearly grazed me. I stumbled back onto the curb, tingly with fear.

George kept going. I stood there for a while, unable to move, realizing, *I don't belong here. I don't belong anywhere.*

George eventually noticed I had not kept up and he didn't come back to get me. He called back in disgust as one would a dog, "You coming?"

We didn't get plates that night.

CHAPTER 20

Dumb Foreigner

THE FIRST TIME HE hit me, I didn't swing back.

It had been a work night, one month into our marriage. Getting home at seven thirty, I didn't feel like cooking so suggested we do pizza. I had already changed out of my work clothes into sweat pants, and George declared I couldn't go out to a restaurant dressed like that. I argued that I was only picking up the pizza. I was not going to put my skirt and high heels back on. If he didn't like how I was dressed, then *he* could go pick up the pizza. But he didn't feel like getting dressed presentably either and was embarrassed that I even dared ask if the pizzeria offered take out (*zum mit nehmen*), a rarity in Switzerland.

"You're such a rude fucking American."

I started to walk away from him. I wasn't going to listen to his insults. His fist caught me in my chest, knocking the wind out of me.

I walked out of the apartment into the hallway to get away from him.

After a minute, when I tried to go back into the apartment, George slammed the door on me, trying to keep me from getting back in. I kept my thigh wedged between the door as he pushed harder, our voices getting louder, until we both heard the neighbor below open her door into the hallway. *Click.* The Swiss, and George in particular, are a private people, and you should never let anyone hear you fight.

George let go of the door and let me back in. Then he left.

I thought of Pat. She would have swung back. When her one-time fiancé, an Englishman she had met while studying abroad in London, swung at her in a bar in London, Pat broke his nose. It was her father who later called off that wedding. Pat saw things in black and white. "Never let a man hit you," she once told me. A good, simple rule. But what do you do when it's your husband? What if the hit doesn't break anything or draw blood? George's blow didn't even bruise me. It only winded me.

I would only leave if it left a mark, I told myself. In later months when his "tickles" left black and blue thumb prints up my thigh, I convinced myself it was not intentional. Those marks didn't count.

The next morning when I went to work, George was still not home.

By day three, I called his mother. George was there, of course. She hadn't realized we had had a fight, and I didn't want to be the one to tell her. She was happy to have her son home and had been cooking him his favorite meals.

I spent the weekend in St. Gallen alone. I tried to pass the time by myself with the usual chores of food shopping, laundry, cleaning. I went to the movies on my own. I walked the dark streets of St. Gallen on my own, trying to push aside the loneliness. *The Accused* with Jodie Foster, a movie about a girl gang raped in a bar with nobody to help her, was probably not the most uplifting choice, but it was the only one showing in English.

At work, I put on a brave face. I tried to laugh at lunch time with the other ladies in the office. George had strict rules about privacy. We didn't discuss differences or fights with anyone. But after several days, I needed a shoulder to cry on. I wrote Donna a letter and faxed it to her, asking her to call me when she could. Donna was the only one I ever shared the ugliest parts of our relationship with, and only when I couldn't handle it any more on my own. I needed to be drowning before asking her to throw me a life raft.

George came home after a few days. He had to for school. He never apologized. In our three years of marriage, he never once apologized. In America, he had been attracted by my independent streak. In Switzerland, it was a part of me he needed to squash. I blamed myself. I needed to learn to read him better, to understand the Swiss ways. My own family didn't want me. Now my husband didn't want me. What did that say about me?

When I wrote home, I never told my father about our fights. He would have said, "I told you so." Pat too would be smugly satisfied. Instead, I sent cheerful notes about work, about fun weekend trips in a foreign land.

On my long commute to Zurich, I had plenty of time to think about my family. Once during my two year re-acceptance into the family, I had told Dad that I was afraid he would disown me again, that the whole Michael thing was just an excuse for him and Pat to push me away. Dad had scoffed. There was no heart-to-heart discussion about my fears or about why I had been disowned in the first place.

So I kept communicating. I thought if I kept writing, maybe, just maybe, they would realize they missed me.

I didn't tell them about how dreary the winters were. The low fog stayed November through April. When I walked to the train station in the black mornings, I sometimes wore a plastic handkerchief over my head just to keep my hair dry, the kind women used to wear over their hair rollers in the sixties. It was a good thing George was still asleep when I left. He would have been mortified.

We did have some happy times. When George was happy, he treated me like royalty. It was Lauren Saraisky who spotted this pattern in our relationship. During our first trip back to the US in October 1989, George got to play some rugby with Steven Saraisky at Dartmouth. George was happy after that game, and as Lauren watched how he doted on me, she could see how I would live for those moments.

I wrote to my father that George and I would be vacationing in the US that October. We had planned to fly into New York to see Donna and the Saraiskies, then down to Florida for a few days. When would be a good time to visit? My father didn't write or call back.

I wrote again saying I would call when I got to the US to fix up a time to visit. In the year that I had lived in Switzerland, I had only heard from my family once, a card at Christmas, signed only by my father. He had included an ad for their new horse farm, Painted

Acres. I had sent a box of gifts that I could not afford. I included
Dad's favorite—Swiss chocolates filled with liqueurs.

We were staying in Connecticut, at Gregg's grandfather's house
along the coast. Gregg was Donna's college boyfriend, eventually her
husband. The house was full of their friends from college. George and
I were the first in our age group to marry.

I went upstairs to a quiet room in the house to call my father. It
was a Saturday, his only day off. I cradled the black phone to my ear,
thankful that it was a rotary, the whir of each dial delaying what I
dreaded would be another rejection.

Pat answered the phone and quickly passed it to my father.

I imagined him sitting at the kitchen table, coffee cup in hand.
I forced myself to be upbeat, cheerful, plastering a smile on my otherwise crumpled face. "So I was wondering when would be a good
time to visit?"

His voice was light hearted, as if he was talking about a baseball
player's smash hit to the outfield. "It's best you don't come."

I knew it would be a difficult conversation. Still, I was not prepared for this. I wanted a reason. I wanted to know why. I bit my
cheek hard to stop the tears. "Why? . . . Why not?"

"It's just easier that way."

"Should I even keep writing?"

"Well, it's nice to know what's going on."

At least he still wanted to hear from me, a thread of hope.

The conversation ended. I sat alone in the room, staring at the
black phone. Laughter from the crowd downstairs drifted up.

George was matter of fact when I told him what my father said.
"Well, now you know."

George was done with my father, done with my family. He could
write people off so easily, just like my father.

The call to my father had consumed all my courage. It was a few
more days before I worked up the strength to call Michelle on campus, phoning her from the airport en route from New York to Florida. I knew her campus address at University of Maryland through
Trish, who knew it through Brad.

I got her voice mail. I tried to picture her dorm room, a new one that had phones in each room. I left a message suggesting a day I could come see her and how to reach me in Florida. She didn't call back. George was quietly glad. It left more time for us.

But time for us alone also allowed more time to fight. In Florida, we drove cross state from Miami to the Gulf Coast intending to see Naples. Instead, George stopped talking to me when I couldn't find the street that would lead us to the beach. So we sped back across I-75, driving the two hours in silence. We only made up the next day, after *I* apologized, even though I wasn't the one who had the hissy fit.

A few days later, we walked through Everglades National Park, and I didn't dare complain about the blisters on my toes from walking fifteen miles in cheap sneakers. I would trade blisters in exchange for harmony with my husband.

Despite the non-conversation with my father, I continued to write home but less frequently. The little news I got about my family was primarily through Trish. She was the only one who ever wrote back.

Three and a half years passed. I continued to write bright letters to my father and sister. I never wrote about the unhappy parts of my life, the struggle to keep my husband happy. Our third anniversary marked a different challenge. George had failed his final exams and couldn't graduate. His failing had nothing to do with how smart he was, but mentally, he hadn't prepared. Some days, I'd come home from work at seven at night and he'd still be in his bathrobe, having played computer games most of the day. The idea of "subconscious sabotage" still comes to mind.

None of George's dreams were coming true, while my career at Dow continued to go well. I was listed on a supposedly secret high potential list. I got several raises, awards, and promotions. George was simultaneously proud and resentful. He liked how much money I was earning, but my income became one more source of conflict. He decided we could never have children, because in his view a mother must stay home full time (a lot of Swiss men shared that view), and no way would he give up my salary. After George failed his first exam and Dow had closed the downtown Zurich office, we moved out of St. Gallen so I would be closer to the new office location along the lake of Zurich. We had a spacious apartment, in the quaint town of Richterswil, with a view of the lake and the Alps. All this, George said, we'd have to give up if we had children.

I was clear on one thing: I would never bring a child into our home with our ugly fights.

We always fought about *things*, and George always got his way. Spotting a beautiful antique secretaire, George coveted it. "We don't have the money," I said. We were saving up to go to Donna and Gregg's wedding in the fall. Instead, George chose to buy the secretaire rather than join me at my best friend's wedding.

I argued that we needed to go *together* to Donna's wedding. George declared the trip offered nothing tangible, only a memory, while the secretaire had permanent value. He constantly challenged my way of thinking.

Christmas Eve 1991, our fourth Christmas together, George was not speaking to me, again. I played Christmas carols on the stereo and encouraged George to come decorate the tree with me. I chose the Mahalja Jackson tape, a gospel singer and George's favorite, instead of my favorite, The Carpenters. Anything to get him in the spirit. He hung one or two ornaments, then gave up.

"Why should I pretend? Just because it's Christmas?" then left the room.

Well, yes, because it's Christmas.

I didn't consider divorce an option. I thought, *I chose this life. I need to make the best of it.* And my father's words haunted me. *You know if you marry, you'll only get divorced.* If I couldn't make my marriage to George work, what did that say about me?

A few months after my loneliest Christmas, George and I were sitting in the kitchen at our café-style table. He was supposed to be helping me with my German. At work, I only had to speak English, but I needed German for getting around town and for when we were with George's friends.

"*Ich vergesse. Was bedeutet Bise?*" I forget. What does "bise" mean.

"*Bise! Denke! Du weisst!*" Think! You know!

"I don't know." I stared at the words in my book. "To bite?" I asked hesitantly.

He broke into his German curse words about how stupid I was. "*Blued! Gottfadammitnachmal!*"

I shut my book and stood.

He grabbed my arm. "Where do you think you're going?"

I yanked it away. "I'm not listening to you call me stupid. It doesn't help me learn German."

He pushed me into the wall. "You don't walk away from me when I am helping you."

He spat angry words into my face, and as I turned my head away, his hand clamped on my jaw to force my face toward him. I refused to look at him. He could break my fucking head off if he wanted to, I would not look at his ugliness.

I struggled to get away as his other arm pushed me deeper into the wall, the stucco cutting into my back. The rest is a blur.

Duke, our dog, his dog really, a Boxer with droopy eyes and floppy ears, started barking viciously, a warning. While Duke was George's dog, he was most protective of me, something that drove George mad. Oh, how I loved Duke!

It was only the next morning as I was getting dressed for work, that I realized my back had been scraped open. The bra strap rode just over the open wound, gooping it with blood and ooz. The bruise beneath my jaw could pass for a shadow, if I tucked my chin in. Nobody at work would notice, and I would never tell. So. He had drawn blood. What did that do to my black line now?

Bise, by the way, means alpine wind from the north. It is a word I have never since forgotten.

I did nothing different after the fight. I went to work and put on a smile, despite the pain on my back. At the weekend, we went on a hike with another couple, scheduled long in advance. George and I pretended to be happy in front of them, and remained icy toward one another as soon as they went home. It had been our way of life for three and half years.

We didn't talk for days, and there was never an apology.

George wondered if we should separate. It was I who said no. I suggested marriage counseling, to which he replied, "I'd rather put a gun to my head."

The Swiss are a private culture, not open to talking about conflicts and feelings. I still had a kernel of love for George, a bruised love by now, but I suspect what I needed more than love, more than not being hurt, was for someone, anyone, to want me. So no, I didn't want a separation.

CHAPTER 21

Breaking Up and Out

REALITY WAS NOT THE happy romance I had envisioned, so I cheered myself in my daydreams. There were times when I drove down the highway, and my thoughts drifted back to John from the video store. John with his eyes that twinkled and his beard that tickled when we kissed. Was he happy?

Sometimes my daydreams turned to a new person in the office, Keith Howson. I didn't know then that one day I would marry him, never imagined more than a fleeting flirtation.

I had first met Keith a few years earlier, when he worked in the UK office and was visiting his boss in Zurich. One of the executive vice presidents, Alan Wilson, had called me into his office and introduced me to him. Keith stood six foot five, with reddish hair and bright blue eyes. A jolt had run through me as we shook hands. Then he spoke, with his deep British accent, and well, what girl wouldn't swoon? He was eventually transferred from London to Zurich. Office gossip revealed he had been married, divorced, and was a ladies' man. Rumor had it his girlfriend would be moving to Switzerland with him.

I was working early one morning when Keith popped his head into my office.

"Hey, is George still playing Rugby?"

"Not so much now. He didn't like that some of the games were three hours away. Why? Are you looking for a team?"

His eyes were distant. *Pained*. "Yep. I need to make a life here."

There was a crack in his voice. I later heard that his girlfriend had abruptly changed her mind about moving to Switzerland and broken up with him.

I didn't know Keith, was never in meetings with him like I was with some of the directors and executives, never had to work with him on a system design. I only knew him as a business manager who traveled throughout Europe a lot. We occasionally said hello to each other at the coffee machine or had a light-hearted exchange when his computer was acting up.

Keith once told me he saw me at one of the rugby games, when George was still playing. But I didn't notice him there, and he hadn't said hello to me. I wasn't looking for him.

Yet I started to daydream about him, about this person I didn't even know.

I scolded myself for thinking about him, then told myself it was okay, it was just a harmless daydream. In these dreams, we'd laugh, we'd flirt, we'd talk. I didn't dare fantasize further. *I have sinned in my thoughts.* I told myself it was no different than day dreaming about Kevin Costner or Robert Redford. They weren't real. They were simply necessary escapes from a growing sadness, a sadness, because I never laughed with my husband anymore, because we wanted different things, because he hurt me. *Because my father had been right all along.*

Premilla, an Indian business analyst in our department, was turning forty and the office was planning a party at Mr. D's, a local restaurant and dancing bar. Everyone loved Premilla, with her "don't give me any grief" attitude that seemed incongruous with her beautiful silk saris and the red dot on her forehead. Spouses were invited to Mr. D's, but George didn't want to go, even though I had gotten him a job interning with Premilla the summer before. I tried to coax him out; we needed to laugh, to dance, but he wasn't budging, too deep into his depression about failing school.

That day at the office, Wytze, another business manager, and Keith and I were chatting. Keith was at his desk, while Wytze stood inside his office as I stood in the doorway. The conversation started over Premilla's birthday party, then Wytze turned it to children. Wytze is Dutch and direct. He would tell someone they were a screw-up or overpaid or an asshole if he thought so. So Wytze said, "Why don't you and Keith get together? You both want kids."

My face turned deep red. "Uh, I'm married, remember, Wytze?"

Wytze waved his hand dismissively. "Aachh. Minor problem."

Keith was laughing at my mortification.

"I have a younger sister. She's single," I offered as an alternative. Few in the office knew the situation with my family and that my sister had not spoken to me in three years.

Keith replied. "If she's anything like you, I'll take her."

"She's pretty and spunky."

Wytze jumped in. "How much younger? How old is she?"

"Twenty-one. Senior year of college."

Wytze waved his hand dismissively. "Too young!"

Keith was in his late thirties, ten years older than I.

Wytze continued. "Lose that Swiss guy, and then you two can get married and have children." Most of the department knew George from his internship and the annual Christmas party. Premilla was one of the few people in the office who liked George, and I suspected the managers thought no student had a right to be that arrogant, no matter his potential.

I didn't think the conversation was funny anymore. It was hurtful. "Okay, right, I have a conference call I'm late for." I smiled and walked away and lost myself in emails.

That night at Mr. D.'s, I was one of the last people to arrive. I went by myself. George still hadn't changed his mind.

I drove through the narrow streets of Zurich trying to find a parking spot and got lost. I hurriedly walked along the dark streets to Mr. D.'s, relieved to see that dinner was not yet finished.

I plopped down next to my friend Ruby, a blonde from Long Island who had recently separated from her Swiss husband. After dinner, the band started, and Ruby and I danced together. I danced with husbands and wives and coworkers. And laughed. At one point, I danced with Keith. Nothing slow. Just twirls and shimmies to the pop music. When we sat back at the table, he sat across from me.

I said, "Wytze went a bit too far today, don't you think?"

Keith looked at me intently with his blue eyes and responded slowly. "No, I think he was right." He wasn't smiling. He wasn't flirting. He wasn't joking.

The room seemed to spin around me. My gaze shifted to Helen, seated next to him. I tried to bring her into focus. She looked back and forth to us, smiled, and blurred. I looked back at Keith, the ladies' man and said, "You're an asshole."

I stood and went to the restroom. Someone from the office was throwing up in the toilet. Her boyfriend was holding her hair back. I dawdled, offering to help, wanting to do anything than go back to the table. Back to Keith.

When I went back to the table, I sat in a different place, as far away from Keith as I could. I needed to leave, but I didn't want to storm out. I tried to laugh with Ruby, but the evening had been ruined. It was almost midnight and tomorrow was a work day.

I stood and said my good-byes. When I got to the door, Keith was behind me.

"I'll walk you to your car."

"I can find it myself." I replied tightly, "and it's twenty minutes away, back near the office."

"Even more reason you shouldn't walk alone."

I didn't want to cause a scene, but I didn't want to be alone with him. I walked out and ahead of him, not waiting. I couldn't speak.

He said softly. "Don't be like this."

"Like what?" I hissed. I wouldn't look at him. "What do you want? You want an affair?"

We marched along in silence. At five foot seven, I was shorter than Keith's six foot five, yet he barely kept pace.

"Are you happy?" he asked.

"That doesn't matter."

When we got to the car, I told him, more calmly, more quietly. "I don't believe in affairs, and I don't believe in divorce."

I thought of how Trish's affair, which I still believed to be the truth at that point in time, had destroyed my father. I would never do that to a man.

Keith's voice was soft. "I'm just saying, if we had a chance, a . . . " He shrugged, not finding the words. "I think it could work. I think there is something there."

I don't know why I revealed my heart to him, this person I didn't even know. I had called him an asshole. I knew this wasn't true. I sensed his kindness ran deep and that he had his own wounds he protected.

I looked away from him, down the dark and narrow street, dense with parked cars on either side. "It makes no sense. I don't even know you . . . yet, sometimes, when I drive down the highway . . . I daydream about you." My voice was small.

"Let me kiss you."

"No."

"Just one kiss. I promise. Nothing more."

"No. Come on. I'll drive you back to the restaurant."

Neither one of us moved to getting in the car. "A hug?" I whispered.

And with that, he took me in his arms, enfolding me like a warm blanket until my head rested on his heart. The world stopped spinning, hurting, if only for that solid moment of warmth. I pulled away and climbed in the car.

I drove Keith back to the restaurant. I waited in the car and watched him walk away. But the door to the restaurant wouldn't open. Eventually, I got out and banged on the door too. The restaurant had closed. Everyone else had already left. The problem was that Keith had left his jacket with his wallet and house key in the pocket. One of the staff thought the blonde girl took it home for him. Which blonde? Ruby? Helen?

I was in disbelief. "Are you fucking kidding me?" I used the f word a lot in those days.

Keith thought it was mildly amusing. "Guess I have to sleep at your place."

"Uh, un. No way. No fucking way."

Keith chuckled, not used to hearing me curse, then suggested he could find a locksmith or a cab or something. But he barely spoke

German, and I wasn't cold hearted enough to leave him alone on the streets of Zurich. I called George from a pay phone, explaining how Keith had walked me back to my car and was now without his wallet and house key. Could he look up Helen's address and try calling her?

I put Keith on the phone to George for directions. Helen lived on the opposite side of the lake from us. Of course. It couldn't be five fucking minutes down the street. It would be an hour, there and back, through the streets of Zurich, to the outskirts on the opposite side of the lake, to get to Helen's who just *might* have Keith's jacket and key—or not.

In the phone booth, Keith laughed with George about whatever wild night George was having, an excuse George had asked me to give to Premilla and the Dow folks for his not coming out with me. All he had done was sit home alone, miserable and angry at life.

I really thought God was testing my resolve. To Helen's and back, we were in the car together for an hour. We had no choice but to talk.

I repeated my belief again. "I don't believe in divorce. Marriage is a choice. You either work at it or you decide to give up."

"But if you're not happy, what's the point?"

"We have happy times." I added defensively. "I can be happy." I was glad to have the road to concentrate on.

"Look, I think it would be wrong if you and I started having coffee together every morning at the office, and I'm not saying I'll wait for you or anything, but you only pass through this dirt ball of a planet once, so it should be with someone who makes you happy."

I tried to steer the conversation to a lighter topic. "Brothers? Sisters?"

Keith spoke of his sister. How she would say it was fate that we met. He shared the demise of his own marriage, five years ago, as he and his ex-wife grew apart, more so when she decided she would never want children. *Like George.*

Helen indeed had taken Keith's jacket and key (thank God!). By the time we finally pulled up to Keith's apartment, there was little left to say. He again asked if he could kiss me good night. I again said no. We both sat there, waiting, for nothing, for everything. Finally,

I turned my head to look at him, a subtle permission. It was not a passionate kiss. It was hesitant and gentle and filled with a longing that could never be filled.

When I pulled away, I would not look at him. I stared ahead at the dark street, the empty cars parked along the road. He stared at me and finally said good night. He opened the car door, waited, then finally climbed out. I said nothing and drove home to George, to my husband.

At work the next day, Premilla brought in Indian samosas, her specialty, instead of the traditional birthday cake. As we gathered to sing happy birthday to her, I felt Keith staring at me. I refused to meet his gaze. In the weeks that followed, I tried to avoid him. At some point, I heard he had a new girlfriend, and I told myself the rumors were true. He didn't care for me as a person. He just wanted me as another one of his conquests.

Regardless, that night with Keith was a wake-up call. Did George love me, really love *me?* I deserved to be happy.

I began making small changes. I joined the Berne Writers Workshop. It meant I'd be away one Saturday a month. George didn't approve. When George didn't feel like going for a run or going to the gym, I went anyway. Before, I would have kept him company in his misery. These little changes put me in control of my own happiness. It also drove a bigger wedge between George and me.

It was at a conference in Frankfurt, alone in a hotel room, that I realized I was happier alone. Alone meant nobody to pinch me, to call me fat, a cunt, a rude fucking American, or to scold me for messing up the carpet tassels. It also meant there was nobody to love me in return. But I was slowly accepting that perhaps I didn't deserve love. I didn't deserve to be treated badly, but love, the kind of love I believed in, seemed not to be real. If my family didn't love me, and now George didn't really either, it just meant there was something not lovable about me. I was better off alone.

The thought formed slowly, but once glimpsed, it was a light at the end of a tunnel. Perhaps I needed to leave George.

I thought about something Pat had said in her first year of marriage to Dad, "I would never kick a man when he's down." I would wait for George to find a job.

Every disagreement after that confirmed my decision. When our little Fiat Uno needed major repairs, George wanted to lease a Mercedes for 700 Swiss Francs ($500 a month). I argued it was an extravagance beyond our means. He leased it anyway, and I was the one to pay the bill.

One day, he flat out asked me, "You're going to leave me after I find a job, aren't you?"

We agreed to a trial separation, makeshift at first in which I house-sat for Ruby for a couple weeks when she was on vacation, then George went to the South of France with his mom to his parents' vacation home. Eventually, George found me an apartment with a month-to-month lease in downtown Zurich. It irked me. Why couldn't he go stay with his parents? Why did I have to pay the rent for two apartments? But George's father didn't want our dog Duke at their home all the time. The apartment was a studio, in a dark corner of the city, a furnished one set up for traveling executives. While George got to enjoy our sunny apartment in Richterswil, I was being banished to the bowels of the squalid part of the city.

When George told his parents we were separating, it was George's father who suggested marriage counseling, something George had refused to try any time I had previously suggested it.

I was hopeful, thinking that we would find a way for our love to be beautiful and kind again. I had never been to therapy or counseling before, and the brightness of the room surprised me. It was filled with plants, with things that required nurturing to grow, so different from the dark office of the court-appointed psychiatrist when Dad had gotten custody of us. At the end of one of our first sessions, the counselor told us each to say something nice to each other.

I sat next to George at a white Formica table and turned to face him. "I want you to be happy."

George replied, "I want you back home."

The marriage counselor pointed out, "What is there for Cindi?"

I wrote home to Dad and Pat that George and I were separated. It was Michelle who wrote in reply, the first letter from her in three years.

I sat alone in the dim apartment in Zurich, reading her letter. The penmanship was frighteningly perfect. Her words lashed out at me, like a scalpel cutting into my weakest parts, *You are a slut just like Trish. Your reputation as a slut at the University of Maryland is still going strong. . . . I hope you never move back to the US . . . You hurt my father!*

That night, I had a nightmare. I was in a dank room, like a cellar with cobble stone. I had fallen and was on all fours. Pat and my father were kicking me. Michelle delivered the swiftest kick, leaving me splayed flat on the ground. I turned my head, my cheek on the cold stone to see my brother Brad standing there, watching, doing nothing. I woke in the rental apartment's bed, clammy, unable to shake the lingering pain of the dream that had felt so real.

I had never once called in sick to work, but the next morning, I couldn't go. Was I a slut? I had kissed Keith and that was wrong, but wouldn't others have let it go so much further?

I allowed myself to cry for a day.

The marriage counselor scheduled sessions separately for George and me. I told her about Michelle's letter, how they treated me so meanly. What was I doing wrong? And my gut had tried to warn me about George. So why did I marry him anyway? How much of my rush to marry him was influenced by my father, or by moving to Switzerland so that I didn't have to confront our family problems? In marrying George, had I run away from my father?

The marriage counselor said I took all the blame with my marriage and my family, while they took none. She suggested my love for my family was stronger than their hatred. She surmised Michelle's letter was motivated more by her need to win favor with my father than actual hatred.

Twenty years later, I am still trying to figure out if the strength of my love for them is a blessing or a curse. My father and sister have thrown the worst at me, and yet I did not shut them out of my heart. I have resolved to accept heartache is sometimes the price of unconditional love.

For the three years that George and I were married, I had blamed myself for every little fight, convinced myself I needed to try harder, to understand him better. It was a dangerous new thought to consider how he was culpable.

I saw Keith occasionally in the office, but we rarely spoke. One morning when I had borrowed the car for work, as I parked the Mercedes, Keith pulled up next to me. My heart fluttered, but I reminded myself that he was not real. He was just a fantasy temptation.

He commented on the new car. "I guess things are going better for you and George."

I tried to laugh it off. "It's not my car."

"You look quite classy in it."

Always, the flirt.

We walked into the building together, with nothing more to say. I didn't tell him about the separation. It would have given him false hope, and I would not lead him on.

My boss was one of the few people who knew about my separation and my rental apartment in Zurich, mainly so he understood I once again had to work according to the bus and train schedule. "I wish I had met you twenty years ago," he lamented.

I ignored his remarks until one evening he asked me if I'd like to join him for dinner.

I pointedly replied, "Will your wife be joining us?"

"No. She's out of town."

I stared at him with all the loathing I could muster. My experience with my boss Steve at the video store had taught me not to trust older men offering to comfort me.

The final blow that would destroy my marriage was, as usual, about money. George and I had a joint banking account into which my salary was directly deposited. He still maintained his own bank account for his military pay; while my salary was shared. When I got a bonus at work for a project, I bought myself a new outfit. This idea was not mine. The marriage counselor told me it was my money to spend, to treat myself.

The bonus was not a secret, but George and I were only seeing each other weekly and I hadn't gotten around to telling him about it. So when he picked me up at work to meet with the marriage counselor, he asked about the extra money in the account.

It was the lunch hour, a sunny summer day. I climbed into the front of his leased white Mercedes.

He looked me up and down with disgust. "What's this new suit?"

"I got a bonus for a project."

He pursed his lips and glared. "How much?"

"1500 Swiss Francs."

"What else did you buy?"

It was as if I had murdered someone. I should have known this was coming. It was a change from how we had handled money before.

"Well, I needed a beach towel and a back pack."

"YOU . . . STOLE . . . FROM . . . ME!"

"No, George—" But he didn't let me finish. He sped out of the parking lot, whipped onto the Seestrasse, and through the narrow streets of the village toward the marriage counselor's office.

Two teenagers were crossing the street as George sped down the small road. He did not slow. I closed my eyes and gripped the door handle. Only at the absence of a scream or a thud did I know he hadn't hit them.

"You can pull this shit when we are divorced," he hissed, "but this is not the kind of behavior I will tolerate from my *wife!*"

He walked in and told the marriage counselor he would not be participating and sped off. I cried through the entire session. She tried to convince me I had done nothing wrong, but I knew George wouldn't accept this kind of change, and I wondered, how much did that matter to me?

I was twenty-seven years old, and I had never broken up with anyone in my life. I had always been the one dumped. I could keep provoking George to a point he would not tolerate. But it seemed important that I had to be the one to end things; I had to break this pattern, of letting the man decide to leave me. It felt as monumental as trying to veer a star onto a new trajectory, into a universe not yet discovered.

It was a rainy Sunday when I wrote my letter to George, the letter to end my marriage. I said a silent prayer, begging God to help me be brave.

When I was done, I had promised myself I would go for a run to keep my spirits up, to avoid sinking into depression.

I hated jogging in the rain but resigned myself to running in the torrent. I started out along the dark cobble-stoned alley ways, and ran to the park, along the river. As I jogged, the rain stopped and some rays of sunshine peaked through. I wondered if God was trying to give me a sign of encouragement. But He's much too busy for such signs, isn't he?

I called George to ask if we could meet. I suggested a spot by the lake, a place I could get to by train.

We sat beneath a lush tree on a lake-side bench. The Alps were picturesque in the distance. I handed George my letter, explaining that it was hard for me to talk.

He read the letter, then handed it back to me. "Is that it?"

"Yes," I replied weakly.

He handed me a piece of paper. "This is a list of our belongings. You are legally entitled to fifty percent. I have divided it. If you fight me, you can get a lawyer, and I will request alimony."

My mouth fell open in shock. So, he had decided it was over too.

I looked over the list through blurry eyes. He assigned a value to my furniture that I had bought myself in the US and divided it by two, gave himself the china platters and crystal serving dishes that the Saraiskies had given us as a wedding present. He assigned me the 700-Swiss-Franc terra-cotta plant pots I hadn't wanted. The fucking secretaire, too, that he bought with money we needed for airfare to Donna's wedding.

He replied coldly, "You have a week to look it over," then got up and walked away.

I sat on the bench trying not to scream, trying not to rip the list to shreds. *Alimony?*

After a while I took the train to Ruby's apartment. She poured me a large glass of wine.

George and I haggled over the list for a few weeks. He assigned me the deposit for the apartment and assigned himself all the cash in our bank account. This meant I wouldn't have any free cash to fly home for Donna and Gregg's wedding. George wasn't willing to negotiate.

My friends wanted me to fight George's list, but what did I know about the Swiss legal system? I also had no fight left in me.

Whenever somebody has expressed shock at how famous, successful women let their husbands treat them badly, I understand those abused women perfectly. My image of myself was the one my father had shaped.

It's not easy to get a divorce in Switzerland. A lawyer decides if a divorce proceeding can begin. It is a back and forth of written complaints and reasons why the marriage should end that culminates in a hearing in front of five judges.

The hearing was scheduled for October, when I was due to be in the US for Donna's wedding. I had it rescheduled to November.

All through the separation, I had promised myself that I would not run away. I vowed to myself that if I was going to begin breaking patterns, I needed to stay in Switzerland for a year. I needed to face George. After that, I would decide what to do. I needed to hang on until October, a three-week vacation in the US for Donna's wedding, when I would be surrounded by the Saraiskies, and friends, and laughter. I would let myself collapse then.

After my trip to the US, George and I both had to sit in front of a panel of five judges and present our sides as to why our marriage should be dissolved. The trial was in German. The judges said they had never had a couple so constrained, so civil. Were we really sure the marriage was over?

George had to answer directly, had he hit me? Had he left for days at a time? He acknowledged that he used to leave, but not in the last year. I was not allowed to add my two cents why—he had stayed for Duke, our dog.

The divorce was granted. As we walked back to the car, I asked George if he wanted to go for coffee. Even after everything, I did not hate him.

He replied quite emphatically, "No."

So we got in our separate cars. I sat in mine, shaking, saying good-bye to a life I had once believed in.

CHAPTER 22

Love, Finally

I WAS NOT READY for Keith. I felt safer alone. I needed time to think. To heal.

One day at work, before my divorce was final, but after George had divided our belongings, Keith and Premilla came into my office to talk about a new system we were implementing. I noticed Keith was not listening to me. His blue eyes were fixed on my hand, now ringless.

Premilla left and Keith started to leave too, then turned and said, "You're not wearing a ring."

Work was my only escape from the chaos of my life. I needed desperately to compartmentalize. "I can't talk about that now."

"Did—"

"I can call you later if you want, but not now."

So that evening, we went for a walk. He picked a trail on the north side of Zurich, a place I could get to by tram. I didn't want him seeing where I lived, in the dark apartment, in exile.

The evening started out sunny but a storm loomed. I wondered if it was an omen that God did not approve.

We sat in Keith's Land Rover, a symbol of his British pride. "I'm not going to tell you I love you," he said.

"Of course not. You don't even know me.'"

We bantered over what constitutes a "date." Sitting in the car in the rain? We referred to it as a conversation only, not a date.

Was I willing to have dinner? "In a few weeks, maybe."

This time, it was I who asked if I could kiss him. It was a kiss that had been waiting for months, perhaps years. His car was a cocoon against the lighting strikes and torrents of rain.

I was worried about getting hurt. I thought back to the time with John from the video store. Would I rather risk getting hurt or risk losing a chance at a deeper love?

Keith seemed genuine. Yet if my sole attraction to him was as a rebound relationship, I would be just one more woman to scar him. He would be broken. I warned him about all this. He still chose to see me.

So I established rules, rules we chuckle about now. One. We could only go out once every two weeks, and only on a weeknight, so that it would be a short "date." Two. There would be no fooling around. I didn't want an unleashed physical attraction to cloud my thinking.

On our first "date," as Keith drove down the highway, he kept stealing glances at me. I watched his profile. His eyes met mine.

"I was wondering what you were doing for Christmas?"

His gaze held mine and my face warmed.

"Christmas?! . . . Uh." *So much for taking things slow.*

We both laughed. Adhering to the "rules" would not be easy.

The first few dates with Keith were filled with quiet wonder. I had learned to feel my way of thinking was wrong and my character flawed. Yet Keith and I shared similar views on things that mattered most, like family (he called his mother weekly), friends (I don't have to like all of his, he didn't have to like all of mine), and money (best spent on a memory, like a shared bottle of wine or trip, that will last a lifetime rather than on a material thing, easily broken). Keith thought it important that I do fun things, hobbies, even if it meant time away from him. He *liked* that I went to a writer's workshop once a month. When I won my first-ever writing award that fall, Keith drove me to the ceremony and listened to me read.

In the early weeks of our relationship, Keith lamented that I would go to the US for Donna's wedding and never come back. He did not know the strength of my resolve to stay in Switzerland for a year, to prove to myself I was not running away; it was my determination to avoid repeating any mistakes, any patterns.

I had never taken a three-week vacation. In the US, I planned to nurture myself with friends, first Donna and the Saraiskies for her bachelorette party, then Bob in Maryland, then my cousin Paul in California, back to New Jersey to see my childhood friend Jill Parker, and finally Donna's wedding.

My visit with Paul was yet another downer about my dad. The last time I had seen my cousin was Christmas 1979, the year Dad had lost his job as a disc jockey at WABC. Paul and I had written each other over the years.

When I got to Redondo Beach, I found a cheap motel. Paul thought it odd I was staying at a motel, but I didn't want to impose.

At The Cheesecake Factory, the restaurant buzzed with a young crowd. We finished dinner, and Paul picked up the bill. I reached for it. "No, I'll get it."

"That's just dumb. You fly all the way here. I ain't gonna let you pay for dinner."

I threw some money down.

He pushed the money back to me. "I don't want your money." We laughed at our argument.

"If you pay, my dad would probably say I was just using you." I meant it to be sarcastic, but the smile left Paul's face and he was quiet.

"That's exactly what he'd say."

Paul's words cut into me. "He told my mom and me not to see you. Warned us against you."

"Warned you?"

"Crazy shit."

The next night, after Paul assured me I was not using him, I stayed in his guest bedroom. The next day, he, his girlfriend, and I took the ferry to Catalina Island and rode our bikes, my heart healing amid the sea and the sunshine.

By the time I visited Bob in Maryland, I knew not to call my

Dad, even though he was only a few miles away. I headed to New Jersey to help Donna with last minute wedding preparations. Donna's sister, Lauren, was taking a class on the metaphysical and learning to be psychic. Her teacher, Nancy Weber, had done police work, and Lauren suggested I do a reading with her to see if she had any insight about George and my family.

I had never been to a psychic before, except for the occasional palm reader on the boardwalk. It was not what I expected. Nancy sat in a chair across from me as I sat on a worn sofa. She didn't wear a turban or gypsy clothes like the boardwalk psychics, and there were no dangly beads or crystal balls. She looked like a woman I'd pass in the supermarket.

She held my hands for a few minutes, breathing deeply. Then opened her eyes and allowed me to ask her questions. She told me my father and I would never speak again. She could see me speaking to my sister, though. It didn't matter. I didn't believe in psychics.

I returned to Switzerland at the end of October, optimistic about a fresh start. It was just as well that Keith wasn't even in the country when I returned; ironically, he was in the US, in Texas for work.

When he finally returned to Switzerland, we greeted each other with both shyness and anticipation. He was surprised I had returned at all, and I was surprised by my resolve to give this relationship a chance.

As my welcome home gift, Keith had bought me a new duvet cover in England, with bright yellow daisies. He helped me make my bed, a new brass bed with no previous memories, and we giggled at the domesticity, laced with lust, of our reunion.

When it felt like I was falling in love, too fast, too hard, I pushed Keith away by filling my calendar to be busy when he was in town. He traveled a lot for work.

Slowly and steadily, he would coax me. I argued rationally that he was a good person; but in my gut, I was terrified. I didn't really know him. And I could feel that my gut was permanently miswired.

My inner compass had led me astray before. Or was it my overthinking brain that messed me up?

My gut told me Keith was my soul mate, but should I listen? I kept warning him away. He did not give up.

We had been dating just over three months when I went to England with Keith for Christmas to meet his family and to join him at his best friend Nick's wedding. We drove through Europe, spending hours together in the car, to catch a ferry from Rotterdam, Holland, to Hull, England. In France, at a roadside rest stop, I embarrassingly had to ask Keith how the "toilet" worked; the "toilet" was like a shower stall with a hole in the middle. "Just squat!" he amusingly instructed.

I wasn't prepared for his mother. She wouldn't even look me in the eye. He had never brought a girl home before, not since his wife, whom he had divorced five years ago. Keith, a typical guy and typical Brit, had told his family nothing about me, only that I was an American. His dad at least gave me a cheery, "Hello, Love," pint of beer in hand at midday. I warmed to him immediately, an older version of Keith; flush cheeks, largish nose, mostly bald but with a touch of white hair on the sides of his head.

After a few days of his mother avoiding me, in a house too small to be avoided, while I helped dry the dishes in the kitchen, I asked her outright, "You're scared I'm going to hurt him, aren't you?" I had not taken a cultural course in the etiquette of British subtlety.

She still didn't look at me, but paused from washing, took a deep breath, and sighed. "Well, yes . . . I don't want my son to be hurt."

"I don't want to hurt him either. I can see he's a nice person."

I could see it by the way he called his mum every week, by the way he shopped for the perfect handbag for her at Christmas. By the way he let me go slowly as long as I gave him chance, any kind of chance.

I could not envision that fifteen years later, I would be helping his mother into a hot bath, gently scrubbing her back, the only person willing enough to set aside such modesty to bring her this small bit of comfort after her husband died and she was too frail to get in and out of the tub on her own.

I wasn't sure how to handle his mum, and was even less sure how to behave around children. So when Keith's three-year-old nephew Thomas pretended to shoot me with a toy gun that Santa had brought him, I pretended to fire back with my finger. Thomas, with his chubby cheeks, blond hair and bright blue eyes, burst into tears and wailed to his mother, Keith's sister, "The baddy shot me!" My only glint of hope was later that night, when Thomas would only go for a walk if I went along too. It seemed the baddy had potential!

At Nick's wedding, I had to be polite to Keith's ex-girlfriend (the one who at the last minute abandoned moving to Switzerland with him). I pretended it didn't hurt when he kissed her hello. His friends drank a lot. So did he. If the movie *Four Weddings and a Funeral* had come out sooner, I would have been mentally prepared.

I never felt my Americaness more keenly than in that first trip to Northern England. I couldn't handle the cold, damp houses; the drippy showers that only made me feel colder, with too little pressure to rinse my long hair; or the drinking culture. At twenty-seven, I had finally learned that love was not enough to conquer all differences.

I was quiet on the drive back to Switzerland, not sure of anything, except that I loved this person—but was love enough?

It took a few months, but Keith and I both learned about the differences that mattered and the differences that didn't. So when the lease on my apartment was expiring that June, he suggested I move in with him. When he first suggested it in March, I laughed and pretended to ignore him. The second time he raised the idea, a month later, I replied, "It's too soon!"

"It's not too soon when you *know*." He tried to lighten the weight of his suggestion by adding, "Really, you'd be doing me a favor. Your car will fit perfectly in my heated garage." Keith had signed a three-year lease on his apartment, with the heated garage (Swiss ingenuity!), only to learn that his Land Rover was too big for it.

It was too fast for me. How could I possibly commit when we had only been dating for six months?

In May, at Keith's third suggestion that I move in with him, with only a few days for me either to cancel or to renew my lease, I countered, "I don't believe in living together as a trial."

To which he replied, "It's not a trial."

We both let the weight of those words fill the silence for several weeks. Eventually, we worked out the details, the terms of this arrangement, and yes, I moved in with him.

I thought he would formally propose to me that first weekend I moved in, June 1993. When he didn't, I worried that he had tricked me. Was it a trial to him? Then he left the next day on a business trip to Texas.

So I was alone, baking a cherry pie for his return, and accidentally spattered his (*my*) new white kitchen cupboards with cherry juice. Nobody had warned me it was hard to remove cherry pits with only a potato peeler.

Keith officially proposed three months later, in early September. We were on vacation in Beaune, France. We shared a wine tasting trip with his friends from England and then were on our own in Bourjet du Lac. We enjoyed a romantic dinner in an old restaurant with a fire roaring in the background. Keith stared intently into my eyes. I stared back at him through the candlelight, willing him with my mind. He didn't propose.

After dessert when he still hadn't asked, insecurity crept in. I contemplated proposing to him or I would move out. I would not live in limbo like this.

Such were my thoughts as we walked quietly back to our hotel along the lake, the moon shimmering on the ripples. Keith told me to slow down. A few people were walking in front of us. When we had the sidewalk to ourselves, he stopped me, touched my elbow, and turned me toward him. "Just wait."

By now I thought something was wrong. Perhaps he had left something back at the restaurant.

He took both my hands in his and stared into my eyes. "Cindi Michael . . . will you marry me—"

"Yes—"

"—stay with me forever . . . Start a family with me—"

"Yes—"

"—next spring, before June."

Before he could finish his full proposal, I chuckled. "Are you done?"

"I am done."

"Yes, Keith Howson, I will marry you and love you forever and start a family with you. Before next June."

I wrote to Dad and Pat that I was engaged. I told them about Keith and asked them to let me know how they wanted to be involved in the wedding. Did they want us to marry in the US? I never got a response.

I had explained to Keith as much as I could about my family. Of course, I had left out the ugliest parts. It was bad enough my father didn't speak to me.

Keith couldn't understand any man who would do this to a daughter, but God bless Keith. He has never outwardly criticized my father, keeping his exasperation to himself. He could see, too, how close I was with the Saraiskies, how they were a kind of surrogate family.

At this stage, I blamed my father less for our estrangement than I blamed Pat. Before Pat was part of our daily lives, Dad and I were closest.

This latest rift had started with Pat and the spilt sugar. It was she who didn't tell Dad I was thinking of selling the car. Her opinions were so strong. I believed she had brought out the bad side of my father. I needed to keep trying to reach him. One day he would want me in his life, again.

Keith and I married in New Jersey, at the Saraisky's house in Oakland, the town where I had lived when my father and I were closest. We also planned parties in England and Switzerland for a larger circle of friends and family who couldn't travel to the US.

I did not ask the Church for an annulment from my marriage to George. Instead, I believed that God wanted me to learn some lessons the hard way and had sent me to Switzerland to meet Keith.

Our wedding was an intimate, outdoor ceremony on a sunny

day, April, 1994. Keith's parents, his two best mates Nick and Dave, and Nick's wife Vicki flew over. My high school friend Bob came up from Maryland and some friends from Switzerland who now lived in Connecticut, about thirty people in all.

Mr. Saraisky again offered to escort me down the aisle; an "aisle" that was through the kitchen and out the back door across the deck. I declined, as I had five and a half years earlier: my father belonged next to me.

This time, though, I didn't wonder what my father was doing at that point in his day. Instead, I heard the birds singing and thought only of Keith, the steadiness of his hand as we said our vows, and *oh my God, is that our wedding certificate blowing away?!* The best man dove for it before the wind whisked it away.

CHAPTER 23

Repeating the Cycle

WE HAD BEEN TRYING for more than a year to get pregnant, and finally on Fourth-of-July weekend, we learned I was pregnant. Coincidentally both Keith's parents and Mr. and Mrs. Saraisky were visiting us in Switzerland. We broke the news to them while touring in Lake Como, and we all affectionately starting calling the baby "junior." We didn't know if "junior" was a boy or a girl, but if a girl, her middle name would be Michelle, after my sister. Keith understood that I needed to make this statement: that my love for my sister, for the Michael family, would never fade, no matter what had passed between us.

I wasn't ready for a baby the last Monday in February, 1996. My due date was still ten days away. Keith and I did not want to raise a family in Switzerland, and with Dow, getting promoted meant moving to the US, which was just fine with me. So we were getting ready to move to Houston, Texas, where Keith had already started his job, commuting between Texas and Switzerland every two weeks. Dow didn't want to risk moving me until after the baby was born, so I had been working in Switzerland and was on my own for the birthing classes. Then, instead of coming home and getting up to speed with the birthing classes he had missed, Keith returned to Switzerland Friday, and went off skiing with his buddies from England. I understood it was their last boys' weekend in Europe, before we moved and before fatherhood, but still, I was annoyed. Normally, Keith was so protective of me.

So, it was a crappy weekend and I suffered agonizing cramps, while sorting out details like selling my car, acquiring baby things, and working overtime for a big project at work.

By Monday morning, when Keith was finally home from skiing, I said I didn't think I could go to work. I had only ever skipped work once in the six years I had been at Dow. Still, Keith suggested I go into the office ("What about the people who flew over to meet with you?") and to call if I needed him. I was pissed at him, a rare feeling in our then-two-year relationship, and I didn't want our child to arrive in the world when I was angry. It would be better if Junior picked another day to arrive.

I had spent a lifetime of putting on a brave face, so on that Monday in the midst of all day meetings, whenever I felt a sharp pain, I went into the bathroom until the cramp subsided. By four thirty, I called Keith to tell him I couldn't take the pain anymore and wasn't able to drive myself home.

He came to get me. We went back to the apartment, not realizing I was in full labor. My birth instructor had a rule for ensuring it wasn't false labor: sit in a warm bath before going to the hospital. If the contractions stopped, it was false labor; if they continued, go to the hospital. Rule follower that I am, I ran a bath, climbed in the tub, suffered through two more contractions, and could barely climb out of the tub after the second one.

The video the birth instructor had shown me of a drugged up baby, post birth, was more than I could bear. So I was determined not to have pain medicine until after the baby was born, come what may. At the hospital, just as I was beginning to lose my resolve about no pain medicine and begged desperately for something, the nurse told me it was too late anyway. "*Zu spaet! Zu spaet! Es kommt gleich!*" We were only in the hospital an hour when Junior arrived. Even as a baby, Megan came fast and intent into the world, ahead of her time.

When they told me it was a girl, I whispered to Keith, "Your mother will be so happy." This was her first granddaughter.

As the nurse placed Megan Michelle in my arms, my daughter

looked up at me with big blue eyes and a thick tussle of dark hair, which soon turned blonde in the Houston sunshine. She was quiet and serious, studying me. I spoke softly to her and it seemed as if she thought, *Oh, I know you! You're the voice I've been hearing from inside.*

I thought of my sister Michelle and the first time I had seen her, in the car when we had gone to pick her and my mother up from the hospital. My sister's eyes had been closed.

I sent a birth announcement to Dad and Pat, along with a letter explaining our upcoming move to Houston. I included a photo of his first granddaughter and a note saying that if he wanted to meet her, I would bring her to Maryland. If he didn't want to see me, then Keith could bring Megan alone to a meeting place. Despite whatever anger he held against me, if my dad wanted a relationship with his grand-daughter, I would make that possible. Surely my father would want a relationship with his only granddaughter, wouldn't he? His issues with me could not possibly extend to this helpless little baby, could they?

Dad never replied. Neither did my brother or sister. Trish again was the only person ever to reply to my letters. Through her, I learned that Brad had a son and had eloped a year after his son was born. Rumor had it Dad didn't like Brad's wife, so I can well imagine why he married after the fact . . . and why he had eloped. I sent them a congratulations card and money as a wedding gift. It was Brad's wife who wrote the thank you note, but even so, I viewed it as an important opening.

Keith, Megan, and I left Switzerland on Good Friday 1996, seven and a half years after I had first moved there. As I was still under Swiss employment, I had three month's maternity leave, most of which was spent house hunting in Houston, car shopping, and setting up a baby room. After a few weeks in corporate housing, we finally settled in a suburb in Sugar Land. Donna and Gregg's first daughter, Jennie, was born six weeks before Megan, and they flew to Houston for the babies to meet one another.

When Mr. and Mrs. Saraisky flew down the following weekend, they asked if it was okay if Megan called them Nana and Pop. The question was bittersweet. My father should have been the one she would call Pop. Finally, I said it was okay, as long as she knew that my father and Trish were her real grandparents.

I didn't know what a mother was supposed to do. Trish was not the kind of mother I wanted to be, and I couldn't remember my father dealing with Michelle much when she was a baby. I read books like *What to Expect,* looking for answers. Should I work or stay home? Full-time or part-time? Nanny or day care? Donna had opted for part-time and hired a nanny, so I did the same. It seemed safer to follow her path. She had all the confidence in mothering that I lacked and a good role model in Mrs. Saraisky.

While Keith's job was in Houston, mine was along the Gulf Coast in Freeport at one of Dow's manufacturing sites, more than seventy miles south of the city. The Freeport plant worked a nine-hour day; with the commute, that meant three days a week I saw Megan only in time to put her to bed at night. My heart longed to stay with her.

Keith tried to encourage me, reminding me that my job helped to support us. In the last year, we had witnessed two close friends lose their jobs with no warning, no notice, no cause. My job was a cushion in case Keith got laid off too; his dad had been forced into early retirement, so Keith lived in fear of the same.

My new job in Freeport was boring. I resented that a global job in my expertise went to someone else, a man, who was less experienced. Before, I had always liked the sense of accomplishment. Now, I had an unfulfilling job that took me away from my daughter.

I understood that for a mother to have a gap in her resume is a death sentence, particularly in my field, information technology. But I started to think that if I could explain that gap by something like a master's degree, perhaps I could get time off with my baby and improve my resume at the same time. So a year later, I resigned from Dow and enrolled in a local MBA program.

I played all summer with Megan, and I guess Keith and I played a bit too, because I hadn't even started my MBA when we learned I was pregnant with baby number two. No matter—the baby might just arrive during the school's spring break, barely disrupting my class schedule. Gosh, what a clueless mother I was!

When I was seven-months pregnant, Trish told me Brad's wife went into a coma following an asthma attack. They didn't know if she would survive. Over the years, Brad's wife had continued to write thank you notes, for gifts at Christmas and birthdays. They now had two sons. I needed to visit my brother. He had left Maryland after college, shortly after I moved to Switzerland, and moved to southern Florida. Trish later followed Brad to Florida. If his wife died and I hadn't even met her, I would never forgive myself. My doctor approved the trip.

Trish met us at the airport, dressed in neon green disco pants, carrying a stuffed panther for Megan. Megan, not yet two, immediately gripped Nana Trish's hand as we made our way through the airport. I had seen Trish only twice in the previous eight years, fragile visits each time, my struggle to forgive all the harder because she could never acknowledge she had ever done anything wrong. Keith had met her once while we visited the US, before we were married, and the three of us went out for dinner. When she kept leaving our table to check if her former boyfriend (who owned the restaurant) would join us or not, it pained me to watch her at the bar, waiting pathetically. After dinner, all Keith would say to me was, "She seems massively insecure."

I drew my line of forgiveness of Trish at my children. She could meet them but never would I leave them alone with her.

The four of us spent the day at the beach and met Brad and his family for dinner that night at a restaurant along a waterway. I was nervous. I hadn't seen my brother in almost ten years, except in the pictures Trish had sent.

Brad didn't rush to embrace me. During dinner, we made polite, safe conversation. His wife had come out of the coma, her voice hoarse from the incubation tubes. She had come close to dying.

After dinner, we went back to Brad's house. He had done well for himself, a house on a waterway, a pool in the back yard. He had his own boat, and I thought back to all the boat shows Trish had taken us to on our weekend visits with her as kids. Brad's sons put the raft in the pool, and Megan climbed in with her cousins, her blood family.

I have but one picture of the three of them in the raft, and it hurts my daughter, now sixteen, that she can't remember that evening. She has a cousin, who is a lifeguard like her, a swimmer like her, has a love for the sea like her, but he is not a part of her life. Our families are divided but connected.

Nothing changed between Brad and me that night. I continued to send cards and gifts for the boys' birthdays and Christmas. His wife continued to write thank you notes. I reasoned that Brad was never much of a writer or talker.

It was Trish who told me what happened after our visit. One of Brad's sons had mentioned in front of my father that they had seen me. My father lashed out at Brad, "Whose side are you on?" and threatened to cut him out of the will too.

Too. So I had been cut out of the will, again.

Our son Sam was born on a Friday, March 1998. Unlike Megan, he took his sweet time. The trade off to no painkillers was that I had quite a gutter mouth during the delivery. At nine pounds, nine ounces, Sam was a big boy, like his father.

I sent a birth announcement to my father and Pat, without a personal note. I was losing hope.

In those early years of motherhood, I worried I would not be good enough for Megan and Sam. I would think about my father and how he was with us when I was little. He used to say he didn't want to be like his own father, who had beaten him with a belt. My father had hit us a couple times when he lost his temper, but he never used a belt. I didn't believe in spanking, yet when my children pushed me too far, I spanked. Was I like my father?

Keith could not understand my fears. He watched me cradle each child in my arms and read to them. Megan's smile peeked out behind her pacifier to *Owl Babies*. Sam chuckled to *Good Night Gorilla*.

I pureed fresh carrots for baby food, worried about all the chemicals in jarred food. I joined a playgroup and did outings to the butterfly museum, the space center, the zoo. I loved them, that much I knew. I had to learn how to be a mother, through books and friends.

I knew Megan and Sam needed me, their mother. They loved me, blindly. But I worried I would pass on whatever defect I had to my children. My father, stepmother, sister, and brother had shunned me. Clearly, I was the one with the problem. If the Saraisky family knew me better, they too would see something was wrong with me. Keith was blinded by love.

Our life had such a blissful quality that I was certain tragedy would suddenly wipe the happiness away. I feared something terrible would happen.

Working on my MBA let me have summers to be a full-time mother, at least that part I got right. Yet, I could not stop overachieving. I had a 3.8 grade point average, and was given an award for being one of the top ten students in the class. As a mother of two, simply finishing school should have been enough of an achievement. It's only now that I can see how driven I was, so much like my father and still trying to make him proud.

Keith was being considered for a lobbying job with Dow, which would move us to DC. I interviewed with a consulting company there, but the final, on-site interview pushed me to the edge. We liked the idea of living in the Northeast, the seasons, and being within driving distance to the Saraiskies. But it was DC. My father's town. How could I move back there and see my father on TV every night? What would I tell my children?

The night before the interview, alone in a hotel room in DC, I turned the TV to the news. I told myself not to look, but there was no stopping me.

I sat on the edge of the bed, my heart racing as 6:20 P.M. loomed closer. *Turn it off, Cindi, just turn it off. Don't do this to yourself.*

Jim Vance did the intro. "Wally Bruckner is in tonight for George . . ."

Thank God. I flopped back on the hotel bed, letting out a breath I hadn't realized I was holding. I would not have done well in the interview if I had seen my father.

I turned off the TV and flipped through the *Washingtonian* magazine. There was a mention about sportscaster George Michael losing his temper in a department store. He ripped up a new suit when the tailoring had not gone right.

Fortunately, I never had to decide about the job in Washington. The company didn't want me, because I wasn't willing to travel; and Keith's lobbying job never materialized either.

So I found a consulting job in Houston. Even though the company got awards for being the best place for working mothers, I still felt it was too much. I wanted to stay home with my children, but was embarrassed to say this. Motherhood was never a role my father had held in high regard, so I hadn't either.

The following year, Keith was offered a job in Dow's headquarters in Midland, Michigan, a company town with nothing else for miles around. We would have the seasons, and I would have a convenient reason to quit working, as there would be no jobs in my field. With Keith's raise, we could get by on his income alone.

It felt like such a relief to have this decision made for me—work or stay home? Yet, I was silently ashamed of myself. Dad would see me as a failure.

I should have foreseen, too, that after so many years of working, having too much time for reflection would bring me to a darker place.

CHAPTER 24

The Letter

Megan and Sam baking bread for the first time

THE YEAR I TRIED to be a stay-at-home mom is the closest I have ever come to ending my life.

Megan trick-or-treated dressed as a witch, in our close-knit neighborhood in Sugar Land, Texas. The next day, we moved to Midland, Michigan, where it snowed three feet that month. We had left behind eighty-degree humidity; the kids didn't even own snow boots or coats.

Nothing had prepared me for the cold, gray winters. My vision of being a stay-at-home mom was based on our lifestyle in Texas. I imagined taking Megan and Sam to the park in the sunshine every day and riding our bikes through the neighborhood. With less stress from juggling work, I would be a happier, better mother. Maybe I'd even play bunko with the ladies in the neighborhood and have energy left for an occasional date with my husband. Instead, Keith routinely traveled two and three weeks at a time to places like Kuwait, Egypt, and Zagreb.

In Michigan, the days were so cold it was dangerous to go outside for only the briefest of walks. The battle to get Sam into layers of warm clothes usually ended in a meltdown, sometimes his, sometimes mine.

One night while Keith was away, I desperately needed adult company so I was determined to go to a book club. I called eleven babysitters and gave up after the twelfth. I felt so alone.

In Houston, we'd had a nanny and our choice of babysitters. In Midland, teenagers were busy with sports and theater. I felt like a single mother, without any support. It wasn't the lifestyle I had bargained for.

In those first weeks in Michigan, I took Megan to ballet class and struck up a conversation with another mother, who told me she was a senior executive at Dow. As soon as I told her I was newly a stay-at-home mother, she stopped talking to me. Literally. She just walked away and never spoke to me again. There was a pecking order in this corporate town, and I was learning it wasn't just my father who looked down on motherhood. My shame grew deeper.

Without the daily grind of a job, I had more time to think about my father and my family. Too much time. My thoughts kept turning to Big Betty, my father's older half-sister. Her name was never mentioned until that one reunion in St. Louis when I was in eighth grade. That terrible cycle had been repeated with me. What if I repeated it with my own children?

During this time I saw a show on *Dateline NBC* about children of divorced parents who were estranged from one parent. I was thinking it would help me understand why I struggled to forgive Trish. I learned about memories and how a parent can shape them, making a child believe anything. In the show, one father told his boys their mother had run away and didn't love them anymore. It wasn't true; the father had kidnapped the boys. When the mother eventually found them years later, the boys could still not reconnect with or trust her. It made me wonder what Michelle remembered about me as her sister, a different version of me that I presumed Dad and Pat had painted. Did she not remember how much I had taken care of her, how close we were?

The wall of family pictures in my home included a picture of me with Michelle, taken on the first day she snuck out of the house to see me when I was disowned during college. In the photo, I was tired and pale from working so much; in contrast to Michelle's glowing tan and sun-streaked hair. Both our smiles were genuine, though. I also had her high school senior picture on the wall. By then, she had colored her hair to remove the highlights, and her eyes did not have a genuine smile. The photo of Brad was a school picture from fourth grade, somewhat faded, but it showed his trademark lopsided smile.

When Megan looked at these pictures and pointed to the girl in the photo with me or the photo of Brad, she asked, "Who's that?" In Oprah's magazine, *O*, there was an article about when grandchildren didn't know their grandparents anymore and advised we should talk more about them. So, I brought my father, sister, and brother into the lives of my children, so they would know who they are. I did not include Pat; she was not on the wall. I hadn't written her off completely, though; I kept a picture of her, with my father and Michelle, tucked in my wallet.

One time when I baked bread with Megan and Sam, to show them the magic of how the yeast makes the bread mysteriously grow, squishing the dough back down, only to have it rise again, I told them how my father had loved my homemade raisin bread. I didn't tell them, though, about how I once had made him a loaf of bread after he talked about my baking on TV with Jim Vance.

Vance made a comment about women not baking bread anymore, and Dad bragged, "My daughter Cindi bakes me raisin bread all the time." When I heard that exchange, I immediately baked two loaves, one for Dad and one for Vance. The next night, on the air, Dad presented Vance his loaf of homemade raisin bread, and the camera zoomed in to show raisins poking through a golden crust.

I did not tell them that my father was on TV. I didn't want his fame to be his main attraction. Instead, when I took Megan and Sam to *Disney on Ice*, I told them about the times my father had taken Brad, Michelle, and me to the *Ice Capades* at Madison Square Garden. And when Megan rode her Big Wheel, I thought of Michelle riding her tricycle.

Once when Sam threw up all over me, I remembered when I had done the same and my father shouted that I could wash my own damn sheets. These memories I kept to myself, locked in the hollow of my heart. I hid my father's ruthless side.

At three, Sam was a terror, telling me dozens of times throughout the day, "I hate you!" I lectured him through gritted teeth. "You can be mad at me, but you can't *hate* me." But when he bit his sister, I spanked him—and I didn't *believe* in spanking! When my father hit me, he hadn't meant to hurt me, not really. He just lost his temper. I didn't want to be like him, yet sometimes I was. It scared me. I dreaded changing Sam's diaper after one particular spanking. Would I see a blue handprint on his bare bottom, as I had once seen on my sister's arm from my father? I was relieved it was only pink, but that still meant I had hit him hard. My fear grew.

I shared these fears with Keith and told him of my worst mothering moments. He tried to comfort me, reasoning he would have had the same reaction. But truth be told, he never spanked either child.

Increasingly, I pictured driving my car into a brick wall, alone. Megan and Sam would be better off without me.

I reasoned that I was having dangerous thoughts because I was exhausted and alone too much. Donna warned me that I needed breaks. I argued that my children needed me.

The dark voice continued to whisper, *If the Michael family is happier without you, perhaps your children would be, too.*

In staying home, I no longer had any sense of accomplishment. Getting the laundry done did not give me the same joy as getting an award at work. Playing with dolls and trucks didn't distract me from a deep, hard-to-name pain, the same way as solving a computer problem.

I realized I needed to work part-time, for my own sanity, but there were no jobs in my field in Midland, so I looked for freelance work. I could write articles and consult for local businesses.

Then 9/11 happened.

It was the first Monday in many that Keith was not traveling, but was at work in Midland. The phone rang all morning with friends and relatives wondering if he was abroad somewhere. The possibilities of "what if" unhinged me.

Lauren Saraisky had just moved back to New York that weekend, within a few blocks of Ground Zero. Someone had reached her by cell phone. But Steven Saraisky's wife worked at Rockefeller Center and could not be reached. It was late that night we learned all the Saraiskies were accounted for.

In the weeks that followed, Dow instituted a travel ban. Keith was one of the exceptions. His first trip was to Houston. The morning he went on that first flight after 9/11, when I drove Megan to school, she insisted on taking his sweater to keep his smell with her. "No, honey, the sweater stays in the car."

"No, Mommy, I want to keep it with me."

I imagined the other children making fun of her, or his sweater, an expensive one, getting lost. "It has to stay in the car, honey."

"But what if the bad guys are flying Daddy's plane?" She had tears in her wide blue eyes, her delicate mouth turned into a pout.

I swallowed the lump in my throat and smiled bravely to reassure her. "There are no bad guys in Houston. Daddy's not that far away this time." It is one of the few times I have ever intentionally lied to my children, because in those early days after 9/11, nobody could make any such promises. The only thing I knew for sure by then was that we could not go on like this.

By Thanksgiving, Keith was frustrated at Dow and was entertaining the idea of going into business with Mr. Saraisky. A smaller business would let him get his hands dirty again. It would feel more real than negotiating these billion dollar projects that may or may not materialize. With Dow, our family life was not what we wanted, and being a small business owner would give him more time for us.

His best friends in England, Nick and Dave, convinced him to take the leap even though it meant a pay cut. If we moved to New Jersey, friends and family from England could visit more easily. In New

Jersey, there also were plenty of contract jobs in my own field, so I could contribute to our income. However, nothing went smoothly.

First, we couldn't sell our house. Then I had signed a contract to write a computer book, and was doing some freelance writing with tight deadlines. Quotes from movers, fix the roof, play with Megan and Sam, the babysitter was sick, "he hit me!", "she took my truck!", "I hate you!" I was going fucking nuts. I could clearly picture the minivan mangled. I even found a suitable wall.

I told myself to hang on. After the move, things would be easier. But the dark thoughts scared me. I finally asked my OB for a prescription, something, anything.

I was sitting on the exam table in a paper-thin gown.

"Do you have a plan?" he asked, code for, "have you figured out how you will end your life?"

I took his question, however, to mean, did I have a plan for fixing what was making me unhappy. "I have a lot to get through first," I said.

He gave me a prescription for an antidepressant. I chided myself for needing it.

My freelance articles yielded some prospective clients, and someone from the IT department of the *Washington Post* called. Could I come to Washington, DC, and consult with them? I didn't think too much about it. But in all that has happened since, it is enough for me to believe either in fate and some karmic connection between the *Post* and my family, or that God sits up there playing a massive chess game with our lives.

I heard that Michelle was working at WRC, in the same newsroom where my father was a sportscaster. So once again, alone in a hotel room in DC, I told myself not to turn on the TV. But I called my sister. I could not give up on her.

My stomach fluttered. I knew the number by heart. The switchboard put me through.

"Newsroom. This is Michelle," she answered in a voice fourteen years older than the last time I had heard it.

"Hi, Michelle, it's Cindi. Um, I'm in Washington for a day. I wanted to see if you want to meet for coffee or something."

There was a long pause. Finally, she spat, "You need to lose this number," and slammed the phone down.

I didn't cry. I had my first big client as an independent consultant to prepare for, and a happy pill to help me through the pain.

When I got back home, still in Michigan as we had not yet sold our house, I wrote my sister a letter. I reminded her of the times I took care of her. I told her how I had introduced Megan and Sam, her niece and nephew, to her through our happy memories. I revealed my fear that our family was repeating a cycle that I did not want to repeat with my own children. Did she know that Dad's sister Betty had been disowned, just like me? Did she know that Pop used to beat Dad? I didn't realize then that, while I had been working hard to understand my family, my father purposely blocked out such pain. Not only had he not contemplated these things or considered Betty in the last twenty years, he had been busy reinventing himself. As a sportscaster, he was always the center of attention, of adulation, and able to publicly criticize anyone from a professional football player to the owner of the Washington Capitals hockey team. He must have felt invincible.

It was September 2002 when the letter from my father arrived. Keith was in Japan. I had been battling a case of vertigo that the doctor attributed to stress so I had to stand slowly and avoid turning my head. I had also stopped taking the antidepressants, because they gave me nightmares and I wasn't sleeping. Tylenol PM left me groggy in the morning.

Even so, I managed to take my children to a carnival at school, where I waited sitting on the curb. At least it was a warm, sunny day.

When we got home and got the mail, I recognized my father's handwriting immediately, the envelope addressed to "Cindi and Keith Howson." My heart raced. After fourteen years of unanswered cards and letters, my father had finally written back. His handwriting in blue marker was so familiar, like all the notes he used to leave on the kitchen counter many years ago.

A small voice told me to wait to read it. *Wait until Keith gets home.* But I had been waiting for fourteen years; I couldn't wait another two weeks. I was alone in the kitchen when I opened the letter.

Cindi and Keith—

I am sure Keith that you must think Pat and I are very cold mean people. What kind of people disown a daughter? The answer is simple—although painful. We are a happily married couple who realized that we needed to get Cindi out of our lives and family so we could stop the continuous anger and pain caused by perpetual problems and fights. It is not unusual for kids to have problems with parents during their high school years. But the extent to which Cindi changed went beyond belief.

When you came home, Cindi, and told Pat and me that Mr. Bogar advised you not to talk to us because "your parents are mini minds incapable of understanding you" we were devastated. We should have known it was the beginning of the end to the wonderful closeness we had shared since your childhood.

Then came the Dr. T. affair. When we asked Grandma to talk with you, trying to convince you that going out with a forty-one-year-old teacher with three little children was wrong, you told her that the only thing that mattered was that you were happy! An affair between a vice principal and a high school student is an offense that puts teachers in jail for five to twenty years. But when you asked me not to go to the police, I was devastated. I simply could not believe that my daughter did not want me to punish this pervert! The problems caused by your affair with Mr. T. left a wake of destruction that is beyond description. Lives and careers were changed forever! I have the satisfaction of knowing I went to wherever he was a teacher to make sure the school board knew what he had done. Finally, just three years ago, he was kicked out of the Montgomery school system. If you Cindi would not let me get my satisfaction in court, I was certainly going to make sure that everyone would know what he had done to my daughter. You left the family, Cindi, to *live with him. When you left, many of our problems went away—but not the hurt of losing you.*

On October 14, 1985, Dallas, your friend, asked us to take you back. "You needed your family," and so we took you back. Pat was the one who said we should bring you back home—because she remembered how wonderful you had been growing up. It was Pat who said we should buy you a new car. It was Pat who agreed to go to Switzerland with you so she could meet George's parents. It was Pat who bought all the gifts for you at Christmas in 1987 when we didn't really have the money. She wanted you to have the things you said you wanted—she wanted you to be happy! I point these things out so that you can be clear about Pat. She only tried to make you happy. She is not the evil woman you try to portray her as being. It was Pat who actually listened to George's mom about the idea of us paying for you to go to Switzerland to go to school. It was me that said NO! Enough was enough. We couldn't make you happy.

Since the night of Michelle's graduation dinner at Quigleys, when you told us that you were going to Switzerland to get married, I have put you out of my mind. I told Pat that night that I never wanted to deal with you again, that you had caused more pain and heartache than I could tolerate!

Now more than fourteen years later, you write Michelle a letter that is so misguided that I must contact you to set the record straight. I never abused anyone—your accusations are OUTRAGEOUSLY false. Pat and I never brainwashed Michelle. She is a wonderful happily, married, successful, independent woman who is too bright to be brainwashed by anyone. You refer to my oldest sister Betty and claim that it is the family way to disown people. Cindi, you weren't there—you do not know anything about Betty. I will not discuss Betty. But you have no right to talk about her—you were not there!

I truly hate writing this letter because it dredges up so many bad memories buried deep in the past. But when you put a bunch of slander in a letter to Michelle, I must respond!

To you, Keith, I am sorry your wife doesn't have family to refer to. But there are many reasons we are better off staying in our separate worlds.

To you, Cindi, get the ignorant accusations about Pat and I out of your life and mind. Be accurate about the past. Be happy in the life you have created, but make sure that it is a life where you are accurate in what you say about the past. I hope you both have a good life and a good family. Now that you have gotten me to respond to your accusations, please make it a life where you stay away from us—and where you keep the facts from the past clear and honest.

I trust you will not contact us—EVER! —George Michael 9/03/02

I began to fall apart. I had tried for so long to bury any thoughts of that time with Michael, and even so, I had recurring nightmares about him. My father had once said that was all in the past, and that he had forgiven me for that mistake. Now twenty years later, to throw it all at me again? My hands trembled as I skimmed the letter again. My father told me he did not want me.

I pulled at my hair, grasping to hang on. I needed Keith, to hear his voice, but in Japan, it was the middle of the night.

I called my neighbor Sally, happy Sally. "Please, take the kids . . . Please, just . . . please!"

She came right away.

I was raving, howling, "Whyyy?" I had never shared my story with her. I had never shared it with any new friends I had met in the last ten years.

She listened and read the letter. It didn't meld with the loving mother she had befriended in the last year.

I probably shouted, "God does not exist! God would not do this to me right now, not when I am weak, not while Keith is away. JUST NOT RIGHT NOW! Why did I open it? Why did I read it?"

Sally was a person of deep faith. She pulled me back from the brink that afternoon. Eventually I stopped sobbing. She offered to stay the night. I assured her I could get through the evening. I did not want to inconvenience her.

The kids and I were supposed to go to another friend's house for a BBQ. We did. I told my other friend what had happened and I drank enough wine to dull the pain that night. Her husband drove us home.

I put on a brave smile for Megan and Sam. I had a responsibility to my children.

That night, I prayed to God not to let me do anything before Keith got home. I couldn't stand to picture my children finding me in a bathtub of blood. I saw the absurdity of praying to God for help, at the same time I was cursing Him.

The next morning, we went to church, because it was our routine. But I was done with God. Either He didn't exist, or He was flat out cruel.

The pastor talked about the three Ds for solving conflict in relationships: Be direct, discuss, dialogue; if the conflict isn't resolved with the first two, have a dialogue with a third party like a priest, therapist, marriage counselor, or trained professional. The pastor said God is with us in this process, and that if the three Ds didn't work, forget it.

I felt like God was talking to me. That sermon seemed directed at me: God does not want us wasting time on relationships that can't be salvaged. He was telling me to let go of my father, to let go of the Michael family, that it wasn't my fault.

So, when we knelt for personal prayers, the only person in my family I prayed for was my sister. It's the first time I didn't include my father in my prayers.

The sermon that morning gave me strength to go on. When we got home from church, I resumed the antidepressants and accepted the nightmares were a better alternative than suicide.

I hid my father's letter like a dangerous poison, but his words lingered in my mind. Already, I saw the mistakes in his own memory: It was not my friend Dallas who had helped with the first reconciliation; it was my boss from the video store, Steve. It was not Michelle's graduation dinner when he told me he wouldn't come to the wedding; it was my engagement announcement. Living with Michael had been a choice of last resort to avoid being homeless. Why all the defenses of Pat? I hadn't even mentioned her in my letter to Michelle.

When Keith got home from Japan a few days later, I showed him the letter. He was disgusted but not surprised. In our ten years together, he had never once witnessed the good side of my father and didn't understand how any man could treat his daughter this way.

While there were some details in my father's letter that I immediately saw were wrong, there were other facts that I had to check and eventually face. So a few weeks later, alone in my new home office in our drab rental-condo in New Jersey, I called the Montgomery County Board of Education, and asked what were the rules for a teacher dating a student? Is it illegal? They put me through to someone in human resources. After I explained my story, he said simply, "If the vice principal was forty and this event was twenty years ago, you can do the math. Don't you think it might have been time for the vice principal to retire?"

I clutched my desk, squeezed my eyes shut. "Was it legal or not? Was my father right to say he should have gone to jail?"

"Legally, you were eighteen, a consenting adult. But we hold staff to a higher standard." He waited a few minutes for this to sink in then said, "Where was your father when this was happening?"

I stared out the window, a gray mist making it seem darker than it should have for an early afternoon. "He worked nights. He and my stepmother worked together. They weren't home much."

"Don't you think your father bears some responsibility?"

I wrote his question down, a habit of mine when people say things I don't understand, in the hope I might eventually figure it out. "No, I don't. I thought I was in love."

"Maybe you should think about that. These things don't happen in isolation."

There was nothing more to say. I quietly hung up. I sat at my desk for a long while, doodling the question. It was the first time in my life that anyone had ever hinted that the whole fiasco with the vice principal was not entirely my fault. I sat there for a while to get my bearings.

Michelle's letter arrived a week after my father's. It was not hateful like his. And it was typed, so no reading into her perfect handwriting. She remembered how I had taken care of her. "Trish should have been thrown in jail for what she did to us," she wrote. I heard my father's voice in her words. She did not want a relationship with me and politely requested that I not contact her again.

I responded only to Michelle's letter, describing the three Ds and offering to go to a family therapist with her, even with Dad, despite his letter. I told her it would be the last time I would reach out to her, and that I would respect her wishes not to contact her anymore. And so it would be for another seven years.

CHAPTER 25

Going Home

NEW JERSEY HAS A dubious reputation, known for its stinky smoke stacks and obnoxious TV shows. Our particular corner of the state, Sparta, is a rural town with rolling green hills, sparkling lakes, deer, and black bears. When I stand in my front yard on a sunny day, I see lush green trees for thirty miles. Downtown, around the lake, was designed by a Swiss architect, with quaint buildings, turrets, and Tudor facades. On Saturdays, the parks are filled with people, both children and adults, playing baseball, soccer, and football. When a neighbor is in need, we cook for one another. New Jerseyans may swagger, but we look after each other.

Sparta is less than an hour from Oakland, the childhood home of my "golden years." Perhaps it was this proximity to Oakland that dulled the pain my father had inflicted to a throb, a throb that peaked on holidays and birthdays. Letting go of my father quieted his voice in my head. Instead of his voice that was once a constant criticism replaying in my mind like a trailer from a horror film, I forgot the ugliest things he had said.

My healing also began with a conversation with Aunt Jane, whom I hadn't seen for decades. When I told my cousin Paul about my father's letter, he encouraged me to call her. "You should talk to my mom."

But I was afraid, like a child who burns her hand on the stove, any contact with the Michael or Gimpel family risked my getting burned. So I wrote her a letter, to Florida where she now lived. To my surprise, she was happy to hear from me and invited me to stay the weekend when I traveled there on work.

We sat beside the waterway, watching the boats along the Gulf Coast. She couldn't explain my father to me, only saying that he also no longer wanted contact with her and had little contact with Uncle Earl. Aunt Marge, Dad's only full-blooded sister, had died just a few months before he had written me the awful letter. It was as if he just wanted to cut all ties with anyone who knew him from St. Louis, or perhaps more so, who knew him as someone other than the famous sportscaster.

It hurt to talk, but it also made me feel less alone. If my father could turn his back on someone like his sister, a woman I admired, who was good and kind and rescued sea turtles, then it meant I was not necessarily trash either.

Aunt Jane still stayed in touch with my father, but I know it was her initiative not his, and I doubt she ever told him we had spoken. That would have been one more reason for him to shun his last living sister.

We ended our conversation along the water with Aunt Jane telling me to give my pain up to God. I didn't know what that meant or how to do so, other than continuing to have faith that one day we would make peace with each other. It's the last we spoke about my father and the Gimpels, and we spent the rest of the weekend laughing over margaritas, eating Mexican food, and exploring boutique shops.

Meanwhile, Keith and I carved a new lifestyle in New Jersey, again partners in raising a family. At school, people knew me only as Megan and Sam's mom, the volunteer during Friday lunch times. New acquaintances looked upon our family with a mild jealousy at how idyllic things seemed.

I introduced Keith, Megan, and Sam to some of my favorite places from my youth. In summer, we jumped the waves in Ocean City, New Jersey, where they fell in love with the boardwalk. Sam scooped up baby clams with me, staring in wonder at the palette of tiny pink, purple and amber shells, no bigger than his pinky nail.

And then to Dot's Bakery, where Dad had taken me on vacations at the beach. The first time we went to Dot's, I had to fight off the lump in my throat as I watched a child excitedly push the button for his ticket to be served. It could have been me when I was five and with my dad. The sweet smells of sticky buns, of butter cakes, of sugar cinnamon twists wrapped around me like a child's blanket.

I kept my feelings about my father in check most days, except my birthday. I don't like my birthday. Period. It is a bitter reminder of yet another year that my father did not want me.

For years, I also would not watch any American sports with Keith, particularly the Super Bowl. I did not want to be thinking about my father or glimpse him in the press room.

As Megan and Sam grew older, it got harder to explain. If I told them I was disowned, would they worry that I would one day disown them too? If I told them my father was a mean son-of-a-bitch, how could I ever expect them to open the door to him?

So, never did I tell my children that my father was a sportscaster, that in some circles he was famous. When Megan started horse lessons, I didn't tell her he owned a horse farm and bred beautiful paint horses.

When Megan was in fourth grade and had to make a family tree, she put the Saraiskies on her tree for my side of the family. I told her she should add the Michaels too.

"That's your family, not my family," she replied matter-of-factly.

I tried to explain that they were her family, too, even if she didn't yet know them.

"There isn't room. You can only have two sets of grandparents."

"I'm sure some people have stepparents."

She didn't respond and just kept on with her tree the way she wanted. If she were older and doing a gene chart, I would have said, "Your stubbornness comes from my father, your grandfather."

But I understood. My father had never earned a place in her heart.

In telling her and Sam about Brad and Michelle, I tried to explain why we never spoke, why they never visited, but it was all so complicated.

Keith said very little about my family. Fortunately, it was Keith who called me one morning in March 2007. "Your father's on the cover of the sports section. He's retiring."

I never read the sports section. Each day, it went into the recycle bin, intentionally unopened.

I got the paper. Even in the article, my father had twisted his own version. He claimed that his retirement was about budget cuts and that if he couldn't have all of his staff, he would be the first to go. *Baloney.* At the time, I wondered how much his stepping down had to do with a decline in ratings. *The Sports Machine* was no longer the novelty it once was in the 1980s. ESPN was now mainstream. My father had to be number one.

My birthday January 2008, I stumbled across an article on the Internet from *Washingtonian* magazine. My father had mentioned my name, saying Michelle and I had been bridesmaids at their wedding. That my father mentioned me by name seemed to confirm my entire theory that once he slowed down, he would reflect and remember. When he remembered me, he would reach out.

I read that he would be in New York giving a presentation for NPR. I was scheduled to have a business dinner in New York the same day, only a few blocks away. But his words still haunted me. *Stay away. Do not contact me. Ever!* So I stayed away.

The next month, we were in South Jersey for the children's championship swim meet, and only a few minutes from Alluvium, my childhood home when Dad and Trish were married. I had planned to drop Keith and the children at the hotel and drive to Alluvium by myself. Instead, my family joined me. Keith was trying to be supportive; the kids wanted proof of my childhood, so much of it a mystery to them.

Thirty-foot pine trees canopied the sidewalks, lush green in the gray of winter. How big had they been when I first moved here? It looked like a neighborhood in which I would like to raise a family.

We rounded the corner onto Hollybrook Way, the street that had once been my home. All I could see was my little sister from thirty years ago, the flash of blue from the desk lamp as it struck her in the face. Dark memories rose like a tsunami and my throat began to close. I had never told my husband or children about that last awful night in October 1976, when I was in sixth grade. The night when the lamp flew across the room, hitting my six-year-old sister in the face, and how I had grabbed her and run down the hallway to hide from our mother.

I looked out the window at my old home. *I shouldn't have come here.*

"Which one is Jill's, Mom?" Megan asked me excitedly, drawing me out of my dark memory.

I had only ever shared the happy stories from my childhood, usually about fun times with Jill.

I swallowed hard to stifle the growing lump in my throat, and pointed toward the left. "That's Jill's." Then I pointed right, my throat thick. "There's mine. Number 6." I forced a smile, as I always had.

Keith parked along the curb, and we climbed out of the minivan. The sky was a brilliant blue on this unusually mild day in mid-February. I studied the façade of my old home, a Millwood model. There used to be beams that jutted from the edge of the roof above the dining-room window, like a ladder slung on its side. The night our mother went berserk, my brother and I had planned to escape out my bedroom window, dangle from the beams, and drop to the gravel driveway below.

The beams were gone now, probably rotted with the passage of time.

Megan took my hand. "Come on, Mom. Let's walk to the bus stop together!"

Megan had heard so many stories of my brother and I racing to catch the bus, and when we had missed it, we had to run fast to catch it at the next corner. I had never shared the other part, though, that the reason we often missed the bus was because our mother couldn't bother to get out of bed before school.

Even now, with the painful memories nearly drowning me, I kept them in, and instead, took my daughter's hand. For Megan at eleven, walking to the bus stop was still fun; Sam, nine, was bored and complained he needed a bathroom. I hesitated, asked Sam to wait, then joined Megan. We skipped along, because it was a *real* sidewalk, not just the street with no sidewalks like in our rural town.

I studied the names on the mailboxes as we skipped by, wondering who from the original Alluvium families might still live here. I heard players from the Phillies and Flyers now lived in the neighborhood. None were familiar. At the bus stop, I shrugged, saying quietly, "Nobody stays in the same place for thirty years."

Sam and Keith ambled along behind us. My son again whined about a bathroom, so Megan and I turned around, and we headed back to the minivan.

As we came closer to my old house, I stretched to see to the walkway that led from the driveway to the backyard, now fenced. My father had laid the walkway and patio himself the first spring we lived here, crawling along on his hands and knees, lovingly positioning each brick into an interlocking pattern.

Finally I asked my family, "Can anyone tell if that pathway is brick?"

Keith, the tallest of us, said, "I don't think so, hon. Looks paved or something."

Something drew my eyes downward then, and that's when I saw the heart.

My eyes welled up as I stooped. It was thirty-five years ago, and they had just poured the concrete. My father took a twig and wrote in the wet cement, George and Trish, 197_, enclosed with a heart.

"Oh, my God," I whispered, and I reached to touch it. "I can't believe it's still here."

I remembered the day my father wrote this while I played outside. I had been worried he'd get in trouble. Did we own the sidewalk? I had wanted to know. Already at eight, I was a rule follower, a good little girl.

My mind couldn't get around the permanence of the writing or this public display of my father's love for my mother. In all the ugliness that followed their separation, I had only remembered the anger and the fights.

"Can you make out the date?" Keith asked.

I traced the jagged edges of his heart, my hand trembling. "No, it's too crumbled in that corner." It would have been 1973 as the sidewalk was poured the spring after we had moved in.

I stayed on my knees, feeling the full force of the love and hope my father must have felt on that bright day, the crushing loss when all those dreams ended so soon after. It was only a few months later that my mother's supposed affair became local gossip. My father hadn't even lived in this house a full year.

I felt a charge, a secret swirling within my grasp, like the prickle before lightning strikes. It was the secret to understanding my father and why he had disowned me, twenty years ago.

But I couldn't grasp the thought before it flittered away, beyond my reach. Sam's plea for a bathroom was now desperate, so we had to leave. I needed to be a good mother, and not the broken shell of a child still trying to mend. What pain might I have spared myself if only I had stood there a moment, an hour, a day longer?

That fall, Sam was in fifth grade and his football team won the county championships. In sixth grade, they made it to the play offs though they didn't win. But Sam's coaches said he had gifted hands. As tight end, he caught the most passes of the season, even the ones that seemed impossible for anyone to catch. His coaches inspired him, "When you're first-round draft pick, you gonna remember us, Sam?" This single comment encouraged me to daydream about how my son would meet my father, his grandfather.

One of the things that made the *Sports Machine* so popular was that my dad had a knack for capturing the person, not just the plays and statistics. I imagined my father, the sportscaster, trying to interview my son, a pro in my dreams, after a game or a draft pick. Would I let him? Or would I shun him professionally, caught unawares live on air, "No, you may not interview your GRANDSON!"

When I couldn't sleep at night, the image that lulled me to sleep was the one in which my father and I had already made peace. My father, of course, would get the exclusive on the NFL's next role model, a respectful freckle-faced boy with big dreams.

I tell both my children, "Dream. And dream big. It may take years, but anything is possible."

CHAPTER 26

Christmas Eve

WHEN MEGAN AND SAM were younger, we spent Christmas in England with Keith's family. As they got older, we preferred to stay home. Some years, the Saraiskies joined us or Keith's family came over. By Christmas 2009, we were ready for a quieter holiday, just the four of us, particularly after hosting twenty-two people at Thanksgiving.

We put up a fresh Christmas tree right after Thanksgiving, and for Christmas Eve we planned the same buffet dinner as Keith's parents had for their wedding anniversary: mushroom vol-au-vents, pork pies, sausage rolls, and minced pies.

Christmas Eve morning, I went to the butcher to pick up the fresh turkey while Keith waited for DirecTV to come fix an intermittent problem with the dish. I left a plate of homemade cookies with Keith for the repairman.

It was a cold, sunny day. Carols were jingling on my car radio and I sang along. On the way home, I stopped at a drugstore for extra wrapping paper and last-minute stocking stuffers. I called Keith to see if there was anything else we needed. He was abrupt on the phone. He always got grumpy when he had to wrap presents. Later, he would tell me it was because he was scared of what I might hear on the radio.

I pulled up the driveway behind the DirecTV truck.

"Well that was good timing," I said cheerfully and parked alongside the truck.

Keith came dashing out. "There you are."

I proceeded to explain to the repairman that we kept losing the signal. He wanted to look at the cables inside. I showed him the wiring in the basement, then went to the kitchen and started unpacking the groceries.

Keith stands at the other end of the counter. Sam hovers near him. Keith rests his palms on the breakfast bar. "I have some bad news."

I smile wryly. Keith is an online shopper. I surmise that a special gift he ordered for me will not arrive on time. I look at him, about to quip something funny. The silence goes on too long, though.

Was it his mother? She was eighty-two and diabetic. Her health had declined since Granddad's death three years earlier. "Trish called . . ."

I keep staring at Keith, waiting.

"It's George. He died. He's been sick a while."

I shake my head no. *No. No. No.* "Nooo!" I try to breathe, but no air comes in. My groan is like the steel of the Titanic sinking. I reach for something to hold onto and find myself clawing at the hardwood floor.

Keith whisks me away to the bedroom, where I clutch at the carpet on the floor, at my hair, and sob—sobs, I had been holding in for twenty years.

Eventually I called Trish. She repeated what she had told Keith, that he had been sick for a while. Brad had called her so she wouldn't read about it in the paper. So the ex-wife got a heads up, but the daughter didn't deserve that courtesy?

She gave me Brad's cell phone number. He was at the airport on his way to the hospital where our father had just died.

Brad didn't hang up on me when I wailed, "Why didn't you tell me?" It had been ten years since we last saw each other. Eventually, I gathered myself and said, "I'm sorry for your loss."

Brad told me our father would be cremated. There would be no funeral, just a memorial after the holidays. I begged him to let me know the details, to please let me say good-bye to my father. I should have known then that he would never tell me, but even so, I blurted the request.

I went through the motions of Christmas Eve cooking.

Nobody in my life loved my father. There was nobody to commiserate with. I stopped cooking and called Aunt Jane. She told me my father had brain cancer. She had learned of his death from Uncle Earl, my father's only brother, who had heard about his death on the news. Nobody had called them, either.

My family and I went to the early Christmas Eve mass, as always. That night, I was barely able to dress myself. The church was standing room only by the time we arrived. I needed to sit. I insisted on looking for seats, despite the crowd. A friend called out to me, but I kept walking, unable to meet anyone's eyes, unable to wish anyone a Merry Christmas. Finally, I found four chairs together.

Mass proceeded and I felt Sam, eleven then, watching me. I tried to sing, to appear okay for my son's sake, but my voice cracked. Sam whispered something to my husband, then pressed Keith's handkerchief into my hand. Were there tears on my face?

The priest's words about heaven made me think of hell, and I pictured my father burning amidst the flames, because he had died with anger in his heart.

When everyone proceeded to the alter for communion, I moved along with them, dragged along with the current.

When the minister held up the Eucharist, I couldn't reply "Amen." I could barely open my mouth. I choked down the dry wafer. The image of a half-chewed wafer on the floor ensured it would be months before I attempted communion again.

Back home, I was supposed to be tracking Santa on NORAD with Megan and Sam. Instead, I was reading my father's obituary. It listed my father's survivors. My name was not one of them. Neither was my brother's. *USA Today* and ESPN repeated the same error.

I slunk back to the family room and announced that Santa was in Iceland on his way to America. We finished watching *Polar Express*. All I saw was my father's face. When the movie finished, we laid out cookies, milk and sherry, and a carrot for Rudolph.

With our children tucked into bed, I worked up the courage to call NBC. Why was my brother not listed as a survivor? I called from the quiet corner of my office, gripping the edge of my desk.

Matthew Stabley, the author of the obituary, wasn't there. I asked whom to talk to about an error in the news story about the death of George Michael. His name stuck in my throat. Only then did I realize I hadn't said his name in decades.

The reporter who took my call asked who was calling. I hadn't thought how to answer this. I hesitated. But I finally said, "Cindi Michael."

He responded with a hint of panic, "Oh, Cindi, jeez, I'm sorry."

"So you know about me?"

"Yeah, yeah, we know about you."

He explained that my brother's omission was an error in phrasing, as they offered condolences to their long-time employees, my stepmother and sister. My omission, however, was intentional, in respect for my stepmother's wishes.

I wondered, then, was this also my father's dying wish?

I remained somewhat composed throughout Christmas day, for Keith and my children's sakes.

That night, we went to our friends' next door. Teresa had been my closest friend since moving back to New Jersey. I explained the story of my dad and me for the first time.

Jack, her husband, asked, "Why didn't you let go . . . just forget them?"

It was not the first time someone had asked me this. "Because he was my father and I still loved him."

Teresa gasped in her Texas drawl, "Oh, my *gawwwd*, look at your hands!" My hands had turned blue as I had shared my story; my body was giving up. We went to the kitchen sink and ran my hands under warm water, but they remained blue.

I drank a lot of wine, but still I could not sleep. At three A.M. I reverted to a sleeping pill.

The phone calls started the next day. The Saraiskies had seen the obituary in *The New York Times*. I didn't know my father was famous enough for that paper. No, I did not want any visitors. It was enough that I had to be stoic for my children.

My special gift to my family that year was tickets to Cirque du Soleil, Wintuk, at Madison Square Garden, a few days after Christmas. We were all finishing getting dressed up for a trip to New York City. I was in the bathroom, layering on makeup to cover my puffy eyes.

Steven Saraisky called. We had not spoken about my father or the Michael family in years, nor had we ever spoken about any matters of the heart. And yet, Steven had called *The New York Times* and, as a lawyer, accused them of inaccurate reporting. The reporter didn't believe Steven and wanted proof.

"The reporter wants to talk to you," he said.

"Why?"

"It's wrong. It's just wrong. He wants to talk to you. Look, I'm sorry. I should have asked you first."

I bit the inside of my cheek, hard. "It's okay. I know you mean well. You can give him my number, if you want, but . . . " My voice trailed off. What did it matter? What did any of it matter? My father was gone.

Bruce Weber, the obituary writer for *The New York Times,* called me on my cell phone a few minutes later. We were in the car on the way to the train station. He expressed disbelief and asked me for proof.

"Proof of what?" I hissed. "What do you want, a birth certificate? Photos?" I tried to explain, "I loved my father. If he chose not to list me in his obituary, then you need to respect his dying wish."

"If this is true, then Pat lied to me." He sounded mad, like a reporter not used to being misled.

I wondered again, what was my *father's* last wish? I squeezed my eyes and rubbed my forehead. "People know about me. He spoke at my high school graduation. He mentioned me by name in an article a few years ago."

The reporter hesitated and acknowledged seeing the reference. "I thought you had passed at some point."

My mind swirled. People thought I had died? I pushed the thought away and suggested that Mr. Weber leave it alone.

Mr. Weber called again while we were on the train. Pat had not returned his call, but Michelle, my sister, did and confirmed that I was his daughter.

"You spoke to Michelle? What did she say?"

"Just that there was bad blood between your father and you." Mr. Weber apologized for opening old wounds.

How could I explain that they weren't old wounds?

He said they would correct my father's obituary.

My children were entertained at Wintuk and I was grateful for the dark venue as we watched the performers flip and twirl and dangle from dangerous heights, exactly what my mind was doing.

When we got home that night, the voice message light was flashing. Caller ID said Michelle. She didn't leave a message.

I stumbled through the rest of the week, and through New Year. It was only after everyone went back to school and to work that I couldn't stop myself from falling apart.

I called our priest, Father Pat, a plump Irishman with a jolly face. I sat in his office and tried to explain my story. I forced myself to ask, "What happens to a soul when he dies angry?"

Father Pat reminded me that God is forgiving. "It's in His hands," he said quietly.

"I don't know how to say good-bye."

Father Pat offered some suggestions for a private service. He eventually ended our meeting with a prayer. I thought he would pray for my father, but instead, he said a prayer for God to heal my pain, a gesture that knocked me sideways. I wasn't used to someone praying for me, nor to ask for that. It had never occurred to me that, when life sucks and there's no resolution, all that's left for Him to do is to ease the pain.

The Saraiskies rallied around me, as they always had. We did a makeshift memorial at my house, with a handful of friends. I displayed some pictures, my *Sports Machine* jacket, and a note my father wrote me on my sixteenth birthday, on his New York Islander's notepad:

No father in this world has ever had a better daughter bring him more pride than you bring me. I love you!

I played the songs my dad used to dedicate to me, when he was a disc jockey. Keith read from a poem that I had found tucked in an old diary, written by someone named Henry van Dyke (*an old classmate?*), copied down when I was twelve, in my perfect cursive writing. "Time is too slow for those who wait . . . too long for those who grieve . . . but for those who love, time is eternity."

I was surrounded by love, and yet, when I laid my head on my pillow at night, I kept seeing my heart being sliced in strips. I stared at the ceiling in the dark bedroom, waiting for sleep. I pictured the shreds of my heart like shark bait—bait that Pat and my sister were carelessly tossing in the sea, leaving just a sliver for my husband and children to try to resuscitate. I lay there, listening to Keith's gentle breathing, watching the red number of the alarm clock.

I plowed through old diaries, photo albums, and handwritten notes by my father. Had I imagined my whole childhood, the golden years just a wish?

I struggled to focus at work. I was supposed to write a technical article for a magazine. The blank computer screen stared back at me for hours.

I began to think this was my father's legacy: Sorrow would ruin my livelihood and leave me as an empty shell of the mother and wife I had once been.

I thought more and more about Trish. My mother. Did she really need to lose custody of us? Or had my father sought vengeance? Had he driven her to craziness, as he was doing to me?

By mid-January, I was having a good day. I finished a work day without Googling my father's name. My office manager had gone for the day, and I sat alone in the office.

I wanted to see if an interview I recently did with a computer magazine had published yet. I was still moving in a fog of pain and couldn't remember which magazine it was. So I Googled my own name. I stumbled across a blog post about my father . . . and me. A reporter from *The City Paper* was speculating about a correction *The New York Times* had recently issued on George Michael's obituary, noting that a daughter, Cindi Howson, and two grandchildren had been left off the original survivor list, "based on information from a family member." He wrote about messy family fibs and that "there must be a real sad story in there." A reader added another comment and linked to an opinion piece in *USA Today* I had written at Thanksgiving about how I was thankful for my education and that I hadn't dropped out of school when I was first disowned. Over the years, I'd had several letters published in *USA Today*, on everything from football safety to family meal times. I had used my married name, Howson, for the opinion piece, not Cindi Michael; so I hadn't revealed a link to my famous father. Now, here were strangers speculating about my disowning and my private pain. *What the fuck?*

My fingers trembled as I tracked down the reporter's phone number. Dave McKenna.

"This is Cindi Michael Howson," I barked into the phone. "Need I say more?"

He was silent.

"This entire conversation is off the record. It is a sad story, Mr. McKenna, and it's not a story. It's my life! You need to delete what you wrote."

He claimed he couldn't delete the story. I argued that I knew it was technically possible. I shouted louder. I closed my eyes and pressed my hand to my forehead. I was so very tired. I continued more calmly. "Look, I have two children I need to protect. They didn't even know who their grandfather was until he died. Please. Can't you just do this?"

He asked me if I had seen the reader comment from a few weeks earlier, saying, "'GM was a lousy father . . . a cold and callous SOB.' It's in all caps. Usually a kid writes like that."

A kid? A kid like Megan or Sam?

"What happened?" he asked.

How could I answer that? "I grew up," I replied.

I could not explain our family's dysfunction in a thirty-second sound bite, my father's world.

"You know, you look just like him."

I felt like I was being stalked. *He knew what I looked like?* I had never thought much about whether I looked like my father or not. I had always worried more about how similar we were on the inside.

"So was he really poor?" McKenna asked.

"What do you mean?" I hadn't heard this before.

He asked questions I had never considered before and didn't want to be considering now. I repeated my request for him to delete the story and hung up.

On my ten-minute drive home from work, I screamed at my father in rage. "You stupid fucking asshole. You sonofabitch! How did you not think of this? And Pat, you are stupider than he is! You are both stupid fucking assholes! If you only included me in the obituary, nobody would be snooping."

When I got home, I called Megan and Sam into the kitchen and confronted them. "Are you Googling my father's name?" I demanded.

Sam shook his head no. Megan acknowledged she was.

I was calm in a scary way. "And are you posting comments about him?"

"No," she replied quietly. She didn't seem to be lying.

My anger dissolved into tears. "I know my father was a jerk. What he did was wrong and mean and cruel. But I still loved him."

I told them they could hate him if they wanted, but I would rather they learn the positive from him. I gave them the "dream big" lecture. Only this time, I explained how my father had turned himself from a nobody into a famous sportscaster.

They grew quiet. After my tirade, Megan came over to me and held me.

CHAPTER 27

A Journey

Megan, me, and Sam, Ocean City 2010

I WAS DROWNING IN pain, the rip tide of sorrow finally destroying me for good. I owed it to my husband and children to fight to stay with them. I found a therapist and joined a support group at church, despite my father's voice taunting me, "Don't be so weak . . . you must be crazy like Trish."

A week later, I received a card from Father Pat, saying he would offer a Mass of Intention for my father on February 7th. I paused, recognizing the date. Super Bowl Sunday. A game my father had been at for the last twenty-seven years.

I showed my children Father Pat's card. I wondered aloud about the coincidence. "Maybe it's simply the next available date."

Megan declared with certainty, "God picked that date, Mom."

Sam, my skeptic, nodded, "I think so too."

I contemplated going to the official memorial at the National Cathedral, but Keith, Teresa, and Aunt Jane talked me out of it. It was made clear, indirectly through Trish, who spoke to my brother, that I was not wanted there. Despite my having begged, my brother never called to let me know the details for the memorial. I found them through Twitter and watched the service on Web TV. I clung to the words of the eulogy of one of my father's friends, who repeated my dad's final words in the hospital: "I've made some mistakes. I have to get stronger. There are some people I need to talk to."

Was my father talking about me?

A few months after Christmas, I began to clear out the junk basket in our kitchen—school notices, Christmas cards, condolence cards, an overdue bill, and old church bulletins. I stumbled across the bulletin from Christmas Eve and saw that it included a story from Henry Van Dyke. *Henry van Dyke!* So Henry was not an old school friend, but rather, a priest who wrote, "If you truly believe that love is the strongest thing in the world—stronger than hate . . . then you can keep Christmas."

I showed my husband the bulletin, because it seemed another coincidence. Keith does not share my faith to the same extent, but at this one, he uttered slowly, "*That* is really weird."

2010 was a year of realizing I had so much more to lose. In May, we went to England for the weekend for Nick's, my husband's best friend, fiftieth birthday. Megan vomited that morning and stayed home from school. By evening, she was well enough to fly, but I was still nervous about the long trip. As we drove to the airport, lightning lit up the sky. I was convinced that either God or my father was telling me to skip this flight. My family scoffed at the superstition. No way would we miss this birthday party and the weekend with friends. Then our flight was delayed. With an extra three hours to spare, we had a leisurely dinner at Gallagher's Steak House in the airport.

The food had just arrived when Keith stood abruptly. He could not breathe.

I started the Heimlich, which I barely remembered learning a decade earlier. Keith is six foot five and 230 pounds; I am five foot seven. My arms barely circled his chest. I could not get enough leverage. I threw him over the chair and pounded on his back. Nothing. I started the Heimlich again. I screamed, "Somebody help me!'" A waiter, smaller than I, looked on, unsure what to do.

Megan's voice was distant, an echo down a tunnel. "Somebody help him!"

"Call 911!"

"Slit his throat!"

Finally, Keith's body eased, his hands caught some dissolved bread. I sat and cried. I didn't want to get on the plane.

But we did. And in England we laughed and partied with friends, going to the horse races in the Lake District. But it all felt surreal, like a movie I was watching.

In the summer, we once again went to Ocean City. I wanted to avoid the place, but Keith gently reminded me, "We have our own memories there too."

I didn't want to go to Dot's Bakery. Megan softly insisted. "We have to Mom. It's a tradition."

I learned later, from Trish, that Brad had stood in that same spot only two weeks prior. In my father's eulogy, my brother recalled the joy of riding the waves with Dad at the beach, so I had written to him about our annual trek to Ocean City and to Dot's. Had he too been looking for that version of our father? I still wonder if my father or the universe had tried to arrange our meeting but had been a little off in the timing.

In August, I would again be teaching a class on big data software at a conference in San Diego. Each year, I had thought of calling my father's older brother, Uncle Earl, who lived near there, but Dad's orders never to contact anyone in the family always stopped me. This year, I wrote Uncle Earl a letter telling him I would be in town and was surprised when he called me.

He called my cell phone when we were in the car on the way home from Ocean City. He hadn't remembered that I existed, having only met me the one time at the family reunion in St. Louis in 1979. Still, when he hung up, he said, "I love you, Cindi." The ease with which he uttered these words pierced my heart.

In California, I took a cab to his house and reunited with him and my cousin Cathy. I explained what I could about why I was disowned.

"George and Pop were so much alike!" Uncle Earl declared. The wall in Uncle Earl's living room was filled with family photos, but I didn't see any of the Michaels or my father.

I admired the picture of Pop in his grocery store, circa 1930. "You know, I've never seen a picture of my grandmother," I said.

Earl replied, "I've never seen one of my mother. Pop destroyed all of them when she died. Didn't even know she had died 'til someone came in the store one day, said 'you're Anna's boy, aren't you?' I musta been about seventeen. I said, 'Anna? Who the heck is Anna?'"

Christ. So for seventeen years, Earl, who was on his third mother by then, hadn't even known his real mother had died in a car accident? What kind of father keeps such secrets? Or is that how Pop—and my father—dealt with loss? Remove any reminders of pain.

Uncle Earl, Cathy, and I only shared an evening. He died in January, only a few months after we reconnected, of a cancer that had quickly resurfaced.

Aunt Jane told me about his funeral, saying the church was packed; Uncle Earl had been a church usher and had so many friends.

I was telling Megan about him and his passing away as we were walking together into swim practice, a cold, dark night. We were holding onto each other, being careful not to slip on the black ice on the pavement. "I don't get it. He sounds like someone my father would have wanted more of in his life," I said.

"The same could be said about you," Megan replied nonchalantly. The clarity of her remark stopped me mid stride, and I turned toward her, those innocent blue eyes seeing so clearly what I still couldn't see.

In the weeks and months after my father's death, I wrote letters to anyone I thought could explain my father to me. I wanted to know which parts of his life were true and which were made up. What made him into a father that could disown me, not willing to make peace even when he knew he was dying.

Most people didn't reply. The few people that I tried calling never answered their phones. I suspect they just stared at the caller ID and decided it was a conversation they didn't want to have. I assumed that my father had painted a picture of me as someone who deserved to be disowned. Drug addict? Murderer? Slut? At a minimum, a manipulative liar. Undesirable and unlovable.

Only a few of his old friends were willing to talk to me, and simply hearing about my father from people who once knew him, once cared about him, eased my pain. Each conversation was like a small buoy I clung to. Being able to laugh about some of my father's ways with these people was a thread to the father I once had. From what I could piece together, my dad did not think he would die. He thought he could beat his illness, and it is this fact that makes me think my father ran out of time.

I tracked down our old babysitter, Jane, from Oakland when Dad first got custody of us. I asked her what she remembered. Was my father really such a good father or had I romanticized that time? She confirmed my memories were real. I had not imagined the golden years.

"He was too hard on Brad, though," she said. "I remember the time your father told Brad he had to have the whole driveway shoveled by the time he got home from work. Brad was only thirteen and out in the storm for hours. I told him not to go back outside, that I would stand up to your father. Brad was so worried."

I had forgotten that Brad once had it worse than I.

Trish offered her own answers, but I never fully trusted her nuggets of information. When I mentioned an article in which Dad said his mother had died when he was a teenager, Trish contradicted this, saying his mom had died when we lived in Downs Farm. Why should I believe her? I wondered. But why would she make up the memory?

So, I contacted the Missouri Bureau of Vital Records. A copy of my grandmother's death certificate confirmed she died when my father was twenty-nine and I was four. Why had my father lied about his own mother's death? I started to doubt everything he had ever told me. I wondered about the custody battle. Were my memories false?

I tracked down court documents and affidavits, spanning seven years and hundreds of pages. Some of it was worse than what I remembered. It hurt to picture me as a child with no winter coat, and how when I got one, apparently from a thrift store, my greatest pride was at being able to sew buttons on it so I could button my coat. I admire that little girl's resourcefulness and her optimism. I would have liked to have found the transcripts from the court psychiatrist, Dr. Yaskin, but I never found those or the doctor himself.

I journeyed to St. Louis, my father's childhood home and my birthplace. I could not say how much I was looking for answers or simply looking for a way to spend time with my father, to walk the sidewalk that led to him cutting me out of his heart forever.

I went to the church where I had been baptized. The priest thought it was so nice that I was paying homage to my father. Is that what this trip was? Homage?

I asked about the private high school my father went to, St. Louis University High School, wondering whether my dad had grown up poor. The priest told me not to judge my father. "Maybe he felt poorer than he really was."

I had found a newspaper article in which my father said he was the poorest kid in school. In an NPR interview, he claimed to have grown up on the wrong side of the tracks. These were stories I hadn't heard. Saint Louis University High School was a private boys' school, where some of the wealthiest families send their sons. I went to the school, its impressive grounds and gates like the entrance to a royal estate. I looked through my dad's high school yearbooks, pictures of a youth my dad had hated. I visited his childhood home near Tower Grove Park. I drove past the beautiful park and pictured him playing baseball there. I had written to the present home owners ahead of time, asking if I might walk around the backyard. I stood on the sidewalk and studied my father's home. With stained-glass windows, so similar to our house in Oakland, New Jersey, the one with the façade my father designed himself.

I rang the doorbell, to ask if I could walk in the backyard, and mentioned that my grandfather was Joe Gallagher, an assistant chief of police in the 1960s. The owner recognized the name, a cop himself. He and his wife invited me in.

I hesitantly stepped inside. They showed me around the house and an upstairs bathroom in its original condition. The toilet had a pull chain; the original white ceramic tiles still lined the floor and walls. Aunt Jane once had to scrub that floor with a toothbrush. We walked onto the back porch and I remembered one of Dad's stories. His mother would wait at the back door. If any of the kids were late, Pop would give them the belt, a lash for each minute they were late. Dad didn't cover for his sisters—divide and conquer, the Gimpel way . . . and now the Michael-family way.

Next, I went to the university where my parents met, to find out for myself if Dad had played soccer or not, another discrepancy debated in the press. The local PBS had just finished a documentary on that first soccer team at St. Louis University. In 1962 they had won the NCAA championship. My father's name was not listed on the roster. The librarian helped me go through old yearbooks. My father was not pictured on any team. The librarian, a soccer fan himself, called a few players who were part of the documentary. Nobody had heard of George Gimpel. They of course had heard of George Michael, the sportscaster, but didn't know he was a SLU alum.

"He's one of ours," the librarian proudly said into the phone, as I sat there waiting and hoping for someone to verify his claim. The only proof of his playing soccer was from high school, his senior year as second string goalie. I could argue that the press had gotten confused. If you are not from St. Louis, perhaps it is easy to mix up SLU High School and St. Louis University. To the end, I still want to give my Dad an out. We believe the lies we need to believe, when the truth is too painful to face.

I went to the cemetery where my grandmother and great grandparents were buried. I laid flowers and a heart-shaped stone made of unakite, a green and pink granite that my yoga teacher said is supposed to heal the past.

I sat in the cemetery, the sun shining brightly, picturing my father standing here forty years earlier saying good-bye to his mother. Pop was not buried here, nor was my dad's only full-blooded sister, Margaret; though her name is inscribed on one of the tombstones, 2002, the year my father wrote me that horrific letter. I wondered if Pop and Aunt Marge were not buried here because they were cremated, or because the last wife did not want to lay Pop's ashes near his first three wives.

The Gimpel tombstone is massive, suggesting a greatness I hadn't known. I spoke to my grandmother's spirit, a woman I never met, asking what she had done to my father when he was a boy, when had he lost his heart? I don't normally talk to the dead, but it seemed that the only hope left for me was for things to right themselves in heaven.

My final stop in St. Louis was to my father's favorite childhood bakery. When Dad last came to St. Louis for Pop's funeral in 1982, he returned home with coffee cakes to freeze.

I searched the phone book and the Internet for bakeries and caramel coffee cakes, but I couldn't find any that seemed right. I asked locals who suggested I try a bakery on Gravois Street. I crossed the River Des Peres. It seemed familiar with its distinctive white walls along the river bank. Couldn't be. Wasn't this river near my Nana's house, Trish's mother? I reached for my old brown phonebook Dad had given me in third grade so I would have a place to write the address for his new apartment after he moved out. I looked up Nana's address and used my BlackBerry to do a MapQuest to her house. I never knew Trish and my father had grown up close to one another, just a few miles apart.

I drove the few blocks to Nana's house, the place we stayed when I was four, and stood on the sidewalk. I could remember sleeping on the sofa on her porch, a breezeway. I could see my brother Brad, taunting me in her dining room with the biggest bubble gum bubble, until I finally popped it, the bubble bursting over his eye glasses. I remembered feeling love.

I had seen my Nana only once during the custody battle and never again. She had called my father a few years later to track down Trish. He promised Nana would get to see us, but we never did.

Now I stood on the sidewalk, a lump in my throat. I never got to say good-bye to her, and in that moment, I realized that in my parents' divorce, I lost more than my childhood. I took a few pictures to send to Trish, then climbed back in the rental car.

Eventually, I found the bakery, Federhofers. The caramel coffee cake was worth the trip. I bought some to take home, hand carried back on the plane. I sheepishly explained to a puzzled TSA agent that it was my father's favorite, my father who had recently died. The TSA agent relaxed then, telling me to take extra care of it, and we both smiled at one other, an understanding of both the love and grief bound in that bakery box.

In St. Louis, I felt like I had spent a weekend with my father, with the person he once was.

CHAPTER 28

Letting Go

I THOUGHT I COULD control my grief, compartmentalize it the way I had addressed every challenge throughout my life. So I gave myself a year to grieve, with Fridays as my dedicated day for reflection and tears. But life has a way of saying "enough already," and so in September, I almost lost my son.

The school called me at work to come immediately; Sam was writhing in pain, but they didn't know what was wrong. I rushed him to the hospital, and on the way there, he had a kind of seizure in the backseat of the car.

He screamed, "I can't feel my hands! My lips are tingling."

I looked in the rear view mirror, his face contorted. The hospital was still ten minutes away. *How long does it take to go from tingling to not breathing?* I called 911 and drove faster, barely able to explain what was happening or where we were, as I struggled to hold back the tears. *My son will die,* I thought. I could save my husband from choking but I couldn't drive and do mouth-to-mouth at the same time. *No!*

I drove over a barrier to make an illegal U-turn, flooring it onto the highway.

An ambulance met us in a parking lot near the highway off ramp. The EMT attached an oxygen mask to my son and whisked him to the hospital a few blocks away.

Sam had an emergency appendectomy. He would be fine.

Aunt Jane came to visit us the following week. "I want to meet the rest of my family," she declared. I understood that with my father gone, she didn't have to worry about how visiting me would have pissed my father off.

We were eating dinner in my kitchen with the bay window, like the bay window in Dad and Pat's dream home in Oakland, and like the one in my father's childhood home in St. Louis, when Aunt Jane asked Sam who his favorite football team is. The Packers! Utterly and completely. I cannot explain my son's passion for this team as we have never lived in Wisconsin. It unnerved me when Sam posted a quote from Vince Lombardi on his Facebook page: "Winning is not a sometime thing. It is an all-time thing," a quote my dad had on a plaque in my childhood living room. I had forgotten that my father once lived in Milwaukee and supported the Packers when my brother was born. Was it all a random coincidence, or was I wishing for a connection—no matter how ethereal—between my father and my son? Would Sam have even liked my dad or found him to be too much of a blowhard?

Around the dinner table, Aunt Jane warmed to Sam's enthusiasm and to his photographic memory of everything football. Sam left Aunt Jane speechless with his statistics and strategies for the upcoming game. I imagined my father seated on the chair next to his older sister, trying to challenge my son—his grandson—on the game plan, the likely outcome, reveling in the conversation. Was it my father's presence I felt . . . or his absence?

I wished Aunt Jane could have visited later, after Sam had recovered, so she could see one of his games, but we both felt time cornering us. And within a few weeks, my husband had his own medical problems: back problems from a herniated disc. In the days leading up to Keith's surgery, I cradled him in my arms, thinking he would surely die from a heart attack from the unabated pain. I thought of Pat, then. She must have held my father, weakened from the Leukemia. No matter her role in furthering the rift between my father and me, I understood how hard it would have been for her to see my father reduced to a broken version of the man she loved.

As I paced for hours in the waiting room during Keith's back surgery, I bargained with God. There wasn't any more time to grieve for my father. My family needed me. *Just let them be okay, and I promise, I'll move on.*

But then there was Trish. Her younger brother, an uncle I had only met once when I was four, died in August, and she asked me to go with her to the funeral. I asked why couldn't Brad or her boyfriend go? Brad was unavailable. "Emotionally or physically?" I wanted to quip but squelched the remark. Her boyfriend was a recovering alcoholic, so a funeral could be dicey. That left me.

It had been several years since I had seen her. As I sat in the airport in St. Louis waiting to meet her for a connecting flight on a small propeller plane to Quincy, Illinois, a flight attendant brought her in a wheel chair. Her frailty gnawed at me.

We talked about her brother and his fear of flying, the reason he had never visited us in New Jersey. She spoke of Dad carefully, controlling her anger over the old hurts. She was embarrassed about the *Washington Post* obituary, in which my dad was quoted saying she had "run away to Mexico with an eighteen-year old." It was an ugly story, uglier that it wasn't true. I looked at her now in the wheel chair, with a nebulizer for her emphysema. I was stronger than she.

A couple months after her brother's funeral, just before Thanksgiving, I contacted the *Washington Post* for Trish. I felt as if my father were working through me, trying to right an old wrong.

My request to the *Post* was simple: delete the reference. Just delete it. If they didn't want to trust my own memory of events, I had the court documents to prove she had not run away to Mexico. She had only taken a three-week trip to start a boutique import business. The *Post* claimed they had to investigate. They never followed up. So I left it to Trish to resolve, if she wanted to. She wrote them a letter. Eventually, the *Post* issued Trish's claim as a "clarification," which made it sound like she was making things up. In another show of insensitivity, the *Post* ran the clarification on Christmas Eve, the anniversary of my father's death.

On Christmas Eve, I thought about going to the crematorium to see if my father's ashes were there. I doubted the place would hold his spirit and decided instead to pay my respects by visiting my childhood home in Oakland, the home of our golden years, the one on Breakneck Road. I went December 23rd, determined to be fully present with my family on Christmas Eve.

I rang the doorbell to ask if I could walk around the backyard, to see the place where my dad once taught me to throw a softball. Instead, the owner invited me inside and showed me the mirrors my father had once hung on the cathedral ceiling.

I went next door to Mr. Voitle's then. I had brought him Christmas cookies, in remembrance of his wife who had taught me how to make the perfect, chewy, chocolate chip cookie. I spotted Mr. Voitle outside; the leaves crunched beneath my shoes as I called out to him. We talked across the little stone wall.

"I was sorry to hear about your father," he said.

I nodded, unable to speak. So few people knew him as my dad, just my dad.

The owner of the house on Lee Way, the house that should have been Dad and Pat's first dream house, scared me. The young owner had tattoos running down his muscular arms, and I think I woke him, even though it was after noon. But I must have seemed like a crazy lady, ringing a door bell of a home that was no longer mine. When I asked if I could walk around back, explaining that my parents had built this house, he shrugged, *whatever*, then slammed the door. As I headed around the drive, he opened the door, calling after me, "Hey! Is that their names in the garage floor?"

I shrugged. He met me in the garage and showed me the heart, *George and Pat*. There was no date on this heart, but it would have been thirty-one years old.

The writer in me wanted to attach a meaning to this, how the heart Dad wrote with Trish's name was crumbled, while the heart with Pat's name was in perfect condition. When I told Keith later, he saw the truth so clearly: The heart with Trish was for all the world to see. The one with Pat was only for them, hidden from the outside world, with no room for others.

The house on Circle Avenue in Franklin Lakes, next to Oakland, was when I still lived with Trish, before sixth grade when Dad got custody of us. It was the house Dad had bought for Trish in the hopes they would get back together. Now it had a highway running through its backyard.

I felt like my home visits were enough to mourn my father and to allow me to celebrate Christmas with my family.

On Christmas Eve, we arrived at the church early enough to be sure we could get seats. It seemed we still were not early enough, and when the usher suggested we could listen from downstairs in the cafeteria, I said, no—I needed to face being in the main church, even if it meant standing in the back. As we found a spot along the wall, one of the ushers said she found four chairs in the front. Did we want to sit up front? Keith hesitated. Up front and church didn't agree with him, particularly this year, in case his back started bothering him. We walked up front and noticed the seats were cushioned. I declared that this coincidence was directed at Keith, and he rolled his eyes at me. The kids teased him too, agreeing with my view.

I focused on my children's voices as they sang carols, and squashed any flashbacks to the nightmare of last Christmas Eve.

On Christmas Day, we prepared our usual feast, just the four of us. Megan and Sam set the table with our finest china and lit white candles in the center of the table.

We dined with carols from Winchester Cathedral and said cheers to each other.

I held my wine glass up. "May I?" Keith nodded, knowing I would want to do this. "To my father. May he rest in peace, and—" My voice clogged.

I took a breath and tried to continue. I had made it through Christmas Eve, through so many days, without shedding a tear, but now they spilled over unabated.

Keith raised his glass. "To George. For all he did right, to make you the kind of person you are . . . for you."

We clinked our glasses in memory of my father, the person he once was—the man my husband and children never knew.

Epilogue

Keith, me, Megan, Sam getting ready to
host Thanksgiving, 2014

SOMETIMES STARING AT THE truth is too difficult. It was only after my father's death that I could write the harder parts of my story and I wrote more furiously. Some of the memories helped me heal. Revisiting the harder times nearly broke me, again.

During this time, Keith patiently stood by, watching me cry, listening to me toss and turn in the night because so many nightmares, long dormant, returned. My husband would have preferred that I only look forward and bury the past, but he has known me long enough to accept my belief that the past—a difficult one anyway—can only be laid to rest when we have examined and understood it. Burying the past, without such understanding, risks allowing it to contaminate the present. I continue to believe that was my father's greatest downfall.

This is the great irony of my father's gifts to me: I am strong and tough and determined. I can wish for an idyllic childhood, but that life would not have led me to Keith and my children.

So this book started with the purpose of opening my father's heart; I had a vision of a happy ending in which I would give him this book, and he would remember our golden years and see what was still possible. Instead, writing it helped me understand him—and myself—more fully. In choosing to publish this memoir, a part of me wanted to set the record straight. There is something about being a secret that is soul destroying.

I wish I could protect my sister and brother from whatever fallout this book will bring them. I admire my brother, doing what he loves: selling boats. I know little of my sister's life, as she wants it that way.

My mother and I talk occasionally by phone, and I try to visit her when I am in Florida. Our relationship is a work in progress. She is my memory of a happier time in my childhood. In recent years, she has tried to do things differently.

It was only after my father's death that I learned he had narcissistic personality disorder (NPD). People with NPD lack empathy, see their children as an extension of themselves, have a false sense of reality, and never admit wrong doing.

I think my father's NPD made his success possible, because narcissists have to be the center of attention. I also suspect his fame made it worse.

But there are no do-overs, so I can only continue to heal and to recognize when I am falling back on some of my old baggage.

There are periods of time in my life when I am confident and happy with the life I have lived, the family I have created. I have a husband I am madly in love with, Keith. Megan and Sam are my life's blessing. What more could a person want?

Sometimes I still hear my father's hurtful remarks. That negative voice doesn't fully disappear, but it quiets to a whisper, and that's enough for me.

Acknowledgments

THANK YOU TO MY husband, Keith, for supporting me in writing this memoir, bringing it to publication, and ensuring I held on to my heart when the process threatened to break me. Thank you to my children, Megan and Sam, who tolerate my baggage, support my beliefs, and are the blessings of my life. I have told them to dream big, and they have told me to do the same.

Thank you, Laurel Marshfield, part writing coach and part muse, who helped reawaken my creative writing skills. Kerstin White was one of my book's first readers, who introduced me to Julie Maloney and Women Reading Aloud, the first group in which I bared my soul and shared my story. Brian McLaughlin, I thank you for the friendship and reading the rambling first draft. Thank you to Cullen Thomas and my writer's group at Gotham Writers Workshop for helping me hone my skills. Editor Charol Messenger made the book into a more focused memoir. Thank you do my dear friend Kris Farnsworth who keeps a better photo album than I and who provided the cover photo for the book. Robin Schwartz, friend and photographer, has always made sure my author photos look good, but for this book, she also was my sounding board for the change in title. For five years, the book was my sentimental and symbolic Cracks in the Sidewalk. It was a tough pill to swallow when the publisher suggested the new title, for a multitude of reasons, but I think Brooke indeed got it right. My Westgate book club has kept me reading and laughing; they provided the spark of an idea to tell my story when we read *The Glass Castle*. They also were supportive early readers.

I have to thank the team at She Writes Press for bringing the book to market. Thank you to Megan Rynott for her attention to detail in the final edits and getting rid of so many so's. Brooke Warner is a trail blazer for authors, seizing the shifts in the publishing business. Cait Levin has kept the project on track, and publicist Crystal Patriarche and Taylor Vargecko worked to allow my book book to reach beyond family and friends.

Lastly, I have to thank Father Pat for telling me to share my story. May he rest in peace.

About the Author

AFTER MOVING FROM MARYLAND to Switzerland to Texas to Michigan, Cindi Michael now lives in rural New Jersey, not far from where she spent the golden years of her childhood. She's happily married to an Englishman and is a die-hard football and swim team mom. Her day job as a technology and big data expert takes her to clients around the world, and she is the author of five business and technology books. She holds a BA in English from the University of Maryland and an MBA from Rice University. She has won two creative writing awards for her short stories.

Reading Group Questions

1. The theme of family patterns is mentioned throughout the book. What were the patterns in the family that were positive? What were the negative ones that Cindi was trying to break? What are the patterns in your own family that you wish you could change?

2. Cindi talks about steeling her heart to survive and how work numbed her to the pain of losing her father. Is this a positive coping technique? What would have been better? Worse?

3. George holds on to grudges. How did this affect his first marriage? His relationship to his daughter? The lives of Brad and Michelle?

4. Many families have rifts without full disowning. What are the rifts in your immediate family and what are the root causes? What are the root causes of Cindi's disowning?

5. How much do you think fame influenced George's change? Is it inevitable that famous people must choose between family and fame, normalcy and dysfunction? How does this affect their children?

6. After her father's death, a friend asks Cindi why she never wrote her father and the Michael family off. Should she have held on to her hope for a reconciliation or would she have been better off forgetting about them?

SELECTED TITLES FROM SHE WRITES PRESS

She Writes Press is an independent publishing company founded to serve women writers everywhere. Visit us at www.shewritespress.com.

Don't Call Me Mother: A Daughter's Journey from Abandonment to Forgiveness by Linda Joy Myers. $16.95, 978-1-938314-02 -5. Linda Joy Myers's story of how she transcended the prisons of her childhood by seeking—and offering—forgiveness for her family's sins.

Accidental Soldier: A Memoir of Service and Sacrifice in the Israel Defense Forces by Dorit Sasson. $17.95, 978-1-63152-035-8. When nineteen-year-old Dorit Sasson realized she had no choice but to distance herself from her neurotic, worrywart of a mother in order to become her own person, she volunteered for the Israel Defense Forces —and found her path to freedom.

Fourteen: A Daughter's Memoir of Adventure, Sailing, and Survival by Leslie Johansen Nack. $16.95, 978-1-63152-941-2. A coming-of-age adventure story about a young girl who comes into her own power, fights back against abuse, becomes an accomplished sailor, and falls in love with the ocean and the natural world.

The Beauty of What Remains: Family Lost, Family Found by Susan Johnson Hadler. $16.95, 978-1-63152-007-5. Susan Johnson Hadler goes on a quest to find out who the missing people in her family were— and what happened to them—and succeeds in reuniting a family shattered for four generations.

The Coconut Latitudes: Secrets, Storms, and Survival in the Caribbean by Rita Gardner. $16.95, 978-1-63152-901-6. A haunting, lyrical memoir about a dysfunctional family's experiences in a reality far from the envisioned Eden—and the terrible cost of keeping secrets.

All the Ghosts Dance Free: A Memoir by Terry Cameron Baldwin. $16.95, 978-1-63152-822-4. A poetic memoir that explores the legacy of alcoholism and teen suicide in one woman's life—and her efforts to create an authentic existence in the face of that legacy.